oth father and son began their careers at Deptford Dockyard as shipwrights and draughtsmen
nd John Cleveley Junior studied under Paul Sandby who was drawing instructor at Woolwich
cademy.
he panel provides a fascinating picture of the Common Quay and the River Front as seen from
he high ground above Stoke Bridge. It also shows the Old Custom House with its colonnade;
his gave place to a new building in 1845 now occupied by the Dock Commission.

SEAGATES TO THE SAXON SHORE

SEAGATES TO THE SAXON SHORE

by

KENNETH WENHAM STRUGNELL

TERENCE DALTON LIMITED
LAVENHAM   .   SUFFOLK
1973

Published by
TERENCE DALTON LIMITED
S B N 900963 20 4

Printed in Great Britain at
The Lavenham Press Limited
Lavenham   Suffolk

© G. K. Wenham Strugnell 1973

Contents

Index of Illustrations

TO MY WIFE, without whose loving patience and encouragement
this book would have probably never been completed.

Acknowledgements

In preparing a book of this nature the degree of kindness, sympathy and help which is so readily afforded to the Author is such that any expression of thanks may easily appear invidious; nevertheless I cannot but express my deep indebtedness to all who have given so much of their knowledge, time and patience to satisfy my persistence and importunity, compared with which that of the widow in the parable must seem mere social pleasantry.

I am grateful to the Library Staffs of Colchester, Ipswich and King's Lynn, and most especially to my good friends, Mr Wilfred James of Lowestoft and Mr Alfred Hedges of Great Yarmouth and their assistants, as well as to the Essex County Archivist, Mr K. C. Newton and his Staff.

The Ladies and Gentlemen of the National Maritime Museum, the Scott Polar Research Institute, Cambridge, the Hydrographer of the Navy, the Royal National Life-boat Institution and the Royal United Service Institution have all been most helpful in answering my inquiries in their respective spheres. Also by the same token I am grateful for the help of Miss Patricia Butler, Curator of the Ipswich Museums and Miss Mottram of King's Lynn Museum as well as to the Revd. Leo Hammond of King's Lynn for his help in securing for me photographs of that especially difficult subject, the Red Mount Chapel.

To Mrs Winifred Cooper, Secretary of the Harwich Society, Mr Donald Wallace of the Ipswich Dock Commission, who have so generously helped me to clarify special matters of doubt, and to Mr Jack Mitchley of the Port of Lowestoft Research Society my thanks are equally due.

I cannot let slip this opportunity to recall in affectionate memory the late Miss Elsie Redstone who received me so graciously at the Seckford Library, Woodbridge, and placed at my disposal without stint and with such charming hospitality all the wealth of information stored in the Library and Redstone Archives, as well as supplementing that information from the rich fruits of her retentive memory. It was a privilege to number myself in humility among the vast host of her friends, united in a bond of grief for her recent passing.

Lastly I record with gratitude the kindness, help and encouragement of my old friend Dr Reinhold Regensburger of Cambridge, especially in the matter of Teutonic and Scandinavian origins and antiquities.

G. K. Wenham Strugnell,
Leiston.
June, 1972.

Introduction

SO OFTEN did Lord Macaulay shame his readers by recounting the many titbits of knowledge which every schoolboy is supposed to have at his command that he has been credited with the invention of this infant paragon. Macaulay himself was a voracious snapper-up of other men's trifles and it is therefore no surprise to discover that the phrase had been in use for at least two centuries before his time and possibly even longer. To those pedagogues who have grown grey in discovering what every school-boy does *not* know the tag must taste a trifle sour; anyone who doubts this should take another look at some of his old school reports.

Those of us who by much application — and not a little physical persuasion — managed to acquire even a modicum of the Latin tongue will remember that we early learned to distinguish between *porta,* a gate and *portus,* a sea-port. That the two words were doublets related to the verb *portare,* to carry, was a pedantic trifle of little consolation to the erring wretch who found, too late, that he had backed the wrong horse.

In addressing ourselves to the subject of this modest essay we find that the kinship between these Latin words is not altogether irrelevant. It is however important to define by limitation what exactly is a 'port'.

Once upon a time when ships were small and easily manhandled it was usually sufficient for them to be hauled up on any convenient shelving beach as is done with smaller fishing boats today. When the sea was less kindly than usual they could be hauled up higher still out of danger and, moreover, roofed over for further protection.

As the size of craft increased they would be anchored offshore or in some sheltered inlet where they would escape the full force of wind and wave. Such an anchorage was afterwards known as a haven and it would not be long before men would improve on natural conditions by building staithes, or hythes, which would afford at one and the same time moorings for the craft and an easy method of embarking and disembarking both men and merchandise. Soon there arose around these staithes sheds for the merchandise and houses for the men. Thus the Haven became a Port.

Thereafter it was a natural and necessary phase of development for roads or packways to be formed linking these coastal settlements with inland towns, themselves linked with other towns, thus making a network of communications over countries and continents. Occasionally it might happen in reverse and men from inland would seek an outlet for their goods to be embarked; but the tactical *sine qua non* was a safe and convenient shelter for ships and for this reason the pattern of coastal settlement would be fixed by maritime necessities rather than vice versa.

Sometimes the growth of the port would be such that from a very early date it became a large and important town in its own right; but it would have little validity without landward communications and usually land-looking defences. In any event it soon assumed the twin meanings of the old Latin words and then it was indeed a 'gate' — a sea-gate, through which all must pass in or out. Here in Britain, "bound in with the triumphant sea", these ports achieved a power and importance rivalled by few other towns, not only in their own country but throughout the known world. From such roots sprang Hull, King's Lynn, Great Yarmouth, Ipswich, Harwich, Southampton, Bristol.

As the natural haven developed into a port so by the same token did the port become a harbour. It is by a strange twist in the use of words that whereas 'haven' has from the beginning been connected with shelter for ships and only by simile has come to bear the sense of protection so that we can describe a home for old people as a 'haven of rest', its synonym 'harbour' had first nothing at all to do with ships on the sea. It is composed of two Icelandic words meaning, respectively, an armed host and a shelter. Thus the common place-name 'Coldharbour' meant originally a place of shelter where no fire was provided and the traveller had to find his own. Similarly it is an offence to 'harbour' a criminal.

Today the words are often so closely allied in use as to be almost synonymous; but there are still many 'havens' up and down the coast where there is not, and never has been, a 'harbour' in the ordinary sense of the word. Some are now merely geographical names with a shadowy memory of past use, such as Wadgate Haven,

Minsmere Haven and many more. They were little distinguishable from 'roads' where ships could lie at anchor.

It is characteristic that the English language, so beautiful when written, so musical when spoken, so subtle in its idiom, is also singularly imprecise at times. This is often due to the wide variety of its origins; and as will be seen, the pursuit of word-derivation is a chancey business, beset with many pitfalls.

The total coastline of Essex, Suffolk and Norfolk is a long haul, of the order of two hundred miles, not taking into account all the estuaries which at some time or another in our history have afforded shelter for ships and where maritime trade flourished. Today there are seven major ports still in operation with a further two or three still in business in a more modest way; others have changed their character and would be completely forgotten except for some amount of yachting or fishing and yet others have so faded on the pages of history that they cannot be discerned at all except by the skilled archivist searching the records and the equally skilled archaeologist working in the field. It has manifestly been impossible to cover every inch of the coast in a book of this kind which has posed the old problem: not so much what to put in as rather what to leave out. Nowhere has this problem been more difficult to resolve than where the pattern of town and port is closely interwoven. It has been a difficult and sometimes invidious task to unravel this tangled skein. To change the metaphor: the author has done his best to steer a fair course in the middle ground.

1

The Land and the Folk

MOST people if asked what they understand by East Anglia will reply without hesitation: "Norfolk and Suffolk". Others may hazard a guess that the term should rightly include Essex or Cambridgeshire or even parts of Lincolnshire. In one sense or another all these answers are partly right: and none is entirely wrong. As a well-known and irrepressible don — now alas! no longer with us — would have said "It all depends on what you mean by . . . . . ."

Many years ago the London Society of East Anglians gave its blessing to a flag designed by Mr Langham, one of its members from Suffolk. Superimposed on the red cross of St George was a blue 'inescutcheon' bearing three gold crowns, or — as some would have it — three ducal coronets. The flag soon became recognised as appropriate to this part of England and King Edward VII accepted one from the Society, as also did King George V at whose command it was flown on the tower of Sandringham Church on 12th July, 1919, when the whole country celebrated the Proclamation of Peace after the First World War.

There has been some difference of opinion as to the significance of these crowns. They have been variously attributed to Bury Abbey, St Edmund, King and Martyr, or even the Royal Arms of Sweden. The first two conjectures can be dismissed on the ground that wherever a crown is symbolic of St Edmund it is usually transfixed by two arrows 'in saltire'. The hypothetical connection with Sweden is a very shaky one; for although the Wuffings, or Uffings, the original East Anglian royal house almost certainly hailed from Sweden, this was long before the consolidation of that realm under one monarch and most certainly before the days of heraldry; moreover the Swedish arms display the crowns differently. It is of course true that the mediaeval heralds were ready to assign arms to saints and folk-heroes who had never borne them in their lifetimes — if indeed they had ever had any real existence at all. It all helped to keep the artists and craftsmen busy! But why three crowns for one kingdom? Let John Lydgate the poet-monk of Bury, writing in English five hundred years after St Edmund's martyrdom suggest a rationale:

> "This other standard field sable of colour ind
> In which of gold be notable crowns three.
> The first token in chronicle men may find
> Granted to him for royal dignity,
> And the second for virginity,
> For martyrdom the third in his suffering:
> To these annexed faith, hope and charity,
> In token he was martyr, maid and king."

The idea is a pretty one and it is no more far-fetched than much that passed for truth in mediaeval heraldry; and even that is generously excelled by the romancing of the heralds of Tudor times — and since!

So let us fly the East Anglian flag with panache and pride, not overmuch worried by pedantic scruples but rejoicing in our ancient heritage. The simple fact is that East Anglia is a locality without exact territorial boundaries; in this respect it resembles Snowdonia or Connemara or the Peak. Wherever the term is used in a legal or official context it usually has to be qualified by a 'definition clause' and its precise meaning has an exasperating habit of changing according to the circumstances in which it is used. When East Anglia was a subordinate kingdom of the Anglo-Saxon Heptarchy, its ruler was known as King of the East Angles, thus witnessing to his complete involvement with his people rather than laying claim to sovereignty over any particular slice of the earth's surface. This relationship was both natural and inevitable in those days, as we shall see when we come to consider the people, whence they came and what they had come to be. For the purpose of this story we shall first look at the land itself and in that connection shall think not only of Norfolk and Suffolk and those parts of Cambridgeshire which, consisting chiefly of river and fen, lie between Cambridge and the Wash, but also of the coastal regions of what is now Essex, bordered by the North Sea and Estuary of the Thames which for reasons hereafter to be seen is regarded as stretching from Tilbury to the Nore. Both historically and geographically this large area of the English mainland has in its component parts much in common, although circumstances have combined to give each of these parts a distinctive idiom of topography, folk-speech and the local vagaries of its inhabitants.

It was not always so. Up to some twenty centuries ago or thereabouts — for geological time is an open-handed measure caring little for historical precision or the niceties of date — the various land-masses and their satellite islands which nowadays go to make up the British Isles were part and parcel of what is now Europe. The first to separate was Ireland and then, some ten centuries later, the last land-bridge over which early man had found his way during the Old Stone Age gave way to the perennial pressure of the Atlantic swell and what we now know as the English Channel and the Straits of Dover were born. Thus Britain became, geographically, an island.

For some centuries this watery zone, forever in restless motion under the impulse of wind and tide, must have seemed as a savage and impassable barrier over which man could pass only at his peril. However with the lapse of time and the growth of skill and enterprise which marked man from the lower animals, people of successive races and progressive cultures found their way here. Not until about three thousand years before the Christian era would there have been regular communications by sea with the European mainland. This is not the place to particularise between the early inhabitants of Britain: the small dark Neolithic folk who were in the fullness of time succeeded by the taller men of the Bronze Age, themselves in turn to give way to the Goidelic Celts or Gaels who brought iron here about 600 B.C. They also brought with them their speech, the first language to have contributed anything permanent to that complex tapestry which is the English tongue today, the tongue of Chaucer, of Cranmer, of Shakespeare; which despite the debasing effects of modern mass media survives and flourishes — a proud tongue fit for freemen and heroes, an articulate speech which, until recent years, has rejected the mouthing and mumbling of the barely anthropoid.

It is true that the development of man is tied up with the nature of the land wherein he lives and the interaction and reaction between the land and the folk is deep and lasting. One can observe how all through history those western parts of Britain, founded upon the great bastions of rock which have withstood for countless ages the pounding fury of the Atlantic surges together with their inland foothills, have also been the last refuge and stronghold of past cultures, past social orders, past faiths. On the other side of the country, the soil was more fertile, more rewarding to those who tilled the land or raised flocks and herds. Life was easier and men tended to value a quiet and settled way of existence. This was the 'Invader's Shore' and more vulnerable to newcomers who coveted the possession of such a land. One physical consequence of being surrounded by water was that the climate avoided those extremes of heat and cold which obtained on the mainland of Europe and Asia. It is difficult even today to realise that Britain lies between the same parallels of north latitude as Moscow or Kamchatka, as Newfoundland or Hudson's Bay. Nevertheless the weather in this country has for centuries been as erratic as it is today. Incredible as it may seem to men of our time, there is reason to believe that in the years before the Roman occupation the weather may have been intensely cold and wet, the greater area of forest encouraging a heavy rainfall. Where there were large tracts of fen there was a degree of humidity which must have encouraged malaria or — as it was known to our forebears — fen ague.

By the time that Britain attracted the attention of the Romans, then well-established in Gaul, the Channel was very much as it is today. It could easily be crossed by ship, provided the mariners knew their job; and it must be remembered that here, as in the Mediterranean, the sea was a factor in the growth of civilisation which united rather than divided the peoples living on its shores. It was in the days of the Tudors when for reasons which do not concern us here England had withdrawn from the main stream of European culture, that men tended to think, as Shakespeare in *Richard II,* of:—

> "The silver sea
> Which serves it in the office of a wall
> Or as a moat defensive to a house
> Against the envy of less happier lands"

In earlier times however, to the inhabitants of Britain, the sea was the highroad on which men passed and re-passed on their lawful — and sometimes not so lawful — occasions. Over that same sea travelled statesmen and scholars, churchmen and merchants, pilgrims and craftsmen. Phoenicean merchants came here first from far-away Syria and later from their western colony at Carthage for the tin which has always been esteemed as a metal of great price. They it was who called this land the Isles of Tin and it has been said that this was a device to conceal the precise whereabouts of their source of supply. Hence too went the British craftsmen in enamelling and fine metalwork.

During the Roman occupation several Emperors came here. In A.D.43 Claudius, hoping perhaps to acquire an aura of that majesty which had so eluded his unhappy and ineffective self, paid a visit of a bare sixteen days punctuated by repeated acclamations of 'Imperator!' Even in this short period he may have learned to love this outpost of the Empire; for after his visit he assumed the surname Britannicus; and one of the nobler occasions of his wretched life came seven years later with his magnanimous freeing of the captive Caractacus. In A.D.208 came Septimius Severus, the African who proved himself one of the wisest and best of the Imperial Caesars. He too assumed the surname Britannicus, which had a certain melancholy fulfilment in his death at York three years later.

In A.D.306 Constantine, while with the army in Britain, was for the first time acclaimed Emperor in succession to his father Constantius Chlorus. As the first Christian Emperor — although in fact he was not himself baptised until just before his death in 337 — he liberalised the official attitude towards the Christians who could thereafter profess their faith without persecution or hindrance. In Britain the Imperial edicts against Christianity were rarely enforced even under Constantius Chlorus and this might well be due to the influence of his wife Helena; but the old story that she was the daughter of Coel, who has been identified by some enthusiasts with King Cole, is probably apocryphal. Most authorities have always agreed that she was born in Bithynia, although there is a very faint possibility that her son Constantine was indeed born in Britain. The mediaeval heralds accepted the tradition of Helena's British birth to the extent of including a stylised form of the True Cross in the arms of Colchester; but not even the most credulous have pretended that her discovery of this holy relic took place in Britain!

Other Emperors too are known to have visited Britain, although some were stationed here prior to their assumption of the Purple. It is very evident that this country was an important and fully integrated part of the Empire and the narrow seas were a constant highway linking Britain with Europe both then and thereafter. Over this encircling sea in 597 came Augustine to preach the Faith to the pagan Jutes in Kent and over a century later Boniface, the west countryman, set out to convert the heathen tribes of Germany. Although Christianity had been overwhelmed by the Teutonic incomers after the Roman occupation it still lingered in the north and west and this resulted in some conflict with the Augustinian mission over certain canonical matters. This is however no part of our story.

That same sea which served both as moat and highway could at times prove an unruly ally. All through history and indeed up to our own time the eastern coastline has changed and changed again through the action of tidal currents and shingle drift, about which more hereafter. The origin of this is to be found in the tidal pattern of the British Isles. Away in the broad bosom of the Western Ocean the tidal flood sweeps outwards until it meets the Continental Shelf which has the effect of magnifying its strength. As the Atlantic breakers meet the hard teeth of our western coastline they divide into two arms, one sweeping up the English Channel through the narrow neck of the Straits and into the North Sea, the other turning north up through the Irish Sea and the network of the Western Isles, hurling itself in fury through the Pentland Firth and so down our eastern seaboard until it meets the southern surge at the Kentish Knock.

Many years ago Hilaire Belloc reminded us of the part played by the rivers of England in the pattern and history of the whole country. In that context he was writing chiefly of the two longest rivers, the Thames and the Severn, each of which rising far inland, developed considerable estuaries with major tidal characteristics, each nursing a considerable port and centre of maritime trade. The size of these estuaries invited 'visitors', whether friendly or otherwise; but of the two the Severn is not of any especial significance in this story. The Thames as it flows into the German Ocean laps a large part of South Essex and historically the southwest corner of the county lay at the confluence of the Lea and the Thames; but for reasons which will become apparent we shall regard Tilbury as the farthest Essex port to concern us.

The general trend of the tidal flow on the East Coast is southwards which produces both scour and shingle drift which combine to create continued erosion of the softer cretaceous tertiary layers as well as the accumulation of long shingle banks. Natural 'nesses' or promontories are eaten away thus leaving the way open to yet further drift and further erosion. The exact movements of this process which has been going on for centuries are complex and are still not fully understood; what is clearly seen is the build-up of long spits of land such as those at Gorleston, Orford and Landguard, the full consequences of which will be considered later. Let it

suffice at this stage to say that these natural processes have made —
and unmade — many ancient sea ports and so have contributed in
no small measure to the history of our land and the people who
dwelt here.

The estuarial shape of Essex is different from that of Norfolk
and Suffolk in one important respect. Due to the lessening of the
shingle drift as the coast line recedes towards the Thames Estuary
the rivers have tended to spread lazily over large areas of marsh
and saltings which at low tides are barely covered with water and
even at high tides there is rarely much depth away from the known
and marked channels. These huge stretches of marsh, with their
myriads of wild-fowl, offering little resistance to the incursions of
the wind and tide, have served as much as entries for the sea as
outfalls for the rivers. William Camden, who besides being
Clarenceux King of Arms was a prolific and informative topo-
grapher, wrote of Essex in 1607: "the Ocean windeth itselfe into
it". A glance at a map shows even today how the sea seems to have
eaten its way right to the farthest part of the county. This of
course created a perennial problem for those who live in this
corner of England. Ever since Roman days man has been concerned
to erect defences against the inroads of the German Ocean and yet
his best efforts have often been unavailing.

There are however compensations. The hazards of finding a safe
way into these estuaries of little depth and beset with sandbanks,
the risk of being neaped at low tide and the lack of good landward
access or egress, even if a landing were effected in the face of
opposition by the inhabitants who were by no means at a disadvantage when fighting on foot; all these factors helped to keep the
land inviolable by Norseman or Dane, by Frenchman or Dutchman.

It is however also true that the inhabitants have sometimes
found that these advantages carried in themselves much of disadvantage. Smuggling has never been so rife in Essex as in Suffolk
because even where local knowledge would have helped to 'run' a
cargo ashore, there was no quick get-away such as was afforded
by the lonely stretches of heathland in the more northerly county.
Moreover the difficulties of approach from both sea and land have
militated against the development of the ports of Essex which —
with the exception of Harwich — have never at any period attained
the status of those of Suffolk and Norfolk. The deep curve inland
increased the length and difficulties of regular trade with the main-

land of Europe. It must further be remembered that Tilbury, which for size of ships and volume of traffic is unequalled on this side of England, is of modern growth and is still less than a hundred years old. But of this more anon. Enough of the geography of our book: let us return to the story of the folk.

Some three centuries after the arrival of the Goidels another influx of people of Celtic stock, the Brythons, began to settle in Southern Britain. They were already grouped in well-defined tribes, the names of which have come down to us and are part and parcel of British history. They had attained a high degree of civilisation and were sufficiently numerous to thrust the Goidelic Celts to the north and west. The speech of these newcomers, although Celtic in character and with some affinity to that spoken by the Goidels, was yet quite different. From Brythonic have grown the Cymric tongues, Welsh and Cornish, which are thus closely related to Breton, itself of Brythonic origin. From Goidelic, or Gaelic, we have Irish, Highland Scottish and Manx.

One of the most powerful tribes was the Iceni who settled over the whole of what is now Suffolk and Norfolk. To the south their territory marched on that of the Trinobantes which was broadly speaking, co-terminous with our Essex. According to the pundits the tribal title of these engaging people meant 'battle-stabbers' and it would seem that in their difference of opinion with the Roman legionaries they lived up to their name. It is clear that Essex was a distinct kingdom in pre-Roman times and to a certain extent this autonomy was retained so that when in later years the Teutonic invaders arrived they naturally fell into a distinct grouping on the same territory. To the east lay the sea — to the west the great man-made barrier of the Devil's Dyke reared its gigantic bulk for seven miles between the Fens and the Essex heights. Exactly when this rampart was made is a matter for conjecture; but even today anyone who essays to scramble up its western face must realise how formidable a barrier it could be, towering an average height of eighteen feet above the surrounding ground level and thirty feet from the bottom of its ditch. It may well be that it was there before the Brythonic Celts moved in, and if so the dyke, together with the natural escarpment of the Essex heights extending southwards, must have been a material factor in the choice of 'lebensraum' by both the Iceni and the Trinobantes. Each was formidable in war and what better formula for peace than a mutual alliance within the defences so readily provided by the lie of the land.

The picture of these 'Ancient Britons' as a savage half-naked people clothed with skins and crudely daubed with blue woad is a false one, much of it based on the clipped terse style of Caesar's Commentaries. They have much in common with the adventures into literature of a prominent military personage of our own day and one may be tempted to suspect that much of this over-simplification is somewhat of a gimmick. Caesar himself was not here long enough to penetrate the territory of the Iceni; with the Trinobantes his experience was chiefly of their harrassing guerilla tactics and he found it convenient to negotiate a tacit kind of *modus vivendi.* Later, when the Romans were here in greater strength and especially when under Claudius a serious attempt was made to incorporate Britain in the Empire, the Iceni were even disposed to be cautiously friendly. A few years later however the Roman procurator was guilty of some shameful breaches of faith and blatant exploitation of the British tribes and both the Iceni and Trinobantes rose in revolt led by Boadicea, queen of the Iceni. Hideous massacres took place on both sides and before peace was restored over 150,000 persons, Romans and Britons, had perished in circumstances of unbelievable savagery.

What of these Britons? What kind of people were they? When they overwhelmed the Roman garrisons by sheer weight of numbers and gave themselves up to frenzied cruelties which sicken us even today, were they just a horde of wild beasts in human form? Primitive they were as regards the lower classes. Their huts were clustered for protection within a banked stockade and life was perhaps no better than that which within living memory was normal in a Zulu kraal; but within that close community the social structure was stable and clearly defined. The tribal chiefs and their families would be well-dressed and richly adorned with gold and enamel ornaments and the women would wear gowns of well-woven materials in bright colours. Many of their household goods would have come from the mainland of Europe where the Belgic Celts enjoyed an even higher standard of living and had already come within the influence of Roman culture and social customs.

After the blood-bath of the Boadicean rising a kind of peace ensued, following the usual Roman pattern. As the Caledonian general said before the battle of Mount Graupius some twenty years later, "They create a desolation; they call it peace".

The majesty of the Pax Romana had been flouted and although many Romans were fully conscious of the corruption of the colonial administration which had provoked the Britons to revolt, the natives had to be taught their lesson and that lesson was ruthless and bloody.

Gradually the ruined cities, Colchester and London, were rebuilt, the amenities of colonial life were restored and the new amalgam of Romano-British culture settled down to a period of development which was to endure in its results for another three centuries. In some ways it must have been a precursor of what prevailed in the days of the British Raj in India; but with important differences. In the first place the Roman Imperium knew no gulfs of race or colour; the effective barrier was between the Roman citizen with his clear-cut heritage of legal rights and social status and those who were not — and could only with difficulty become — Roman citizens. This distinction is especially important when it is remembered that the Imperium in Britain alone lasted for an epoch at least twice the span of our own Imperial rule in India.

In other respects there were many points of resemblance. It was part of Rome's colonial policy to take the sons of the British aristocracy and send them to Rome to be educated and 'conditioned' as Romans. Britons of good standing spoke Latin—albeit, perchance with a 'British' accent and the addition of many words of Celtic origin, and they lived in houses which were colonial adaptations of Roman villas. Gradually Roman Britain became more self-sufficient and many men of Italian, or Mediterranean, stock were content to settle here after their term of service as soldiers or administrators. Moreover many veterans — time-served soldiers — from the auxiliary troops, who were of many races and who therefore could not acquire Roman citizenship settled here with their British consorts — wives in all but name; for none but citizens of that no mean city could contract a valid marriage. In this way there was a steady infusion of Hungarians, Greeks, Germans, Africans and Gauls, all of whom must have had some effect upon the racial make-up of the native community. Perhaps there is some lesson here for us today. It is probable indeed that some of the settlers in our part of Britain were Saxons who thus anticipated the arrival of their kinsmen two centuries later. It must be remembered that the Romans used the word 'Saxon' as a generic term, including the Angles and Jutes of which we hear a great deal later.

Obviously the Roman rule over this important Province of Britain was not maintained without all the occasional disturbances and vicissitude making up the inevitable white man's burden then or now or at any other time and whatever might have been that man's exact degree of 'whiteness'.

It is not relevant to our story to consider the minor incidents which enlivened life on the Pictish or Welsh borders; but there was one constant problem of defence which affected this side of Britain very intimately. All the Saxons were not serving in the Roman auxilia or peaceably settled in Romano-British towns or homesteads. From time to time the east and south coasts were visited by other roving gentlemen from the neighbourhood of the Rhine or the Elbe whose intentions were anything but peaceable. So far did these raiders form a recurrent threat that it was necessary to maintain a fleet to patrol the coast, the *Classis Britannica*. In general the defence of Britain by land and sea was entrusted to a highly placed military person known as the Count of the Saxon Shore — *Comes Litoris Saxonica per Britanniam* — and to afford some solid land defences a line of massive forts was built from *Branodunum*, known to us today as Brancaster, in Norfolk, to *Portus Adurni*, now Porchester in Hampshire. We know a great deal about this line of forts and of the troops who garrisoned them from a Roman official document, the *Notitia Dignitatum*. This lists ten forts in the chain, but there is one other port not in the list — that at Walton near Felixstowe. This has been submerged by the sea; but it is believed to have been of a type almost identical with the others. It is now the subject of fresh archaeological investigation which may yet yield fruitful and valuable data. The three forts which come into our story are Brancaster *(Branodunum)*, Burgh Castle *(Gariannonum)* near Yarmouth, and Bradwell *(Othona)*. The remains of Garriannonum are sufficient to tell us that it was very large and of enormous strength and it is obvious that this was equally true of most of the others. This, coupled with the fact that these northernmost ports appear to have been garrisoned by cavalry, tempts one to speculate on the possibility that they were intended to hold out against an attack until they could be relieved, since the use of cavalry as a 'striking' arm was a late development; not indeed until the Romans had learned by bitter experience from the Goths and Vandals the usefulness of the stirrup. It is no more than a bow drawn at a venture, since the forts of the Saxon shore are known to have been occupied by legionaries as well as auxiliaries. The exact location of the third fort in this part of the coast, Othona, has been disputed; but it is generally agreed now that it stood at Bradwell where the old Saxon church of St

Peter-ad-Murum certainly rests on Roman masonry of massive design. This still leaves the exact site and type of the 'castle' at Walton a little uncertain since, because the sea has overwhelmed it, it can only be examined by divers — who need to be trained archaeologists. Whether these forts ever had any real use we may never know, because their construction coincided with a turn of events in the history of Roman Britain which against the majestic background of Imperial Rome is nothing if not bizarre.

When the raids by Saxon pirates on the Roman settlements in the coastal areas of eastern and southern Britain increased to a degree where they seriously affected stable government and the safety of lives and property in those parts it was decided to strengthen the *Classis Britannica* and one Carausius was placed in command of these sea forces. His was a colourful character. A Menapian, born in what we know as the Low Countries, he was a skilful sailor and in fact he has been described by some writers as a pilot. He had great success in dealing with the raiders and recovering their booty; but this was not sufficient to satisfy his ingenuity. He seems to have conceived the idea of playing a kind of cat-and-mouse game which consisted of letting the Saxons at first get away with their bounty in order that he might then pounce on them and appropriate their ill-gotten gains for his own profit. This policy of 'farming' the wrong-doers did not commend itself to the Emperor Diocletian who decreed his capture which in those days could have resulted in only one painful conclusion to the career of this opportunist. Carausius lacked nothing in cool cheek and accordingly landed in Britain proclaiming himself Emperor of Britain — an early pioneer of U.D.I! He found plenty of supporters with regional aspirations and proceeded to issue coinage bearing his image, which gives us an amusing picture of his appearance; he looks rather like a music-hall caricature of a quarter-master-sergeant. Whether he himself was responsible for initiating the chain of forts is not very clear; but he certainly strengthened the coastal defences and it has even been suggested by some writers that the forts were as much to resist his own subjection by his former Imperial master as to keep the Saxons out. In any event they certainly constituted a major weapon of defence and lasted much longer than Carausius himself who in the middle of a very successful campaign was murdered by one of his own officers, Allectus. Thus perished the first and only Emperor of Britain who seems in his short reign of six years to have set about his task with remarkable energy and efficiency. It is believed that he strengthened the defence along the line of Hadrian's Wall; at a time when the coinage throughout the Empire was debased he restored a silver coinage in Britain; and he so repelled any attempts to displace him by naval action that eventually the two emperors accepted him on some qualified basis of equality. This surprising situation was recognised by coins minted in *Londinium* (London) and bearing the heads of Diocletian and Maximian the two Roman Emperors, together with that of Carausius and with the convivial superscription, "Carausius et Fratres sui" ·— Carausius and his brothers. What a pity that this jolly extrovert was cut off in his prime!

After Carausius and his treacherous slayer had passed from the scene of this short-lived sovereignty the more orthodox rule of the Emperor of the West was restored, although much was happening in the East which was soon to result in the dichotomy of an Empire with two capitals, which was of course the beginning and a prime cause of the fall of that Empire in the West — at least so far as Britain was concerned. Little did the Byzantine East know or care to expend money or men on maintaining these far-off Isles of Tin.

Eventually the time came when no further help could be looked for from Rome who was fighting her last desperate battle against the enemies at the gate, and these great fortresses with no troops to man the walls must have been a bitter sight for the Romano-Britons who were left in what was their homeland, whatever may have been their ancestry or standing in a very civilised way of life.

It is a false and superficial view that so soon as the Legions left Britain the whole Province was reduced to a supine state of terrified inaction. There is abundant evidence that the Romano-British state (for such as it was, in spite of the breakdown in direct administration from Rome) had every ability to put up an effective defence for a considerable time. Nevertheless the knowledge that there were no reinforcements in depth to back up the coastal garrisons must have been discovered very soon by the Saxon raiders. From minor raids of a violent nature they proceeded to settle in this rich land, so much better than their own at home. Up the creeks and rivers of the Eastern seaboard they crept in their not very seaworthy, many-oared craft; for the Angles and the Saxons had not learnt to make any really practicable use of the sail, nor were their ships built on very sophisticated lines. By the same token they tended to hug the European coastline until they reached the narrow seas which offered a quick and easy crossing, after which they worked northwards along the British littoral. The eye-catching pageant with which the first landing of the Jutes in Kent was celebrated some years ago provides a sad example of how a fallacy can be nourished in the laudable cause of civic pride. With great publicity and much blowing of trumpets a colourful replica of a *Danish* long ship was *sailed* across from the shipyard in Denmark where it had been meticulously constructed from the most authentic records and it now stands as a magnificent monument to muddled history to mislead our ingenuous offspring until someone has the moral courage to make a bonfire of it.

So now we have another substantial weft to add to the rich human tapestry of our East Anglian folk. Although the people who settled in what we now call Essex were in the beginning Saxons from that part of Europe which we now call Schleswig-Holstein, the old territory of the Iceni was taken by Angles from the Jutland peninsular. The racial difference between the Angles and Saxons was not of great importance beyond one significant fact mentioned by Bede. It seems that only a proportion of the Saxons left their homeland to settle in Britain whereas for some reason not fully understood, the Angles left their native territory almost untenanted. It may be that they were under pressure from their Danish neighbours or that they could not wring a full living from the soil. Be that as it may, if Bede is correct, it may explain why so much larger an area of Britain was settled by the Angles than by the Saxons.

For another four centuries the newcomers would be known simply as the East Angles for they would take some time to emerge from the primitive tribal, or even family community. Even today our placenames remind us that some thriving town or village was once simply 'Saxmund'a Home', Saxmundham, or 'Hael's Farm', Halesworth, or 'Wahlberhts Village', Walberswick.

The prime urge of these newcomers seems to have been to settle rather than to loot; as regards the Angles in particular they were a pastoral and agricultural people and the well-farmed estates of the Romano-Britons must have offered rich prizes for the taking. Nevertheless they were a rude people and their methods would have been anything but gentle; the Saxons would probably have taken a fair quota of slaves as easily negotiable human merchandise.

To the people in possession grown up in a settled state where the Pax Romana was their only known way of life, the situation was one of gathering darkness as they saw one homestead after another fall into the hands of the raiders. We can imagine them watching from their villas as the smoke rose in a circle drawing even nearer. News would come through of the sack of London and Colchester and those who could accept the inevitable would pack up their portable goods and move inland or at least send their womenfolk and children away in charge of a few trusted servants.

What was left of the Home Forces was by no means inactive in spite of political shilly-shallying and internal dissension between the 'Roman' and 'Celtic' factions. The names of some of the military commanders are by no means unknown, including Ambrosius Aurelianus who may have been of Imperial blood and also that Artorius whose real existence must be admitted, in spite of the apocryphal atmosphere surrounding King Arthur and his knights. The resistance put up by the champions of Roman civilisation against the pagan hordes was chiefly in the north and the west and could do little for the dwellers in Eastern Britain. Over the greater part of the land there ensued that baffling period of the Dark Age until Roman civilisation was re-born phoenix-like from the ashes of its former grandeur. And it is one of the ironies of history that that re-birth was accomplished through the medium of a faith which Imperial Rome had first despised and then feared.

Christianity had been secretly practised in Britain by a handful of believers during the persecution which gave the country its proto-martyr Alban about 303 — the date also assigned to another Roman officer, George, who in far-off Asia Minor was to be hailed as the "Great Martyr" and eventually the patron of mediaeval chivalry.

From being despised and ridiculed the new belief had become almost fashionable to the eventual displacement of Mithraism, although it may well have been treated very much as a social habit by those who would be "with it". With the coming of the heathen it shared the fate of other institutions of Roman origin. The worshippers of Woden and Thor would give little thought and less mercy to such philosophic eccentricities and Christian gee-gaws burnt as well as any others.

The story of the re-introduction of the Faith by the mission of St Augustine who landed at Kent at about the end of the sixth century is well-known and we have it in some detail from Bede who tells us the tale of how Gregory when a young deacon saw some Anglian slaves in Rome. "Non Angli sed Angeli" sounds trite; but whether Gregory meant exactly what is assumed could depend on whether he spoke in Latin or Greek. Although Greek had then ceased to be the official language of the Western Church it was still a polite tongue among educated folk and so the meaning could have been "Not Angles but messengers" — it is just anybody's guess! Be that as it may, the spread of what was to most a new religion was rapid, although not without untoward incidents from time to time. To the East Angles came Felix from Burgundy; to the East Saxons Cedd from Lindisfarne and a crop of monastic houses for men and women sprang up and became an important factor in the development of a civilised way of life.

In one way this may have been a contributory cause of the scourge from the sea when raiding Vikings from Jutland and Scandinavia descended on the countryside to loot the treasures which they knew would be found in these 'quiet fortresses'. In East Anglia the ultimate disaster was when a great force of Danes under Ingvar Lodbroksson descended upon the kingdom little able to make any real organised military effort in reply. Edmund, King of the East Angles, then in his early twenties, seems to have realised that the only way in which he could rally his scattered and numerically inadequate followers was to reorganise on what we should now call a guerilla basis. This he succeeded in doing to such good purpose that he was regarded by the Danes as a marked man and thereafter the war became as much a conflict of wits as of arms.

Eventually the Danes, having rampaged around in Northumbria and Mercia returned in force to East Anglia; but in the meantime Edmund had taken advantage of this respite to gather strength and when the two armies met near Thetford the Angles gave a better account of themselves than might have been expected. Edmund managed to extricate himself; but later fell into Ingvar's hands and having refused to relinquish either his people or his faith, was done to death in the circumstances well-known to history with some legendary embellishments. Whether the site of the martyrdom was, as used to be believed, Hoxne in Suffolk or, as is more usually credited today, at Hellesdon near Norwich is a matter which may be wrangled over by the learned. The outcome was the same, that East Anglia fell into Danish hands and became, together with the greater part of Essex, the Kingdom of Guthrum the Dane, who in the fullness of time, embraced the Christian faith as Athelstan. This was an outcome of the Peace of Wedmore by which the Danes withdrew to that part of England included in the Kingdom of Guthrum, the eastern half of Mercia and that part of Northumbria south of the Tees. This was to be known as the Danelaw and apart from occasional clashes of a local nature, Danes and Angles lived together in a kind of *modus vivendi,* which must have brought about a considerable fusion of Anglian and Danish blood. The monkish chroniclers have a habit of lumping all these Scandinavian newcomers under the generic term 'Danes' and it is not easy to be precise as between Danes and Norsemen; but it is probable that there was an area in Norfolk which in fact was settled by a small enclave of Norsemen, strictly so called.

Meantime the Fens remained very much an area apart, because of the inaccessible nature of this wilderness of small islands surrounded by water and swamp and here there remained a pocket of Gyrwas, or Girvii, who are believed to have been of Celtic stock. They were small dark men who kept themselves very much apart from their Teutonic neighbours and seem to have changed little right up to the present day.

After the union of the whole realm of England under Edgar — 'the Peacemaker' — the Danelaw ceased to have any real significance except for the resulting Anglo-Danish amalgam and when the Saxon kings were succeeded by a Danish king, Cnut, this had little or no impact upon East Anglia, especially because a generation later another Englishman was upon the throne in the person of Edward the Confessor. That same reign however saw the rise of the 'Earls' of the House of Godwin who between them ruled over practically the whole kingdom of England and in this 'carve-up' East Anglia fell to the share of Gyrth. Such was the situation in 1065; but in 1066 came 'All That'. As regards the racial composition of East Anglia, the Conquest had little effect upon the common people. In spite of the horde of rapscallions and adventurers whose support had put William on his profitable throne, they did not affect the lives of the Anglo-Danish majority so long as they were prepared to give up their lands and goods and chattels without a squeak of protest. Whatever may be said about the rule of the Godwins, it would be a favourable comparison with that of those bully-boys, the Bigods. Truculent and treacherous by turns — or sometimes both at the same time — they were a continual thorn in the flesh of the kings by whose grace they enjoyed their lands, until Henry II gave them their quietus. They are remembered today by the ruins of their castles at Framlingham and Bungay and an odd entry here and there in the pedigrees of honest folk who may derive a melancholy satisfaction from this somewhat undesirable ancestry.

Later when Edward III encouraged Flemish weavers to settle here in order to improve the quality of English woollen cloth the fortunes of the Suffolk and Essex clothiers were founded and we can gauge the size of those fortunes when we look at the magnificent churches at Lavenham, Long Melford, Saffron Walden and the other 'wool towns'. Again in 1685 many Huguenots who had fled from France following the revocation of the Edict of Nantes settled in Essex and Suffolk.

The pattern is now complete; and what a rich one it is! Goidel and Brython, Roman — and all the cosmopolitan assembly of races which were gathered in the *Imperium Romanum* — Angles and Saxons. Norsemen and Danes, Normans — themselves a blend of Northmen and Franks — Flemings and Frenchmen; some infinitesimal strain of blood from any of those who bore the torch before us may flow in our veins. Is it surprising that the men of Norfolk and Suffolk, 'Fen Tigers' — and the dwellers in the Essex marshlands — are men set apart by descent and by way of life from their inland neighbours. Kindly and tolerant to the incomer, yet cautious withal until they have found him worthy. Sometimes, although rarely, a crack appears through which one glimpses a momentary flash of the old Adam, as in the dark and savage stories of smuggling days or in tales of piracy and wrecking. As we look at the history of the ancient ports of the Eastern Shore, we shall come upon these characteristics from time to time and lo! the past is at our hand to make clear the present.

2

Tilbury

"To See a Fine Lady Upon a White Horse"

ALTHOUGH the traditional boundary between Essex and Middlesex has always been accepted as the course of the River Lea which enters the Thames at Bow Creek — nowadays a very sad and sordid meeting — so much of each county has been absorbed for all practical purposes in London that it seems realistic to regard Tilbury as our first Essex port.

As one of the chief ports in the United Kingdom it is nothing short of paradoxical that this place should first figure in history, not as a port but as a fort. Of Tilbury itself little is especially worthy of notice beyond the fact that according to Bede, St Cedd from Lindisfarne established a church here in the seventh century, as well as another church at Bradwell which is referred to in a later chapter. It seems fairly well accepted that the placename is derived from *Tilaburh* — Tila's Fort.

When Lord Halifax in the seventeenth century exhorted England: "Look to your moat", the importance of naval power as an essential element of defence had already come to be recognised; but two hundred years earlier this was not yet fully apparent and in the days of the earlier Tudors men still relied on coastal 'blockhouses', some of which — or their successors — are still to be seen in our maritime countries. So it was that in 1539 Henry VIII caused a fort to be built at what is now known as West Tilbury.

It was here that in 1588 a large concourse of troops consisting largely of the Trained Bands of London and adjoining counties was assembled under the command of the Earl of Leicester, not to engage the Armada itself; but as a flamboyant gesture of defiance to Parma's men whom the Spanish ships intended to ferry over as an invasion force. This seemed to be the occasion for a grand gesture by the Queen who was rowed down the river from London to Tilbury. Having arrived, she mounted a white horse and wearing a steel corselet — so 'tis said — and bearing a marshal's truncheon, rode among her troops who cheered her to the echo.

Her speech on this occasion has been quoted so often as to afford food for the ribald:

> "I am come amongst you, as you see, at this time, not for my recreation and disport, but being resolved, in the midst and heat of the battle, to live and die amongst you all to lay down for God, for my Kingdom, and for my people my honour and my blood, even in the dust. I know I have but the body of a weak and feeble woman; but I have the heart and stomach of a King, and of a King of England too, and think it foul scorn that Parma or Spain or any Prince of Europe, should dare to invade the borders of my realm; to which, rather than any dishonour should grow by me, I myself will take up arms, I myself will be General, Judge, and Rewarder of every one of your virtues in the field."

Fine resounding words which stir the emotions nigh four hundred years later. Truth, and a rapid calculation of time and distance, uneasily remind us that when Elizabeth was at Tilbury she almost certainly knew that the Armada, hard-hit by the English gunners and disordered by Hawkins' fire-ships had streamed away northwards without taking a single Spanish soldier aboard. If that had been known to the reluctant heroes at Tilbury, it would have been a major task to keep them all under arms until it was known that the danger had passed its point of no return.

The fort so confidently raised by Elizabeth's father stood until 1667 when the Dutch took advantage of the sorry state of our navy to cock a snook at the Thames-side defences. The Netherlanders were able to do little damage at Tilbury because in the Lower Hope they encountered a small but determined squadron under Sir Edward Spragge. As usually happened whenever they were resolutely opposed they withdrew with alacrity; to appear again three weeks in the abortive attack on Landguard Fort at Orwell Haven.

These events called for a re-appraisal of the existing fortifications and this resulted in a completely new fort designed by Sir Bernard de Gomme, who while still a Dutchman had come to the notice of Charles II during his years of exile in the Low Countries. De Gomme had studied with Vauban, the leading French military engineer of his time, and in his reconstruction employed such sophistications as star-shaped bastions and twin concentric moats. There were moreover riverside batteries outside and in support of the fort itself. As it happened the new fort never had to face up to an attack again; by then we had learned our lesson; this country continued very seriously to look to its moat — at least until recent years!

It may be that England tended if anything to rely overmuch on her naval supremacy; for in 1783 it was noted that Tilbury which in 1766 had mounted fifty-four guns, had by then fallen into a bad state of repair; moreover it was then the only fortified place in the whole of Essex.

Nevertheless nearly fifteen years later, in 1797, the guns of Tilbury spoke in anger when they fired a few rounds at the boats of the Nore mutineers who were rowing round the fleet in an endeavour to raise support among other crews.

Tilbury continued to be an essential part of the Thames defences, although today Sir Bernard de Gomme's fort is but an interesting Ancient Monument of no strategic significance in the context of contemporary national defence. The world-wide fame of Tilbury today rests on an entirely different basis, its character as a port. To trace the origin of this — not yet a century old — one must look westwards up London River to London Town.

Ever since Londinium developed as the Roman capital of Britain its potential qualities as a *portus* were recognised and developed; in fact it may well be that this maritime advantage was one of the factors which brought about the rise of London over Colchester as the capital city of the Province. Throughout the centuries of successive Roman, Saxon and Norman supremacy, the wharves and hythes of early times grew in size and complexity so that at the end of the twelfth century the Canterbury monk, William Fitz Stephen, admirer and biographer of Becket, could write:

> "To this City Merchants bring in Wares by Ships from every Nation under Heaven. The Arabian sends his gold, the Sabian his Frankincense and Spices, the Scythian Arms, Oil of Palms from the Plentiful Wood; Babylon her fat soil, and Nilus his precious stones: the Seres send purple Garments; they and Norway and Russia Trouts, Furs and Sables, and the French their Wines."

In 1661 the first wet dock was constructed at Blackwall, which was capable of accommodating ships of considerable burthen, such as the "brave new merchantman" which Pepys saw a-building there. This opened a new era when no longer would it be needful for ships unable to come alongside the wharves to discharge into lighters with consequent detriment to their cargoes. Other docks followed through the eighteenth and, more particularly, in the nineteenth century thus adding to the city and its environs the great area of 'Dockland'. The dock companies themselves were in constant competition with each other and in 1886 the East and West India Dock Companies joined together to go right outside London down stream to Tilbury and thus the huge complex of Tilbury Docks was born. In those days when the great steamships of the East Indian trade, together with countless sailing-ships including the classic China clippers thronged London River, this competitive move proved an attractive proposition, although it proved anything but beneficial to some of the other London dock companies. The journey up river was shortened by some twenty-six miles and passengers arriving at Tilbury could get to the City of London at Fenchurch Street, and thence to the other London termini, without undue delay. There were no planners in those days to complicate still further the traffic congestion of the capital city.

In 1909 the Port of London Authority was formed to take over the management of the River from Teddington to the Nore and twenty years later in 1929 Tilbury Docks were enlarged, with land held in reserve for yet more expansion in due course. Besides improving the accommodation of cargoes in warehouses as well as bringing the dock equipment up to date, it was possible to improve the river itself to accommodate the larger vessels which modern progress demanded.

To a small boy the sight of these great ships with their evocative names and the brown-skinned Lascar crewmen brought a vicarious sense of the allure of the mysterious East, the memory of which has not dimmed after three score years and ten which an unfeeling Fate decreed that he should spend in the land of his birth, loving her none the less while he nursed the frustration of a life-time.

3

The Isles of Essex

A QUESTION which can always be relied upon to provoke discussion to the point of vehement disagreement is how many islands are there in the British Isles? The answer, according to the best authorities is that there are about five thousand. After the first gasp of disbelief, and after we have allowed the Shetlands, Orkneys and Hebrides to account for nearly seven hundred, there still seems a terribly sizeable gap to make up the balance. The chief difficulty is that no-one appears to have laid down a canon to determine what is an island according to the rules. It presumably must include skerries, which are sizeable rock formations exposed only at certain states of tide; but can this also include mere sandbanks? And what of those areas encircled by water so confined in its channels as to be almost within the extent of the proverbial biscuit-toss? Of these 'islands' there is an abundance and often their insularity is nought but a merry jest among the local wits. An exceptional conglomeration of such islands *honoris causa* is to be found in the region of the Thames Estuary and more especially along its Essex side. Ignoring the Isle of Dogs — which is in any case beyond the traditional western boundary of Essex — we find as the river begins to open out near its confluence with the Medway at the Nore, such islands on the Essex shore as Canvey, Havengore, Rushley, Potton, New England, Foulness and Wallasea. These — with the exception of Canvey — are often referred to collectively as the Essex 'archipelago'; but seeing that they sit so snugly close-gathered, this seems not entirely appropriate. The whole area is more like a delta; but of which river it is hard to judge. The Roach which separates Wallasea from Foulness and the rest here joins the Crouch as a tributary or confluent; but its tidal relationship is such that it must sometimes seem more like a backwater. It is tempting to think that Rochford means the ford over the Roach; but the etymologists will not have it so. It is, they say, 'the ford of the Hounds', there being an Old English word *raecc* which means a dog which hunts by scent. They do not adduce any story to support this romantic theory; but they may well be right, none the less. If they are, the Roach is presumably a 'back formation' even if it is no backwater.

Of all these islands the one which is most prominent in the public eye nowadays is Foulness; and here before we begin to think of the place the name of which is so lightly bandied about as a bone of contention, it might be well to put on record that this name is derived from the promontory at its north eastern end which juts out as the southern tip of the Crouch estuary. In the early thirteenth century it was 'Fughelness' — the ness or promontory of the birds. In spite of this, much play will doubtless be made of the emotively derogatory sound of the name as spelt today.

If the true meaning of Foulness evokes any thoughts at all, they must be sad ones. Once this island was a fertile place with ample grazing for cattle and sheep. Since the middle ages, and perhaps earlier, the ewes had been milked and good cheese made, comparable to the ewes'-milk cheeses of the north country. Through consistent 'inning' of land from the sea, the arable acreage had increased likewise; but in 1855 a change came about which at its inception was no more than the minute cloud which Elijah's servant saw from Carmel. Although the country had barely recovered from the disastrous Crimean War, there were those with the forethought to have a mind to national defence and especially the significance of ironclad ships and the shore-based artillery powerful enough to deal with them. Hence sprang the War Office establishment at Shoeburyness and the development of part of the Maplin Sands as a testing-range. Still Foulness continued as a remote but flourishing farming area, while the guns thundered, although the sea-birds stayed to breed and feed in their ancestral haunts, harassed less by the rumble of the big guns than by the constant activities of the wild-fowlers.

Meanwhile farming went on until the War Office wanted more than the open spaces of the Maplin Sands and sought to acquire the whole of Foulness Island as an experimental area for weapon research. A long period of negotiation followed; for the Lord of the Manor was not very disposed to part with his interest. Eventually authority won and although farming activities have gone on with marked success, the overall control by the War Department with the inevitable restrictions on access have kept casual visitors away.

Now alas! after much rancourous discussion it looks as if the new airport may be situated here together with a huge dock complex on Maplin and Foulness sands. No one will attempt to deny that each of the three inland sites suggested as an alternative would be equally disastrous in its destruction of ancient churches, gracious villages and towns with rich farmlands. But by the same token this wild lovely place with the birds who have lived here for so many centuries and some of whom have annually winged their way here from so far away means the annihilation not only of a place of irreplaceable beauty but the disjointing of a whole facet of the natural order. The land is exceptionally fertile and the standard of its standing crops, to say nothing of the mustard which although considered unusual in 1688, is now of outstanding quality in the world. The wild flora are in some cases unique and will join the other victims of this projected holocaust. Does it really make any sense; or has man developed to a stage where sense no longer has any meaning? The irony of it all is that perhaps almost as soon as the airport is complete, the necessity to have long runways for take-off may be itself as obsolete as the stage-coach. If this be more substantial than a utopian dream the irony will blossom into catastrophic tragedy.

Meanwhile the Isles of Essex still dream in their ancient peace and hard by, the seaward bound waters of the Crouch as they skirt the northern shores of Wallasea and Foulness harbour the very antithesis of the ear-splitting cacophony of the giant jet planes. Here is Burnham, best-known centre of yachting on this side of England, sometimes hailed as the East Coast Cowes.

It was not always so. In the final decade of the last century Burnham was nothing more than a pleasant fishing village offering to the less ambitious yachtsman a congenial stretch of water, and in those days, reasonably accessible from London by train.

Yachting is a strange yet kindly obsession. When in 1661 the Dutch presented Charles II with *Mary* and the *Bezan* they also — albeit without any conscious desire to infiltrate the English language — presented us with a new word. That the emphasis was on racing would appear from the connection of *jacht* with the verb *jagen* — to hunt. Charles was no newcomer to the joy of sailing a boat with skill and pluck — he certainly was never lacking in the latter quality. At the age of sixteen when he was living in Jersey to secure his safety from capture by the Parliamentary rebels, he learned to handle a boat and this love never left him. When two years later a mixed fleet of nineteen ships appeared off the Kentish Coast in an attempt to rescue the King, the Prince was in command and throughout his life both Charles and his brother were as devoted to ships and sailing as they were realistic in their assessment of the nation's need for naval supremacy. From this stemmed the interest in Harwich which three centuries later might so easily have become the equal of Cowes in very truth. Why this did not happen will be told hereafter.

The story of Burnham's rise to fame as the pre-eminent home of East Coast yachting is almost haphazard. Although the town was known as a fishing and trading harbour in late mediaeval times it was not outstanding and the references to it are sparse compared with those relating to other Essex ports. It was only occasionally called upon to find ships for the King's service and while it is probable that a certain amount of wool was shipped out it seems unlikely that this was in considerable quantities. It has also been claimed that it was popular as a landing-place for pilgrims bound for Walsingham; and this is linked with the known fact that such parties passed through Thaxted. It is tempting to suggest that there has been some confusion here with Burnham in Norfolk; but it may well have been attractive for travellers from the Low Countries of Northern France, and in any case there may have been good reasons not unconnected with other mercantile operations. It seems however that the chief interests of the men of Burnham was in fishing, largely of oysters, and where there are fishing boats there are inevitably to be found the men who build boats and who are wise in the ways of handling them. This was of course generally known among the 'pleasure' sailors who knew that part of the coast and they found it a congenial place to sail and also to lay up their craft. Eighty years ago or thereabouts as others, besides this original handful of yachtsmen came to know of this haven of peace, gradually the numbers grew.

As the Crouch waters became better known the trade of the town profited accordingly. Unfortunately the period was not one of undiluted good taste and a due sense of the value of things; indeed such words as environment and planning were unknown in the vocabulary of late Victorian and Edwardian days. In the result the little collection of small Georgian houses and homely clap-boarded cottages, never very formally arranged, have now been swamped by a horde of shop-fronts, the inevitable chain-stores and undistinguished modern overflow. The quay is still functional and dignified by reason of that very quality; but the hugh towering mass of the Yacht Club — however eminent the status of the Club itself — is something which can be neither harmonised with nor subdued by neighbouring development. The river itself is far removed from that haunt of ancient peace which it was to our parents and grand-parents. It is crowded with craft of every shape, size and most important of all, social status. It is true that a man tends to be as much the slave as the master of his boat; but paradoxically the airs and vanities of the owner tend to rub off on to his craft so that his own social aspirations are displayed for all to see and admire or deprecate according to the personal predilections of the viewer.

Once upon a time 'yachting' had one overwhelming bond of union between the rich man in his luxury yacht and the poor man in his little old hooker — they both loved the sea and all that went with it — indeed like Rat in *The Wind in the Willows* they liked "messing about in boats." Nowadays the boat has tended too much to become a Sacred Cow, and not only at Cowes! Too many people have yearned to own a boat because it is 'the done thing'. They regard it as a status symbol to be recognised and duly admired by all the other Joneses. Once it was a common subject for good-humoured jest that yacht owners spent more time tinkering with their craft under the accepted blanket-term 'fitting-out' than they did in sailing or cruising; but at least they had a wealth of fun and most of them did their own work with their own hands and the right honest tools to help. When they came into the bar they might have a few dabs of paint or tar on their hands or their clothes. In the camaraderie of their own sort they discussed how to set about this job or that. With a few notorious exceptions they avoided vain boasting of what they had done or high-falutin' talk of what they were going to do.

Nowadays the balance of money as distributed over the general run of boat-owners has changed and the attitude to the owning of a boat has changed with it. Many races are now sailed over a bar on which the surf never breaks, around buoys of handled glass and where the crack of the finishing gun has given place to the clang of the bell at closing time.

And yet — and yet — naught can rob the ship of her magic. If fibre glass and synthetic stopping has robbed us of the sweet scent of pitch-pine and tarred cordage, the lure is still there; and by and large the folk who own a boat, have ever owned a boat or dream of one day being owned by one are still brothers under their shaggy jerseys and, maybe, even more shaggy hair.

From one thing, however, Heaven preserve us in such a happy band: the barely water-borne dodgem-cars which career about the waters of civilised people, sometimes aggravating their nasty, noisy, noisome antics by trailing moronic clowns on water-skis. They should be banished from all inland or off-shore waters and relegated to some well-buoyed area well out of sight and sound of the outermost territorial waters of every civilised nation. Here they can career around and, with luck, collide with each other until like some aquatic Kilkenny cats they are silenced for ever.

So far we have omitted one island which, although it has been named in connection with the Essex archipelago, is not itself part of the group. Canvey is often regarded as larger than any of the others; but this in fact is not true as Foulness is nearly three square miles larger in area. Like the six other islands it has for centuries been the object of constant attempts to protect it from inundation by the sea and for even better reason than in the case of its neighbours, because its whole extent lies below the level of spring tides.

Ever since Roman times the erection and strengthening of sea walls has preoccupied Kings and Churchmen alike. The Danes established a fortified camp there — and to do this asked permission from no one. In 1622 the Canvey landowners compounded with a Dutchman, Joas Croppenburgh, to carry out the necessary works of sea-defence, on condition that they should convey to him one third of the lands so reclaimed. From this originated the strong Dutch influence on the island which has left its traces in the distinctively 'round' houses still to be seen here and there. For at least a century after this Dutch settlement some Canvey folk lived almost as a Dutch enclave. No ties of blood deterred the Dutch from landing on Canvey when they were rampaging on the Thames and Medway in 1677. Besides looting cattle and anything else of value, they burnt the Church and so went their way rejoicing. It was a shameful time for England, "as dreadful a spectacle as ever Englishmen saw, and a dishonour never to be wiped out". Nevertheless in the years that followed the Netherlands were repaid in full and after their trouncings at sea they had to rely on their undoubted capacity for intrigue to attain their ends — and quite a deal of profit. Far, far older than the Dutch invasion are the 'Red Hills', which have occasioned so much speculation and donnish controversy. They are not peculiar to Canvey and are found in several places on or adjacent to the East Coast estuaries. Several theories have been advanced to account for their origin and purpose, as varied as that they were the remains of early potteries or even 'dumps' of calcined matter to provide the material for coastal 'hards'. Present opinion however leans to their being associated with ancient salt pans. Although the existence of extensive salt marshes afforded brine of a more than usually high degree of salinity it seems hardly likely that in this part of the world the water could be evaporated by the mere heat of the sun. It seems that in very early times the salt water was poured over heated stacks of clay rods — or as we should say 'elements'. This explanation receives some support from the fact that 'Red Hills' are found where salt-pans are known to have existed.

In the years before the First World War some financial opportunists set on foot a great money-raising device whereby hundreds of hopeful souls invested their small savings in plots of land on which there developed an appalling rash of bungalows of every conceivable design — or no design at all. The era of the planners had not yet dawned, so that it argues a certain ingenuity on the part of the settlers that they could create such a degree of hideousness without any official assistance.

Not only at Canvey but in all the coastal regions hereabouts the continual war against tidal inundation by raising and strengthening the sea walls has had this unfortunate repercussion, that wherever the sea has broken through the protective works it has been retained in these precious areas as if in giant saucers, so that the task of recovering the drowned land has been made that much more difficult. At no time in history has there been so much damage and loss, not only of crops, houses and livestock but also of human life as in the 'Great Tide' which devastated the coastal areas of Norfolk, Suffolk, Essex and Kent over those few fateful days of January and February, 1953. So far as Essex is concerned the stark and terrifying drama of this time with all its tragedy and yet courage and heroism is told meticulously by Hilda Grieve in *The Great Tide*. It was a time when all were united in the face of a common peril; when the great bulk of the Yacht Club at Burnham was as it were a citadel offering a store for the essentials of rescue as well as a temporary casualty station and hospital to say nothing of the overall view of a part of the devastated area which thus provided an observation post. The whole saga is a deeply moving story; but will the moral of it all be still alive in our minds when the tempest breaks again — as break it assuredly will?

Just beyond Benfleet Creek which separates Canvey from the Essex shore lies Leigh, nowadays still the home of a busy fishing community, noted for its cockles and shrimps, and formerly also for the inevitable oysters. What it no longer has as a trading port is reflected in yachting and sailing for pleasure. In the past Leigh was of considerable importance both as a centre of shipbuilding and a fruitful source of ships for impressment into the King's service. One of the first Leigh ships to qualify for the Tudor bounty of five shillings per ton was the *Speedwell,* 105 tons, in 1574. A few years earlier in 1565 Leigh was esteemed "a very proper town where commonly tall ships do ride, which town is a common and a special lading place for butter, all manner of grain and other things". That the town was rated as of considerable importance is evident from the statement that Harwich, Colchester, Brightlingsea, Maldon and Leigh did the greatest trade in Essex.

At about this time Leigh was included in a total of 187 harbours, ports, and creeks in the county noted by the Queen's Commissioners who, be it remembered, were concerned that no fish, however small, should slip through their net. Few of these places could be reckoned as ports, being merely the odd creeks or strands where fishing boats could be pulled out of the water. Many of the vessels 'arrested' for impressment would be required as victualling craft or tenders to larger ships and seeing that the total number of ships of all sorts was but 349 with 1196 mariners and fishermen to man them, the picture is seen in truer perspective.

Today Leigh is dwarfed by its huge and amorphous neighbour, Southend, which indeed has not scrupled to swallow up a mere 'fishing village' as a picturesque addition to its tripper amenities. This is the more ironic seeing that little more than a century and a half ago, the mushroom Southend was but the southern end of Prittlewell, a village itself of a more than respectable antiquity. What began as a quiet 'watering-place' reasonably accessible from London — albeit somewhat odoriferous at low tide — came in the grim fullness of time to be what it is today; of which the less said the better!

No mention of Leigh may omit the famous Leigh Bawley, a distinctive fishing-boat with an enormously high top-mast, loose-footed gaff mainsail and bowsprit. She was chiefly used for shrimping.

Although not strictly confined to Leigh another distinctive Thames craft was the Peter Boat. Various theories have been advanced to account for this name; the most readily accepted is that associated with St Peter, the patron saint of fishermen; but whether this is in the general sense or because of the Abbey in London dedicated to the same saint, better known to us today as Westminster Abbey, is something over which the scholars may well be left to wrangle. She was a small double-ended boat of an overall pattern strongly reminiscent of Viking design, semi-decked at stem and stern with a fish-well amidships, very manageable and quick to turn. She was in fact very much on general lines like a chubby form of the whaler. It must be remembered that up to the first quarter of the nineteenth century fish for market were still being taken up to London Bridge and that these peculiarly London boats were well-known the whole lower length of London River.

This was the general pattern of the Lower Thames estuary with ports like Leigh, Barking, Benfleet and the like still carrying on their dual role as fishing towns and a modicum of general trade both taking cargoes in and shipping them out. The whole length of London River was a highway which linked the capital city with the sea traffic not only of the German Ocean and the ports fronting on that historic sea-bridge to Europe but indeed with the whole maritime world.

4

Maldon and its Battlefield

"And Battles Long Ago"

MALDON — *Maeldun*, the hill of the monument — is commonly recognised as an ancient borough and a port and yet either description is both exact and inadequate. The Saxons must have known what the monument was; but we have no trace of it today. It has been conjectured that once the hill on which the town has always stood was crowned by a cross; but it is probable that the heathen Saxons found a name for it before Christianity had become established hereabouts. It could have been a cairn, a heap of stones, the significance of which could have been known only to the men of those days. Or it may have been some last lone relic of Imperial Rome still surviving after the Legions had left and the local Romano-Britons had gone down before the waves of the land-hungry Saxon raiders. Little is known of the *colonia* at what we now know as Maldon; but there is some slight evidence of its existence. Camden believed that this was part of Camulodunum and Defoe in one of his characteristic excursions into history without tears persuaded himself that here Boadicea was subjected to the scourging and humiliation which sparked off the blood-bath of the Iceni rising. The belief that Maldon occupies part of a colony, *Idumanum,* and that the Blackwater is the *Idumanum Fluvium* of those days — later known simply as Maldon Water — is not entirely without foundation.

It was five and a half centuries after the final departure of the Eagles, although only four after the end of the effective Romano-British resistance, that Maldon emerges from the mysterious shadows of the Dark Age.

Much must have happened since those far-off halcyon days when the Roman veterans and colonial officials enjoyed a prescribed and ordered way of life on the high ground looking out across the saltings where the rivers met and lost themselves in the broad waters of the German Ocean. The long twilight that settled upon Britain was succeeded by what has to later generations been an impenetrable night of which we know nothing and can merely conjecture how

the old order died. Of the first century and a half there is no
record and even when the first Christian missionaries appeared to
bring back the Christian message we have to rely on the accounts
of Bede and other early chroniclers who themselves were writing a
century or more after the events of which they told. The whole
period from the end of ordered Roman rule to the full emergence
of an Anglo-Saxon Christian culture was roughly equal to that
space of time which separates us today from the Wars of the Roses.
But during that time the social scene had become something very
different from the dark days when the savage raiders from the
mouth of the Elbe had crept in their cranky boats up the East
Coast rivers to burn and loot and slay. The scholars and craftsmen,
the churchmen and statesmen of England were known and respected
throughout civilised Europe. When Charlemagne was crowned as
Emperor of the West in 800, standing at his side was his chief
minister and architect of the Empire, Alcuin of York, a churchman of noble Northumbrian lineage.

But by now a new cloud had appeared from the North East, the
Vikings from Denmark, Scandinavia and the Baltic fringe. They
professed very much the same dark beliefs as had the Angles and
Saxons when they first came, but they were a far more sinister
foe. In general they came in search of loot, especially the gold and
silver and jewels which they knew were to be found in the
Christian monasteries and cathedrals. In this the Danes exceeded
the Norsemen in cruelty and rapacity. Their longships, using the
sail as much as oars, could swoop upon any desirable target which
would offer them treasure worth the taking. Moreover, — far more
than the Saxons in their day — they took a positive delight in
slaughter, especially in its more uncivilised forms. In 870 the
Danish host had sacked Ely, Peterborough and Croyland and
murdered Edmund King of the East Angles.

Forty years after St Edmund's death Edward the elder, son of
Alfred of Wessex, set about the Danes in no uncertain manner and
took heavy toll of their leaders as well as some English 'quislings'
who had aided them. In 913 he fortified Witham and while the
work for this was going on he took up his quarters at Maldon of
which he made a similar strong point to control the coastal
approaches. In spite of the respite of the Peace of Wedmore and
the establishment of the Danelaw in 991 a mixed force of Danes
and Norsemen attacked Ipswich and then went on to the Essex
rivers.

By this time the Englishmen were preparing to confront the invaders and to whom should they look more hopefully than the great Earldorman, Brihtnoth, a great giant of a man — "viribus robustus corpore maximus" — who stood six feet nine inches tall with a great mane of silvery hair and, in spite of his sixty-five years, could fight and lead. One can judge his kind of leadership from the story that, when marching southward to gather his forces, he sought hospitality for himself and his carles at Ramsey Abbey in the Fenlands. The Abbot, with an eye on the housekeeping problems posed by this request, made polite excuses for not entertaining more than the Earldorman himself and his thanes. To this Brithnoth retorted in high fury: "Tell the Father Abbot that since I cannot fight without my men, I will not eat without them."

The Abbot of Ely, taking the hint from this rebuff, offered full hospitality and indeed rejoiced at the number of his guests. In gratitude for the warmth and courtesy of this welcome Brihtnoth gave to the Abbey some of his Cambridgeshire manors with the promise of even more if the monks would receive his body, should he fall in battle.

What happened when the Earldorman arrived at Maldon is well known; for the whole story is preserved in imperishable verse which, except for the legendary song of Beowulf, is the earliest poem in the Anglo-Saxon tongue. It has been compared to the Iliad and although this comparison has been discounted by some, it makes epic reading whether in Anglo-Saxon, which is not for everyone, or in one of the modern English translations, provided that it preserves the saga-rhythm of the original.

Col. Alfred Burne has reminded us in *More Battlefields of England* that few other battlefields in English history have changed so little over the centuries and it is relatively easy to trace exactly what happened by observation on the ground today. The English having gathered at Maldon, which was itself a fortified town at that time, moved out eastwards to where the Danish army was assembled on Northey Island. At high tide the two armies could only hurl abuse at each other because there was no means of crossing from the island to the mainland except by means of a 'bridge'. It is this mention of a bridge which has bedevilled many historians in their assessment of the circumstances of the battle. The Anglo-Saxon word *brycg* meaning either a stone or wooden span or a hard causeway, has misled people into visualising a situation rather like that surrounding Horatius in Macaulay's poem. In this case it has been assumed by some writers that the Danes approached from Heybridge; but there is no evidence that there was at that date any kind of bridge at Heybridge. In fact the very name Heybridge was not known until the thirteenth century. Moreover the story of the fight goes on to detail the deployment of the Danish forces in a manner which would be impossible unless they could open out while still in act of crossing.

Whichever theory is nearer the truth, the plain fact remains that until the tide went down the armies could not meet. As soon as the Danes could advance they did so; and the story goes on to tell how Brihtnoth chivalrously allowed them to form up before attacking. This accords well with the character picture of Brihtnoth himself, although it is a surprisingly sophisticated act of courtesy for those rough days. The incident is not entirely without parallel in later times as at Agincourt and Flodden; but in those cases it resulted from a challenge in the first case by the French, in the second by the English. At Fontenoy, in 1745 the French are credited with a similar gesture — "Messieurs les Anglais, tirez les premiers".*

When eventually the two armies really got down to business it was a bloody affair. Brihtnoth was wounded by two javelins in succession and fell; whereupon the Danes set upon his prostrate body and hacked him into pieces. Cutting off his head they carried it off, doubtless to be tastefully mounted as a drinking-cup. When the body was received by the monks of Ely they made a ball of wax to replace the missing head and this, together with the size of the bones, helped to identify the warrior's remains when they were found buried in the north choir wall at Ely in 1772.

The words put into the mouth of the dying hero are themselves epic in the simple piety with which he commends his soul to God with thanks for the good things which had given him joy in his life.

For the Danes it was an undoubted victory, although but a Pyrrhic one since they had been so mauled by the English that they could scarce man their ships and made off without any tangible loot. But the overall result was disastrous; for this was in the

---

*Truth compels us to observe that this courtesy was a brittle thing, seeing that the first to fire would have been at a disadvantage. In any case the parallel is hardly worth pursuing, seeing that this battle is not one which the British Army commemorates as a victory!

reign of Ethelred the Unredy — which does not mean 'unprepared' but 'un-counselled' — and in the same year that Brihtnoth died so valiantly at Maldon the first payment of £10,000 was made as Danegeld.

At the Domesday survey Maldon had a population which has been estimated at a thousand or possibly more. It had its own mint and had already acquired a status comparable to Colchester, indeed it scored a point ahead of Colchester by being granted a charter by Henry II in 1155. Colchester, although mentioned as a borough in Domesday did not receive a formal charter until 1189 from Richard I. Although the town had confirmations of this charter from Edward I, Richard II, Henry IV, Henry V, Henry VI, and Henry VIII, as well as new charters from Mary, Elizabeth and Charles II, Maldon still based its fishing rights, as late as 1830, upon the original Angevin charter.

A large part of Henry II's charter is taken up with a long and recondite recital of the various freedoms and privileges conferred upon the Borough. Whether in the original Latin or its equivalent in contemporary English these terms are more familiar to the legal historian than to the general reader. The most important provision from the aspect of the town's maritime history is that which decrees that the Burgesses are to be quit of every kind of foreign service except the provision of one ship when necessary for the King's service for a period of forty days as was done in the time of King Henry I. This obligation would seem indeed to go even farther back in time; for it appears from the Domesday survey that in 1085 besides providing a house for the army the burgesses also contributed to building a ship.

The date of Henry II's charter is not without interest in a national context; for it was executed at Pembroke on 7th October, 1171, a few days before the King set out for Ireland with the intention of consolidating the tentative expedition two years before by Strongbow in aid of Dermot, King of Leinster. Henry had at the same time much else on his mind. His stormy relations with the Archbishop of Canterbury had culminated in the murder of Becket the previous December and he had only just returned to England after despatching a conciliatory mission to Rome, whereby he hoped to calm the wave of horror which had swept through Europe as the result of this atrocious happening. In England his position was precarious and he may well have wished to enlist the support of such towns as could be relied upon to remain loyal in opposition to some of his stormy and dissident barons. On 18th October he landed at Waterford and a few weeks later he contrived to be acknowledged as King. The consequences of that fateful entry into Irish affairs have bedevilled subsequent events in the British Isles ever since.

The town's mint had its beginning over a century before Domesday and the earliest coin known to have been struck there has been identified as of Athelstan's reign — 924-939. It is now preserved at Rome and it has been hopefully supposed that it reached there as a contribution to Peter's Pence. By a similar flight of imagination Maldon coins found in Scandinavia have been associated with the payment of Danegeld. That they could have found their way abroad in the ordinary course of trade is apparently too pedestrian and unromantic to be a tenable possibility.

It has been fancifully suggested that this obligation to supply a ship for the King's service bears a significant resemblance to the Cinque Ports; but the comparison is not very convincing. The scale of their contribution, their close association and their strategic position to command the Narrow Seas are factors to which Maldon can offer no parallel. A further point of resemblance, namely the arms of Maldon with its three lions passant guardant impaling a ship on the waves of the sea, is more superficial than significant. The Cinque Ports used the gold lions of England, passant guardant on a red ground 'dimidiated' with three hulks silver on a blue ground. The character of these arms is unique and unmistakable in meaning and there seems little doubt that — as some heraldic writers have propounded — this design was intended as a Royal naval standard and it was as such that the Cinque Ports used these arms.

In the years which followed the grant of Henry II's charter Maldon grew steadily in maritime status and besides supplying its annual quota of one ship as and when required, the skill of Maldon shipwrights became known up and down the coast. During the Hundred Years War two vessels from Maldon are known to have been included in Edward III's fleet gathered for the siege of Calais in 1346 and over two centuries later a ship was found for defence against the Spaniards. Whether she ever took part in the battle is not certain; and seeing that the Armada was defeated as much by the elements as the English fleet, it is not of much consequence. Brave and skilful as Elizabeth's sailors were, the moments of panic among the Spaniards when the fire-ships were wafted among them, followed by the gale which blew them northwards combined to save the country from this considerable peril. "Afflavit Deus et dissipantur", "God breathed and they were scattered", as the Psalmist exultantly sang.

Perhaps one of the best known ships built at Maldon was *Jersey*, 556 tons, in 1654 during the period of the Commonwealth. Apart from the fact that her builder was one Sterling — who probably called himself Starling — little is known of her early years; but it is noteworthy that her name was not changed at the Restoration. She fought in the 'Four Days Battle' against the Dutch in the Downs in June 1666, the first issue of which was rather in the nature of a 'draw'; but her name as the *Jerzy* has achieved a certain wry immortality by reason of the fact that she was for a short while 'commanded' by Samuel Pepys, in circumstance recounted in the Diary on 13th March, 1668:

> "But that which put me in good humour, both at noon and night is the fancy that I am this day made a Captain of one of the King's ships, Mr Wren having this day sent me the Duke of York's commission to be Captain of 'The Jerzy' in order to my being of a Court-martial for examining the loss of 'The Defyance' and other things; which do give me occasion of much mirth, and maybe of some use to me, at least I shall get a little money by it for the time I have it; it being designed that I must really be a Captain to be able to sit in this Court."

Three days later Pepys, having occasion to go down to Deptford by water on other Admiralty business, saw, but did not go on board, "my ship 'The Jerzy', she lying at the wharf under repair".

The court-martial was at Chatham and once it was over we hear no more in the Diary about *Jersey*. Samuel after chuckling over this short-lived charade, seems to have been content to return to the more congenial world of the Navy Office, although it seems that his knowledge of administrative affairs had a daunting effect upon the gallant sailors sitting with him on the Court.

In 1672 *Jersey* fought in the Battle of Solebay, of which more hereafter, but nineteen years later, in 1691, she was taken by the French who, *horribile dictu,* used her as a privateer and, like Sir Richard Grenvill's Revenge, ". . . . away she sailed with her loss and and long'd for her own." However she was not to die of shame in spite of her enforced bondage under Lettres de Marque: for in

1694 she was in action with a British squadron and sank with honour. One of her opponents was, ironically Resolution, built in 1667 at Harwich; that same Resolution whose flag-officer failed to prevent William of Orange reaching Torbay in 1688.

Maldon seems to have enjoyed Admiralty jurisdiction at least as far back as 1528, which is the date of the first known grant; but it seems fairly certain that it existed for some considerable time before that. The Admiralty seal is still in existence and is a remarkably fine one with its bold design of a ship of early sixteenth century date. It does not seem very certain when the jurisdiction ceased to be exercised; but it may be significant that the civic insignia does not include a silver oar as is usual with most ancient ports which have ever enjoyed such status. The mace, dating from 1687, is exceptionally large and is claimed to be one of the largest in the country, which is true so far as it is within a score of maces of four feet or more in length! It is remarkable that municipalities are so eager to lay claim to a place in this exclusive company. Some of the loveliest and oldest examples of this emblem of mayoral dignity are quite small and one suspects that many such may have been sacrificed in efforts to keep up with the Jones' — or even to excel them. Indeed it is known that many large specimens have been acquired by cannibalising older ones. It has been, as two learned authors wrote many years ago, very much like Aaron's rod swallowing up the rods of the Egyptians.*

The Maldon mace originally bore the initials of James II; but for these there have been substituted A.R for Anna Regina. The original initials of J 2 R for Jacobus Rex II still appear on the crown surmounting the mace-head.

During the eighteenth century Maldon throve mightily, and especially in maritime trade, until in the second half of the century more than half of the town's population was so employed. In 1797 a scheme to link the Chelmer and Blackwater by means of a canal nearly fourteen miles long was carried into effect in spite of the opposition of those who feared that the traditional traffic of the natural Blackwater channel would be prevented from coming to the Hythe. In fact the existence of this link brought fresh trade to the town and two flourishing factories, one a ploughmaker, the

---

*The Corporation Plate and Insignia of Office of the Cities and Corporate Towns of England and Wales. Llewellyn Jewitt, F.S.A., & W. H. St. John Hope, M.A., 1895.

other an ironworks, moved to advantageous sites to their own and the town's advantage.

Another firm, John Sadd and Sons Limited, which now manufactures timber frame-work and builders' materials, is in direct line of descent from an old-settled family of carpenters. Towards the end of the eighteenth century they already owned their own fleet of coastal vessels plying between Maldon, London and ports of Western Europe bringing timber and building materials and they are still in the same line of business today, although now linked with other firms within the framework of a well-known consortium.

The name of Maldon's own river has often given rise to speculation; but although there is obviously some muddy constituent in the saltings spreading each side of the estuary the water is no blacker than anywhere else, the name being derived from the colour of its bed.

Even when it is compared with other East Coast rivers the proportion of salt is very high and this has resulted in the survival of a thriving salt-making industry which flourishes today. The distinctive flavour of Maldon Salt is well-known and recognised, so that is highly esteemed as an epicurean feature on the tables of the discerning.

Actually the upper part of the river is known as the Pant, tradionally pronounced "pont", whence some have essayed to fasten upon it a deviation from the Latin *pontus*, a river.

During the period of the Napoleonic War, Maldon like most coastal towns had to take the usual quota of soldiery and it was during these martial days that a considerable number of the gracious late eighteenth century and early nineteenth century houses were built by officers stationed here. In this respect Maldon is not unlike Woodbridge in Suffolk, where the same thing happened. There is indeed a certain resemblance between the two towns in the general appearance and atmosphere, each very gentle and mellow, welcoming and friendly. There is rather more evidence of industry of that period at Maldon and more evidence of a busy coastal trade at Woodbridge; but they still seem to have much in common — or so it seems to the visitor.

Nowadays the great sailing barges lie at the Hythe as of yore; but no longer on their old ploy. Most are owned by 'yachtsmen', although like many yachtsmen the owners probably spend more time re-fitting than going to sea — or anywhere else. That is the strange joy of being owned by a boat; she is more demanding than a woman, she absorbs your whole love and attention, she never says "Thank you"; — but she never complains, never answers back!

Throughout the ten or twelve estuarine miles which separate Maldon from the point where the Blackwater joins the sea, to which it has made its genial unhurried journey, there is no place of outstanding maritime importance today. Past Northey Island where the Danes and Norsemen had clustered in boisterous assembly before joining battle with the valiant Brihtnoth and his men some of whom may rest, "friend, foe — in one red burial blent", beneath the barrows on Osea Island, hard by.

On the south side of the estuary lies what the geographers are pleased to call, rather grandly, the Dengie Peninsula. It does not really look much like a peninsula and Dengie is a quiet unassuming village situate four miles back from the estuary. Nevertheless at some time in the past it was sufficiently important to give its name to a Hundred and in that same Hundred there lies the pleasant riverside village of Bradwell. In times past it was a small fishing port happily content to mind its own business, culling the harvest of the sea — and maybe, turning a discreetly blind eye to a trifle of smuggling when the riding-officer's attention could be distracted. Today it is overshadowed by the vast cubical concrete bulk of a nuclear power station where, with arrogant expertise, modern man tinkers with the angry atoms to feed his high-speed turbines despatching ninety megawatts to be dissipated in the endless hunger of *la dolce vita*. Visually the structure of the station is tolerable. It is functional and if the alternation of light and shade produce at times a somewhat sinister effect of brooding power, it is one of those things we have to live with until we find some more gracious way to tap the natural bounty of the universe. The wise men tell us that the station will have a working life of thirty years or thereabouts, by which time man may have dreamed up something which will make this place as obsolete as the treadmill.

Not very far away, and indeed almost within sight of the power station, there stands another building of a very different age and order. Apart from a few sporadic interruptions during the last four centuries it has been a power-house of another and more enduring sort of energy for thirteen hundred years and no man has yet ventured to set a limit of a life-span to that which is by any human standards unmeasurable.

To tell the story of the little stone shrine which, under the simple name of St Peter-on-the-Wall, stands fronting the restless grey waves and near enough to be kissed by their spume when the East wind breathes strongly one must go a long, long way back in the web of time.

When the Romans planned the system of fortresses to hold in check the Saxon raiders — that formidable chain reaching from Spithead to the Wash — they sited one at a place which is named in the *Notitia Dignitatum* as Othona (Bradwell). Archaeological opinion has from time to time been divided over the exact location of this fort and this is not the place to set out all the arguments of the learned in line of battle. Let it suffice to say that the final weight of opinion seems to favour a position on the rounded north-east shoulder of land around which the Blackwater sweeps to meet the open sea — at times not without the boisterous bonhomie of old salts.

We know that for most of the time the garrison was a regiment of North African auxiliaries, the Fortenses; but there may have been a dash or so of the various shades of 'colour' which the Roman Army included in its ranks without much racial consciousness. A man stood on his merits as a professional soldier, in very much the same way as he does in the British Army today. The remains of the fortifications are slight and haphazard; but it is fairly evident that it must have followed the general pattern of the other forts of the Saxon Shore. The plan was probably that of a near-square on a base of approximately five hundred feet with walls about twelve feet thick and with solid bastions, the chief functions of which was to provide permanent mountings for the heavy cata-pults which could hurl projectiles of formidable weight at attackers.

The exposed position of the fort has inevitably resulted in con-siderable sea erosion throughout the centuries and no doubt a great deal of the material has been taken for local needs. There was never enough stone to satisfy the more perfectionist of the Roman masons; but as we know in their own words; "We do not meet everywhere such materials as are most desirable, but make use of whatever is available:" following this policy a great deal of septaria has been used here, as well as Roman bonding-tiles.

Some two hundred years after the presumed withdrawal of the Roman forces there came here a Monk of Lindisfarne, Cedd, whose brother Ceadda, was bishop of the Mercians, now better known as Chad of Lichfield. The East Saxons had relapsed into pagan ways and driven out the previous bishop, Mellitus of London. Cedd set about his work with the approval of the King of the East Saxons, who in fact had appealed for a missionary to shepherd his wayward subjects back into the fold.

Unlike his milder brother Chad, Cedd seems to have been a pretty tough disciplinarian — and perhaps needed to be; but he appears to have commanded their love as well as obedience. For him the firm foundations of the Roman fort were a boon. In the main gateway he built his church right athwart the line of the wall and it may be that the excellence of the Roman work is the basic reason for the fact that the church stands today. Whether this is in fact the original one or whether it succumbed to Danish raids and was re-built is not certain. There must have been other buildings to house the little community; but they have not survived. Of the church itself we know that it was longer than the present one and had an apsidal end. In fact there are reasons for thinking that in those far-off days it may have been a harmony in stone, unconsciously representing the three elements of the primitive church, Eastern, Western and Celtic. What was standing in the fifteenth century was used as a chapel-of-ease to the parish church at Bradwell two miles away on the very road along which the Romans marched at their brisk four miles to the hour and Christian worship went on continuously until the Reformation. Thereafter it was used for secular purposes, possibly as a beacon and certainly as a barn, until 1920 when the then owner had what was left restored and the building was re-consecrated by the Bishop of Chelmsford. During succeeding years further restoration was carried out and today it is in active use as a Christian church on 'pilgrimages', and other special occasions.

All this has little to do with the maritime history of Essex and its seaport towns; but no one visiting this place can fail to be moved by the spirit which seems to pervade it. The simple stark simplicity of the chapel is filled with something which is not of this age. In the whole of Britain it can be matched only with Iona or Lindisfarne. The memories of Canterbury, the majesty of Durham, the Marian ecstasies of Walsingham, nay! the mystery of Glastonbury itself — 'the English Jerusalem' — none of these can compare with this sanctuary of surrender and abnegation, the oneness with nature, with the restless ocean and the voices of the sea-birds.

Such is St Peter-on-the-Wall. Like Moses of old we know that the place whereon we stand is holy ground.

5

City of Cymbeline

"It is a proper towne walled and is thought to have flourished in the time of the Romans."

WITH these complimentary yet cautious words John Norden, that accurate delineator of our homeland, introduces what is in many ways one of the most fascinating towns in the whole length and breadth of England.

The very name of the place provides a rewarding field-day for the etymologists. Looking back to the nostalgic fairyland of pure legend, our forefathers sought to derive the name from old King Cole — or Coel — who besides settling himself for prolonged and pleasurable potations also prepared to listen appreciatively to the outpourings of his contemporary 'Group' and may well have been a real person. The chief difficulty to this derivation is that the only British chieftain or general of that name, or something very like it, seems to have confined his activities to the immediate promixity of Hadrian's Wall which was in any event not built until a century after the Romans had already established a *colonia* at or near the town of *Camulodunum*. It seems probable that this word was of British origin and meant the fort or strongplace of Camulus who — give or take a letter or two — appears to have been a Celtic war-god. The evidence that a British King, called Cunobelinus, more familiar to us as Shakespeare's Cymbeline, held his court hereabouts is plausible. Here we are asked to believe that because of the Roman *colonia* the river Colne was thereby so named, which is just possible; for there are other Colnes in the country. On the other hand, since the town was later known as Colneceaster the river-name may be a 'back-formation' from the name of the town. Eilert Ekwall in his *Dictionary of English Place-names* most sapiently says, "The etymology is obscure." How very true!

What we do know is that Cunobelinus was friendly towards the Romans. His neighbours probably regarded him sourly as a 'collaborator' but it must be remembered that Roman culture to a considerable extent influenced the British aristocracy even before the early expeditions by Julius Caesar. Like their kinsmen in Gaul they had been fully aware of the advantages which might accrue from living it up according to Roman colonial standards and no better way was there, not merely to keep up with the local Joneses but indeed to be more than one move ahead of them.

Part of the myth of King Coel is the story of Helena, who is reputed to have been the King's daughter, and who captured the affections of the Roman general Constantius: from this union sprang the Constantine hailed, somewhat superficially, as the first Christian Emperor. It is all a most touching story and on the strength of it, coupled with Helena's reputed discovery of the relics of the True Cross, Colchester today incorporates in the Borough Arms a cross 'raguly'. To murmur that Helena is, by Christian tradition, said to have been born in Bithynia and that her son Constantine, while issuing the Edict of Toleration which protected Christians from persecution, was not himself baptised until shortly before his death, may perhaps be regarded as mere captious criticism.

The *colonia*, the settlement of *veterani*, time-served soldiers, which formed the nucleus of the new town was somewhat higher and to the east of the old British city; but it is evident that it developed on a considerable scale. Besides the usual lay-out and characteristic features of a Roman colonial city there was also erected after the visit of the Emperor Claudius and also, presumably, after his death, a magnificent Temple dedicated to him as being divine, which by then the Emperors had assumed.

The new town speedily became of prime importance in the province from every point of view. It was strategically placed as a place of military importance, as well as governmentally and commercially. In many ways it was deemed of greater dignity than Londinium and it could easily have become the capital city.

Then came the rising of Boadicea. The Iceni and Trinobantes swept down on Camulodunum, overpowered the garrison and sacked the town with great slaughter before moving on to Londinium and Verulamium which they treated likewise. Excavations both at Colchester and London have repeatedly disclosed physical evidence of the fires which accompanied the massacres. Eventually of course the rising was crushed with the same savagery as had accompanied its outbreak and a new Camulodunum arose to replace the old. It never seems to have recovered its former prestige as compared with London; but it was nevertheless always a city of outstanding importance and remained so throughout the remainder of the Roman Imperial regime in Britain.

The walls which had failed to keep the vengeful horde of Britons out were at their reconstruction greatly strengthened and a large part of these walls are standing today. It is not true of course that they survive to a degree comparable with those of Chester, York or Lincoln; but it must be remembered that besides damage accruing from the destructive hands of time, the Parliamentary artillery in 1648 left scars which are ineffaceable.

After the final departure of the Eagles from Britain in 440 and during the Dark Ages the exact history of the town is obscure and most of the little we know has been derived from constant and painstaking archaeological excavation. It is natural and logical that this has concentrated on what remains of the great Roman metropolis; but even of that a great part is buried or laid waste beyond recovery. When the Roman buildings have been submerged by subsequent structures of worth and having an historic status of their own, the loss may be more easily tolerated. It is fairly certain, for example that the *podium* or stone platform of the Temple of Claudius sacked by the Iceni, provided the major part of the foundations of the great Keep built under Eudo Dapifer in the early years of the Conquest. During the six and half centuries after the fall of settled Roman government the town area had been occupied in some sort by the occupying Saxons who seem to have taken advantage of the protecting walls; but in due course the Danes moved in and remained there until they were driven out by Edward the Elder. The Danes were not conspicuously adapted to the fenced-in compactness of the town dwellers and the shape in which they left the town is evident because one of Edward's first tasks was to restore the walls.

It seems likely that there were still traces of the old Roman city still standing and indeed one of the Conqueror's reasons for choosing to build such a massive castle here may have been the vast hoard of Roman masonry and rubble still on the site.

Although a large part of William's castle was demolished in 1683 by a local ironmonger who seems to have been a kind of 'Steptoe' who hoped to make his profit out of the materials, the Keep itself still stands, the largest Norman Keep in the country and reputed to have been designed by Gundulf, Bishop of

Rochester, who is also credited with the design of the White Tower of London. Huge though the Keep — generally known as the Castle — may seem today it was once half as high again as it is now and of course the outworks and baileys would occupy much more ground as well as adding to its total strength. It was occupied on several occasions by various sovereigns and sometimes by other less welcome visitors, as for example, the French troops brought in to support the barons who were in rebellion against King John. This was before Runnymede and Magna Carta, that magic touchstone of the freedom of the Englishman, so often invoked and so rarely relevant to the cause of the common man. In 1157 Henry II had held court here when Thomas Becket was present with his Royal master before the alternating quarrels and reconciliations between them to be eventually resolved so bloodily over thirteen years later.

With the passage of the years Colchester grew in importance until it nearly matched the greatness of the ancient Roman city. Not least of the town's claims to notice was its significance as a port. In 1347 the town provided five ships and 170 men for the fleet mustered for the siege of Calais; but there seems no mention of Colchester ships at Sluys seven years earlier, although five ships had sailed in Sir Walter de Manny's expedition to Brittany in 1342.

Not a little of Colchester's prosperity was derived from its river. Besides providing the town with a direct access to the sea, albeit not always without hindrance as the size and draught of ships increased, Colne water proved to be very suited to the fulling of cloth. The arrival of the Flemings in the fourteenth and fifteenth centuries was due to a combination of reasons. The extensive loss of land in the Low Countries due to the flooding of the Zuider Zee in the twelfth century had resulted in a certain number of Flemings seeking a home and a livelihood in the Eastern counties. Subsequently this trickle became a steady flow when Edward III encouraged the craftsmen from Flanders to settle here with the deliberate intention of improving the quality of English cloth; and so the worsteads and their derivatives the 'bays and says' for which Colchester became famous were born. Whether 'worsted' is a corruption of Worthstead in Norfolk or — as some aver — comes from an old Dutch word 'ostades' a kind of cloth of similar substance is better left for the etymologists to wrangle over to their heart's content. What is certain is that in the villages and small towns of Suffolk and Essex the clothiers and weavers flourished mightily. The motives for combining the production of our excellent native wool with the conversion of that wool into high grade cloth are matters for another story. Edward's fiscal problems, keyed as they were into his insatiable need of money for his French war, do not concern us here. The result of all this was a degree of prosperity which has left behind it the magnificent 'wool' churches, the opulent merchant's houses and many ancient charities which still dispense to aged and deserving people the largesse of those who were gathered to their fathers long since but whose names linger on and deserve the respect of us today. We live in an age when such things may be much better organised, but with less warmth and compassion.

As for the Flemings whose original craftsmanship went to the making of all this prosperity — well, we learn that human nature has not changed overmuch. The attacks on their persons, property and reputation by those who were ultimately to benefit from their skill, displayed a shockingly low standard of 'racial relations' which has a very modern touch!

Much of these new materials was produced in or near Colchester and loaded on to ships at the Hythe for carriage not only to other parts of England but also in many cases to be shipped to European countries whose expatriates had taught us the very skills which had brought these goods forth.

Like most English towns of substance there was a Jewry in Colchester until Edward I decided that the Jews must leave England. The size and importance of the town may be estimated as in most mediaeval towns by the number of churches or religious houses of which there were eight within the walls and eight without in 1594. There were also formerly a Benedictine Abbey, a Priory of Black Canons and two Friaries of Grey Friars and Crutched Friars, as well as the inevitable and indispensible leper hospital. Most of the parish churches survive in some form or another, some mangled as much by restoration as the hand of time. Generally Colchester has been fairly conscious of its old buildings; but Holy Trinity Church, the most interesting from an antiquarian viewpoint, having been found redundant, has been given over to vandals and the pigeons because Authority has been unable to come to a decision as to its fate. This is the kind of thing that happens in many old towns. Piety, or apathy, prevents the demolition of an old building; but if it gradually crumbles into ruin, all is well and Bumble slumbers on until it is too late for anybody to do anything. In the case of Holy Trinity Church there is a Saxon doorway with a pointed head and some parts are probably older. There is also a monument to William Gilberd, Physician to Queen Elizabeth and James I and commonly hailed as the Father of Electrical Science. *Absit omen!*

In 1648 Colchester, although being deeply committed to the cause of the Parliament had a Royalist garrison under the Earl of Norwich. The Parliamentary Forces under Lord Fairfax then invested the town and the famous siege, which lasted eleven weeks, began, bringing in its course great suffering to the defenders and inhabitants as well as enormous damage from the cannonade during which the Royalists had to subsist on their own cavalry horses and the town's cats and dogs. Their ammunition ran so low that Lord Norwich was reduced to firing back the Parliamentary cannon balls for which he paid sixpence each when they were retrieved by patriotic opportunists within the walls.

Eventually the Royalists surrendered on terms; but this did not deter the chivalrous contenders for the liberty of the people from shooting two of the defenders, Sir Charles Lucas and Sir George Lisle. It was believed that for many years thereafter the grass would not grow where this dastardly deed was done. An obelisk now marks the spot.

During this distressful time the affairs of the town do not make momentous history. In time if civil strife there is neither rhyme nor reason for what is done and in the end it is usually found that no one has profited in the least. Meanwhile the port continued to operate despite the continual difficulties of handling ships up the stretch from Wivenhoe through the combined handicaps of erratic depths and ever-increasing draughts of the ships. There were no powered tugs in those days and where there was no room to sail there was no alternative but to quant the smaller ships and warp the larger ones to the Hythe. Defoe wrote in 1724:—

> "This Hithe is a long street, passing from West to East on the south side of the town: at the West end of it there is a small intermission of the buildings but not much, and towards the river it is very populous (it may be called the Wapping of Colchester); there is one church in that part of the town, a large quay by the river and a good Custom House."

At Wivenhoe, now chiefly occupied with yachting and yacht-building, there has always been shipbuilding on a reputable scale. Here was built in Commonwealth days *St Fagan* which, together with *Jersey*, were the first men-of-war to be built in Essex.

In the mid-eighteenth century the colliers could rarely get above Wivenhoe and it was usually necessary for their cargoes to be transhipped into lighters, while at the same time there was a constant demand for sea traffic to take the products of a flourishing textile trade to other markets both at home and abroad. All kinds of schemes were initiated to improve the river but most came to naught. It was obvious that to maintain a constant depth and a non-tidal channel the river must be locked and this was done in 1740 but within ten years the lock was dilapidated and unusable. Meanwhile much maritime trade had passed to Maldon.

Eventually Peter Bruff, that brilliant engineer who was to do so much for Harwich and Ipswich, who has been described as the 'Brunel of the Eastern Counties' submitted a scheme for the construction of a lock at Wivenhoe with a straight ship canal seventy feet wide leading to a dock of eleven acres at the Hythe. But neither Bruff nor any other engineers were taken seriously; for the very men who were charged to safeguard Colchester's sea-gate were merchants who knew that such a scheme would involve locking fees and other dues which would have to be borne by themselves and the shipowners. Meanwhile the muddle went on with delay in handling such cargoes as could reach the Hythe which was still not free from tidal rise and fall, often resulting in damage to the ships themselves.

A further complication was the constant war between the ship-owners and the oyster 'farmers', because the water between Wivenhoe and Fingringhoe and the sea was the centre of what, during a large part of Colchester's history, was its principal business interest.

As far back as Roman times the oysters of the Colne were highly esteemed and exported, at least to Rome and probably wherever Romans were stationed who could afford to indulge their sybaritic taste for that delectable mollusc, *ostrea edulis*. Oysters are of course found in many parts of the world and of various sizes, from the huge ones which were found in the Wash to the tiny 'button' oysters found among the Whitstable natives and which decrease in size after they reach a certain age. It would seem that the Romans still preferred the Colne oysters; for shells have been found in Rome which have been identified as of East Anglian origin. That the oyster has always been regarded as a staple product hereabouts is evidenced by the oyster-gauge which is part of the mayoral insignia. Most famous oyster towns have their own traditional ceremonies at the opening of the season; but the Colchester Oyster Feast has for long been the most famous. It used to be the practice to invite to this dignified junketing a whole galaxy of eminent people in Church, State, Law or Diplomacy and occasionally Royalty was included. It is however now considered that the ancient and civilised habit of selecting the guests according to the wishes of the hosts must cease as this disgraceful display of free-will is 'undemocratic'. That the feast is of considerable antiquity would seem to be apparent. Apart from reference to the Feast at about the time of the Restoration, the fact that it was usually held around the date of St Denis' day would seem to suggest pre-Reformation beginnings. There were several saints of this name but the most probable, the Archbishop of Paris whose name became a French battle-cry "St Denis for France", has his Feast, in both the pre-Reformation and Anglican calendars, on 9th October and if St Denys' Fair has opened a little later in more recent years that is probably due to the change from the Julian to the Gregorian calendar in 1752.

What is more puzzling is that the earliest date on which oysters could be eaten with safety -- and propriety -- in London was reckoned as 25th July, the Feast of St James the Great, and it is said that the habit of London children making 'grottoes' of oyster shells originated in this way. It is perhaps both purist and captious to recall that the symbol of St James as exemplified at his shrine at Compostella, was a scallop shell. The price of these 'early' oysters was based on their scarcity; hence the proverb that 'he who eats oysters on St James's Day will never be short of money'. For Londoners of more modest means the date was 5th August; but here again there is the same hiatus of ten days. Is this also connected with the transition from the Julian to the Gregorian Calendar?

It is not surprising that Colchester was always ready to battle on behalf of the oyster fishery and even the shipping was not allowed to disturb the precious beds. Nevertheless, as will be seen hereafter, the men of Colchester and Brightlingsea were not above exploiting other beds farther up the coast and if the owners were not prepared to come to a commercial understanding then the Essex men would not disdain to indulge in a little nocturnal gathering from other men's waters. It must be added that besides these clandestine coastal trips, English fishermen went farther abroad and less than a hundred years ago they went annually to the Channel Isles as well as to Holland and the Frisian Islands, the West Country and even Scotland. The Dutchmen, Frenchmen and Scotsmen alike all resented these intrusions into their home waters. Nowadays we hear much of the validity of 'territorial limits'; but in sober fact, this has been going on for centuries and the naive belief held by many fishermen that the world is their oyster, so to say, is rarely admitted by the sitting tenants. Nor is this battle of rights confined to the subject of the said mollusc!

Nowadays the Customs House at Colchester is not especially noteworthy for its architecture which is strictly functional; but one of its predecessors was in 1748 the scene of an audacious display of force when thirty armed men raided the Customs House and carried off a considerable amount of smuggled goods which had been seized and impounded by the excisemen.

The relations between Colchester and Brightlingsea do not appear to have been noticeably difficult, possibly because their interests in the oyster fishery were largely identical. Nevertheless there must have been occasions when Colchester resented the status of Brightlingsea, a relative upstart when one thinks in centuries, as a 'limb' of the Cinque Ports. Nor would the situation be eased by the fact that the particular port concerned in this doubtful guardianship was Sandwich, possibly the most piratically minded of the whole confederacy. The fact that Brightlingsea lay down stream from Colchester might easily have put the older town at a disadvantage as happened so often on East Coast estuaries; but there does not seem much evidence of this having been the case. Perhaps the older brother was also so much the bigger brother that it really was not worth while for Brightlingsea to try a tussle. After all is said and done, Sandwich lay a long way off, and Colchester was close at hand. Today Brightlingsea is a busy yachting centre and a favoured place for retired folk who have no use for Fun Fairs and Bingo Halls. There is the usual caravan rash on one side of the town but the whole place is quiet — some people might think it too quiet; as a rule sailing folk like it that way. The traditional pronounciation 'Brykylsea' is alas, yielding to the more sophiscated and tongue-twisting Brightlingsea, but the more homely form can still be heard.

Halfway between here and Colchester lies the very pleasant riverside town of Wivenhoe, also given up to boat-building. It is reputed that under the Commonwealth a man-of-war was built here; but Cromwell's government was not lavish in naval expenditure. Between Wivenhoe and its opposite neighbour, Fingringhoe, there used to ply a ferry, but like many other ferries it has succumbed to 'progress'.

The reason for Sandwich, a 'Head Port', claiming Brightlingsea as a 'limb' or non-corporate member of the confederacy is obscure. It may well be that for reasons of local strategy it suited the Portsmen to have an 'outpost' on the East Coast. Not only would it serve these maritime Bashi-bazouks to have a hidey-hole where they could refit before prowling up and down the North Sea on their not-so-lawful occasions; but this place on the Colne was that much nearer their ancient rivals at Yarmouth — of which more hereafter. Brightlingsea may have felt that as a limb of Sandwich they enjoyed some added status in the matter of ship service for the King. In Ethelred's reign, each three hundred hides had to find a ship for war service, on which basis Brightlingsea would have to join twenty-nine other places to fulfil this obligation — a complicated, undignified arrangement. At Domesday Dover, Sandwich and Romney found ships for the King; but we may be sure that by then the Men of Kent had seen the eventual advantages as well as the disadvantages of having special and private relations with the monarch.

Throughout the Hundred Years War a whole succession of ships were provided, not necessarily or usually ships of war; but rather for transport of stores. It is possible that some of these went to Britanny with Sir Walter de Manny's expedition to relieve the Countess of Hennebon who was besieged in her own town by Charles de Blois whose claim to the Duchy of Britanny was supported by France. The chronicler tells us that de Manny arrived when all seemed lost, whereupon the Countess, coming down from her castle, kissed Sir Walter and his companions one after the other two or three times. "She was a valiant lady." Indeed she was: for women knew then how to take their rightful place in human affairs without the aid of any Liberation Movement or such-like gimmicks.

In 1588 when England was mustering her meagre resources to face the threat of a Spanish invasion Edmund Bocking, Vice-Admiral of Essex, reported that he had 'stayed' — or arrested — seven ships of 30 tons or upwards:

> "There is within this county a town called Brightlingsea, being a member of the Cinque Ports, having good shipping to the same which have stayed and certified as the rest until your honour's pleasure be further knowen therein. 22 were listed at some time or another and we know their names and tonnage and the names of their masters. Seven were fifty tons or over."

During the siege of Colchester in the Civil War two Royalist ships attempted to make their way up the Colne; but the Parliamentary ships hid in Brightlingsea Creek and attacked the Royalists as they came up the river.

The story has not lacked embroidery; for it has been said that the Dragoons who had taken the Mersea Fort to prevent any interference with this manoeuvre rode into the water to attack the King's ships — mounted presumably on sea-horses since the ships must have drawn five or six feet at least!

On the right bank of the Colne estuary facing Brightlingsea Creek lies Mersea Point, the eastern extremity of Mersea Island, which covering about eight square miles and separated from the country south of Colchester by a narrow channel, the Pyefleet, is lapped by both Colne and Blackwater as they unite to meet the sea.

There is clear evidence of Roman occupation and besides the burial mounds there was — until it was overlaid by modern building operations — what may have been the base of a Roman lighthouse, *pharos,* which would probably have marked the channel up the Colne to Camulodunum.

There was certainly shipping activity in mediaeval times; for in 1342 Mersea sent a ship to join in Sir Walter de Manny's expedition to Brittany. In the Tudor survey of coastal defences the vulnerability of the Colne estuary was recognised by the construction of a bulwark at East Mersea and it would seem that this or its successor was the fort captured by the Parliamentary dragoons at the time of the abortive attempt by Royalist ships to succour the garrison of Colchester during the siege of 1648.

In 1801 the threat of a French attempt at invasion was countered to some extent, by stationing river barges carrying four guns each at the mouths of the Colne and the Blackwater.

Mersea has always been an island rather more than by mere geographical nicety; for the folk living there have been very aware of their identity, although all that separated them from 'England' was the narrow width of the Pyefleet crossed by the one road known as the Strood — or Strode — which even today is often impassable by traffic at times of exceptional tide. Here again the oyster has always been an essential part of the island economy, supplemented by considerable yachting activity and boatbuilding. There has been a great deal of building, some of it being of a somewhat pretentious type; but there are still quite a number of traditional cottages scattered about cheek by jowl with the self-conscious ruralism of stockbroker folkishness. Inevitably there is the inevitable caravan rash; but somehow it all adds up to a pleasant blend of honest-to-goodness fishermen and the sailing folk who find it so necessary to assume a species of troglodyte hirsuteness before they can handle a mainsheet or pitch their garboard strake.

Away across the broad bosom of the Blackwater estuary towers the Bradwell power station and contrasting with its grey bulk the tiny chapel of St Peter-ad-Murum, timeless and immutable.

6

Harwich

"But Orwell coming in from Ipswich thinks that she
Should stand for it with Stour and lastly they agree
That since the Britans hence their first discoveries made
And that into the East they first were taught to trade
Besides of all the Roads and Havens of the East
This Harbour where they meet is reckoned for the best."

IN THESE words Michael Drayton, who in *Polyolbion* endows the rivers and towns of his England with human characteristics, sums up not merely the mythical contest of Stour and Orwell but what is not myth but very real history, the continual rivalry between Harwich and Ipswich.

As we shall see, Ipswich, the older and larger and richer port, was constantly handicapped in her maritime development by certain natural deficiencies of the lovely waterway which linked her with the sea. From time to time there were also difficulties in her own body politic, largely of her own making — but that is another story. It is not disputed that Harwich enjoyed the better share of the natural haven formed by the meeting of the Stour and Orwell and to which the latter river gave its name and the fact that the excellence of that haven derived much from the protection afforded by the sheltering arm of Landguard — *lang gar*, the long spear — was not likely to place the practical men of Harwich under any obligation to their neighbours. That was a dispensation of Providence who had so shaped the coastline, so why moralise upon the obvious.

Harwich derived its borough status from a charter of Edward II in 1319 which placed it well behind Ipswich in the seniority stakes; the king did not fail to remind the new town that "greater privileges involved greater obligations". Fine words; and Harwich was probably duly elated thereby. Certainly, the burgesses were apt to stand very much on their dignity. The name of the place is believed to be derived from *Herewic* — the place, or camp, of the army, and from early days there must often have been a militant element about the place; for the Bigods played an important part in its early days and it may well have been a case of "like master like man". In 1253 Roger Bigod, Earl of Suffolk, granted the town a weekly market and that there should never lack 'trade' for that market was easily ensured; for it seems that complaint was made that:

> "neither the said Earl nor his men of Oreford allow the merchants, who wish, to put in at the town of Ipswich with their merchandise; but against their will he compels them by force to put in at Herewiz, which town of the said Earl's, taking their sails, anchors and steering gear and drawing their ships to dry land, taking their merchandise at will and they pay what pleases them for the same merchandise whereby the town of Ipswich is much depreciated!"

In the same manner did the Earl disport himself up and down the coast in true Bigod fashion, despoiling the ships of all who sought to sail on their lawful occasions and treating the whole Haven of Orwell as his private preserve. In 1285 another Roger Bigod, nephew of the aforesaid Earl was called to answer a writ of *quo warranto* with regard to rights of wreck in those parts of the coast. What came of this is not recorded; but it would look as if, notwithstanding the notorious misdeeds of the Bigods, Harwich still stood well with the King; for in 1338 Edward III granted murage to the men of Harwich and in the grant referred to the Port of Erewell, i.e. Orwell, "pertaining to the said town". The significance of this would be that every ship passing through the haven would have to pay this levy in aid of the maintenance of the town wall of Harwich and it is not surprising that Ipswich protested so vigorously that within six weeks the grant to Harwich was withdrawn.

This trifle does not seem to have deterred Harwich; for an inquisition held two years later to determine the exact boundaries of the Port of Ipswich revealed that John But, the Bailiff of Harwich, was still collecting the murage dues, willy-nilly, in spite of the revocation, thereby discouraging merchants from visiting Ipswich.

And so the merry ding-dong between these thriving ports went on to their mutual glee, but with little profit it would seem to either town. In 1513 Henry VIII granted Admiralty jurisdiction to Ipswich to the further chagrin of Harwich and certain unedifying displays of civic dignity ensued as will be told hereafter.

By Edward III's reign Harwich had become well established as a port of high repute. It was from the port of Orwell that the King set sail on the expedition which was to bring about the first English naval engagement, Sluys, of such success that the history books have given sufficient attention to impress it even on the fugitive memories of most schoolboys. During the time that the King was gathering his ships he lay chiefly at Shotley; but the size of his fleet was such that Harwich was more involved than any place on the far side of the Stour. For this campaign the town found 14 ships and 283 seamen which was not only more than from any other Essex port but indeed more than anywhere else on the East Coast, save only such towns as Newcastle, Hull, Boston, King's Lynn and Yarmouth. It was already the largest 'harbour of refuge' on this side of England and so remained for another five centuries.

In 1339 Harwich men came to the help of a Flemish ship which had been driven into the haven and there attacked by the men of Yarmouth who seemed to spend most of their time harassing the ships of any nationality passing up and down the coast. In return for this 'interference' the Yarmouth crews threatened to burn Harwich. The King being appealed to by his loyal subjects of the latter port declared that if the Yarmouth bravoes carried out their threat he would "provide another remedy". Whatever may have been the import of this cryptic warning, the gentlemen from the Yare seem to have taken the hint! It is all rather like a father having to cope with a whole family of naughty boys and the monarch's success in keeping the peace at home had to be balanced against his need to rely on the provision of ships and men when he had a war on his hands.

This was long before the provision of a Royal Navy and the practice of impressing ships and men or alternatively raising a levy out of which these could be purchased or hired had been well recognised since Anglo-Saxon times. It was a two-edged affair; for without ships of war the coast towns complained that the king had left them defenceless, while they were always reluctant to play any part in the provision of those ships. Nor was the obligation to furnish vessels restricted to the coastal towns. In 1461 Essex was 'invited' to join with Suffolk and Hertfordshire to raise a fleet at their own cost against the French and Scots, although Hertfordshire has never been a conspicuously maritime county.

Eventually of course this was to become a great national issue and there are many people today who piously believe that those who refused to pay 'ship-money' in defiance of this eminently practical and commonsense practice are for that reason to be hailed as champions of English liberty! Even the maritime towns themselves were ready to grab at any excuse to evade their responsibilities. When Colchester pleaded that they could not meet their levy Essex refused to help and even when Suffolk was prepared to bear a third of the costs in conjunction with their neighbours this was refused by the towns as insufficient. The situation was often quite unreasonable and not only in the seventeenth century battle between King and Parliament. When the King failed to provide ships to protect the traders and fishermen he was blamed for diverting what ships there were to aid his nephew Rupert in his campaign and when he sought to exact the established levy for the purpose he was held equally culpable. It has been suggested that this maritime issue may have been a contributory cause for the eastern counties standing so firmly against the King when the conflict developed into open rebellion.

With the use of the harbour by ships of war there grew up a flourishing trade in shipbuilding and indeed before the growth of the Thames and Medway yards Harwich was the equal of Southampton. Even when those new centres of industry began to arise they were staffed principally by craftsmen from Essex and Suffolk. In Tudor days the great shipbuilding dynasty of the Petts migrated from the Stour to the Medway and indeed the two greatest Petts of them all, retained their links with Suffolk in a very personal way, as we shall see later.

With this importance attaching to Harwich it was only natural that the harbour should be regarded as especially liable to enemy attack and in 1380 and 1405 active preparations were made to deal with descents upon the haven by combined French and Spanish forces. In 1450 a French ship appeared at night and destroyed part of Harwich, killing nine men, and we learn that this calamity happened in spite of a watch having been sworn to guard the town during the hours of darkness. Moreover it was established that one Adam Palmer,

> "showed to our French enemies the very secret way of our port of Orwell leading their ships in safety to the grave damage of the town against the ordinance and statue of England".

We do not know what defence was put up by this fifteenth century 'Quisling' for his outrageous behaviour; but it must have been good; for a few years later he was one of a crew of a ship fitted out by Sir John Howard. This was the famous Yorkist who later became Duke of Norfolk and fell on Bosworth field with his master, Richard III.

Like the other East Coast ports Harwich was not immune from threats to its self-sufficiency by that perennial source of maritime trouble, the Cinque Ports. Brightlingsea — as we have seen — was rated as a 'limb' of the Ports and this provided an excuse for the Portsmen to interest themselves in this part of the coast. They also passed this way on their periodical excursions to Yarmouth where they claimed the right to sell their fish and dry their nets on the 'strond' — a claim in the exercise of which there was a plethora of broken heads and blood-letting. To interfere with the lawful shipping of other ports was as the breath of life to these rumbustious Men of Kent; indeed it has been suggested that the King regarded the presence of the Portsmen on the East Coast as a useful corrective factor to keep the Yarmouth men in their proper place and vice versa. In 1472 a Sandwich ship was hired for the 'protection' of the fishing and one may fairly speculate on how much safer every one might have been without this help!

The eminence of Harwich as a gathering place for the fleets conveying our armies during the Hundred Years War is frequently brought out in various references of that period and not the least interesting is the part played here in the embarkation of war-horses. We often find that this port or that had to provide ships with a prescribed loading capacity for horses and in contemporary manuscripts the artist's impression of a ship of the period with the horses' heads looking primly over the side inevitably reminds us of a naïve picture of Noah's Ark. But from contemporary records we can learn quite a lot of how this supply operation was accomplished. At Harwich it was necessary to supply gangways 30 feet long and 5 feet wide to lead them on board and, once there, specially woven hurdles were provided in units — or 'modules' — of 9 feet by 6 feet to protect the timbers and planking from damage by their hooves. For their securing to ensure safe passage canvas had to be procured from London and rope from Woodbridge as well as iron staples and rings. In one respect no doubt the unfortunate animals must have suffered as much as horses do today; because the horse cannot vomit, he is in misery when sea-sick. For their sustenance on the journey Essex had to find 30 loads of hay, 120 quarters of oats and 20 cart-loads of litter as well as empty tuns for carrying water.

The Main Gate, Tilbury Fort, designed by Sir Bernard de Gomme to replace the old blockhouse
ilt by Henry III.
                                                                            Essex Record Office

(ii) The Tilbury Blockhouse, built in 1539.

Essex Record Office

(iii) Barking. The Quay with Maltings c. 1831.

Essex Record Office

(iv) Where Brihtnoth fell. The reputed site of the Battle of Maldon showing the causeway whi
is believed to be the 'brycg' over which the Danes crossed to join battle with the Saxon fyr
Essex Record Of

(v) Cockle boats unloading at Leigh. These have taken over from the famous Leigh Bawleys.
Walter A. Blyt.

(vi) Mistley Church showing the body of the Church as built by Robert Adam, c. 1776, and demolished a century later leaving only the towers which remain today. *Essex Record Office*

(vii) 'Quiet Fortress'. The ancient church of St Peter-ad-Murum, Bradwell.

(viii) Colchester Hythe.

Essex Record O

(ix) Trinity House Pier, Harwich.

Walter A. Blythin

(x) 'Misleading lights'. The High Light and the Low Light at Harwich.

(xi) Harwich Crane. This crane operated by a double treadmill is now unique in England. It
almost certainly built in the reign of Charles II and has been erected on the Green whithe
was removed from the Navy Yard just before the 1939-45 War.

Besides the transport of the chargers there were also the more synthetic weapons of war, 1,098 sheaves of arrows and 1,000 bowstrings. There must also have been bows and these would have been made from bowstaves imported from Spain, Italy or Poland; contrary to romantic notions of more recent times. English yew was useless for the making of bows — if the inevitable pun may be forgiven.

Throughout the period from the Angevins to the Tudors men had passed through Harwich to take ship to the European mainland. Merchants and warriors, priests and scholars to say nothing of the thousands of pilgrims to the holy places of France and Spain and Italy. One of the chief shrines which drew the pious was that of St James at Compostella in Spain and from the scallop-shell associated with this fisherman saint is derived the popularity of the 'escallop' in symbolism and heraldry. Although the shrines of England drew pilgrims from all over Europe many pious folk from this country made the long and perilous journey to Spain and Harwich was a busy port of embarkation. When pilgrims passed in piety there was also profit to be had by those who catered for their needs. Sometimes indeed others came on less pious errands such as Isobel, the infamous queen of Edward II, who in September 1326 landed here with her paramour Roger Mortimer and a force of 2,700 men. A year later the King was murdered at Berkeley Castle in circumstances of revolting barbarity. Having shaken off the malign influence of Mortimer and avenged his father's death, Edward III proceeded with his ambitious campaign against France and, as we have seen, he assembled his fleet at Harwich in 1340 on an expedition which opened with the memorable naval victory at Sluys.

Notwithstanding the virtuous behaviour of the men of Harwich in 1339 when they upheld the King's Peace so valiantly against the freebooters of Yarmouth, some of them were not above a trifle of piracy themselves as when in 1400 certain of them hired a boat for the express purpose of boarding and plundering a ship in the open sea opposite the 'clevysende' which is presumably what is known as Cliff Foot. What happened then is not recorded nor how they disposed of the results of this highly irregular behaviour. The whole affair is by no means out of character with what frequently went on up and down the eastern seaboard of this Happy Isle, where the old adage that "dog don't eat dog" very demonstrably did not run.

The other side of the coin must not be forgotten; for in 1328 the ships of a German merchant Albrides of Bremen, one of the Hanseatic towns, were lying peacefully at anchor at Harwich when they were boarded by a party of Winchelsea men led by a notorious pirate, John Lambot, who having thrown the crews overboard, looted a valuable cargo. Eight years previously the same John Lambot had been outlawed for pillaging the valuable wool cargoes of two Flemish ships while on passage off the coast. Looking at the picture with an unjaundiced eye there does not seem much difference between all these rapscallions whether of Harwich, Yarmouth or the Cinque Ports. It was indeed true, as was said on more than one occasion, that on the German Ocean no monarch's laws were effective to protect his own subjects.

By the fifteenth century the English ships sailing to the Icelandic fishery made up a considerable fleet of between 100 and 150 vessels and of these a full tenth came from Colchester, Dedham and the Orwell ports; in 1528 these amounted to a score of ships.

In 1543 Henry VIII visited the port to survey his ships and in 1561 Elizabeth was the guest of the townsmen and lodged at a house in the High Street. It may be that she expected a more magnificent standard of hospitality; for she does not seem to have bestowed any conspicuous token of her royal favour. At that time the regular construction of ships of war was a staple factor in the town's maritime life; moreover in an age when land defences were still regarded as the ultimate deterrent to invasion, attention was inevitably concentrated on the 'bulwarks' and ordnance which could deny a vital port to an enemy.

The strengthening of the fortifications at Harwich and Landguard loomed large therefore and Thomas Cromwell had suggested to Elizabeth's father that the traditional payment of Peter's Pence to Rome might be diverted to the defence of the realm and chiefly in the building of coastal fortresses. Three forts were built at this time at Harwich, the Bulwark, the Bulwark-upon-the-Hill and the Blockhouse of the Tower. Of these one, later to be known as the Redoubt and incorporated two and a half centuries later into the Martello chain, still stands on its hill behind the town today. It is a formidable affair and has never ceased to fulfil some kind of military role even up to the 1939-45 war; it is reassuring to know that the Harwich Society is active in its preservation and restoration.

From the purely maritime standpoint a matter of the deepest concern was the strengthening of the harbour works and for this there was an ample supply of septaria, the stony deposit derived from the cliff front. This natural asset was in fact a frequent bone of contention and when Wolsey had wanted to take some of it to build his new college at Ipswich he found that the Countess of Oxford was prepared to contest his claim with all the protective instincts of any angry and maternal lioness. Eventually however the wily churchman proved the better protagonist and the Lady decided that, with the Ipswich butcher's son at the height of his power, it was better to remain in his good books. Her letter in which she signed herself as his "humble bedeswoman," is very conciliatory. There were however others in Harwich itself who cast covetous eyes at this eminently saleable commodity and because of this the harbour works were retarded not a little by the greed of the townsmen and the ineptitude of their elected representatives.

It seems likely that when Elizabeth paid her visit she was accompanied by Lord Howard of Effingham who in the year of the Armada, 1588, as Lord High Admiral, wrote to Burghley:

> "On Wednesday last I went to Harwich which I had not seen this twenty-seven years. My Lord, it is a place to make much of for the haven hath not its fellow in respects not in this realm and especially as long as we have such enemies so near us in the Low Countries . . . . . . My Lord, we can bring all the ships that Her Majesty hath aground there . . . . . . I know not that we can do so in any place else but here at Chatham."

It is uncertain that Harwich sent any ships for service against the Armada: but there is little doubt that some of those serving may have been laid down there.

It is not all a tale of neglect; for in 1583 attention was focussed on the falling off of maritime trade as the harbour grew more shallow and it was forbidden to shoot ballast or rubbish under the considerable penalty of £5 for each offence. The regulation and its sanction would seem to have had some effect; for two years later Leicester's forces gathered here for his descent upon the Low Countries. The Channel was by then so improved that foreign ships would often venture in without a pilot and by night, although there were still some hazardous banks to be negotiated at the haven entrance.

In June 1553 there put into Harwich three ships, the *Bona Esperanza*, 120 tons, the *Edward Bonaventure*, 160 tons, and the *Bona Confidentia*, 90 tons. These, together with their pinnaces and boats, under the command of their Captain General, Sir Hugh Willoughby, had cruised round from Deptford and after an experimental casting up and down the coast to flex their muscles they finally assembled in Orwell haven from which they set sail on the 23rd June on their adventurous search for a north-east passage to Cathay. These ships were well-found and the expedition planned with care; but they never reached their golden goal: for early in the following year the gallant band perished "for cold" in Lapland.

Three years later another traveller went a-voyaging, one Anthony Jenkinson, whose prime duty it was to escort the Russian Ambassador back to his master in Moscow; but he was also to explore the diplomatic and commercial possibilities of opening a regular trade with that vast land — no less enigmatic than today. Richard Hakluyt gives a long and detailed account of his experiences and from this we learn that Jenkinson was an able and meticulous observer. His description of his reception by the Czar, the customs and costumes of the Russian Court and the splendid and exotic ceremonies of the Orthodox Church is both precise and accurate and this is noteworthy at a time when few men could know anything of the fundamental difference between the Western and Eastern Christian traditions. From the reports of the prospects of trade sprang the Company of Muscovy Merchants and in 1571 Jenkinson himself was appointed Elizabeth's Ambassador at the court of the Czar.

Another traveller who dropped anchor in Harwich Harbour in 1592 was an adventurer of a very different sort. The great Portuguese carrack *Madre de Dios* had been attacked and captured by a force of English 'adventurers' who had been lurking at Flores in the Azores waiting for the richly laden Spanish and Portuguese ships. She was the largest prize which had ever fallen into the hands of these licensed pirates, whose little ships were dwarfed by her towering hull. Among the English ships was the *Dainty* with her captain, Thomas Tomson of Harwich. Although *Dainty* was first to attack, she would have fared badly had not the *Roebuck* and *Foresight* come to her assistance. It is said that the Portuguese ship carried a cargo of jewels, costly fabrics, furs, pearls, ivory and ebony worth £150,000 — a very tidy sum in those days — but by the time the *Madre de Dios* reached Dartmouth she was observed to be riding two feet higher in the water than before she was attacked! What may have happened to the best of the cargo in the interim is a matter of involved and murky speculation; but by the time *Dainty* returned to Harwich her share realised £500 when sold in the first instance, although it is believed that the booty fetched more than twice that sum by the time the entrepreneurs of Harwich town had had their 'cuts'. Hakluyt gives the whole story of her capture, the events leading up to it as well as the carnage of the battle. All in all, it is not a pretty tale and it is not improved by the knavery of the captains and 'gentlemen' which resulted in the disappearance of the greater part of her cargo which is described in great detail by Hakluyt. In spite of the glamour with which these Elizabethan ruffians have been invested, there is nothing in the whole affair to excite our national pride. From time to time someone refers in words heavy with emotion to Portugal as our oldest ally; it is wondrous to what lengths romance can go!

In 1577 Martin Frobisher set forth on his second voyage in search of the north-west passage and again on the same quest in the following year; he fared better than Sir Hugh Willoughby in so far as he returned with much which fed the insatiable curiosity of those who still dreamt of an easier way to China than the long and perilous overland route trodden by Marco Polo three centuries earlier. Englishmen were in fact no nearer the fulfilment of that dream; but much else resulted from the voyages of Frobisher and his fellows and their voyages laid the foundations of the reaching-out of British adventure and enterprise in the great white lands of the frozen north.

By the opening years of the seventeenth century in spite of the years of neglect in Tudor times Harwich had acquired a renewed importance from both naval and military points of view and in 1625 three thousand men of the Essex trained bands were moved into the town. This may have comforted the good people of Harwich — or at least those without eligible daughters — but there was something approaching panic in other parts of the country who felt themselves denuded of defence; or perhaps the loss of the soldiers had disastrous effects upon the licensed trade!

During the Civil War Harwich established a high reputation for naval refits and General Monk remarked on the expedition with which this work was carried out as compared with the Thames and

Medway yards. It is obvious that Harwich builders could bestir themselves when need arose; or were they conscious of competition from their smaller but no less competent neighbours such as Maldon or Brightlingsea or Wivenhoe?

After the fall of the Commonwealth and the Restoration of the Monarchy Harwich might have gone forward both far and fast; for both Charles and his brother were fully conscious of the importance of a well-found yard on this side of the Kingdom, especially with the sporadic outbursts of truculence on the part of the Dutch. It is strangely puzzling that the townspeople were never very enthusiastic. They may have felt that the presence of the King's ships, while giving work to many, discouraged commercial traffic with its greater prospects of substantial profits. Or could there have been a flourishing amount of 'free-trade' on the quiet which could flourish the more without the King's officers taking note of what was going on.

After a short easing-off of naval trade immediately after the Restoration the Navy Commission resumed possession of the yard in 1664 and thereafter a steady stream of ships came off the stocks. The increased depth of water and the ample size of the haven led to a marked tendency to build ships of the larger sort. Within the first thirty years out of sixteen King's ships eight were third-raters and two, the *Sandwich* and *Albemarle* were second-raters.

The activities of the Navy often brought Samuel Pepys to Harwich and the interest shown by the King and the Duke of York encouraged another maritime interest, the building of yachts.

The first time that the word 'yacht' appeared in the English language was when the Dutch presented one to Charles II at his Restoration. The King and the Duke of York were enthusiastic and highly competitive yachtsmen and it was natural that Harwich should be associated with this novel pastime which speedily attracted fresh adherents. Nearly two centuries later the Royal Harwich Yacht Club was founded and in Edwardian days the Harwich Regatta was nearly as exclusive as Cowes in the great days of yachting when the huge 'J' class with their towering masts and great spread of canvas were a normal feature of what was then a rich man's sport. Royalty and nobility from all over Europe might then be seen on the broad waters of Orwell Haven. In July, 1921, King George V brought *Britannia* here in triumph after winning the

'Down Swin' race from Southend to Harwich. Not since the days of Charles II had the King sailed his own yacht in King's Channel and the enthusiasm at Harwich was unbounded. When the King, having lunched with the Captain of *H. M. S. Ganges* embarked in the Royal Pinnace to steam up the Orwell to take tea at Orwell Park with the Commodore of the Royal Harwich Yacht Club and his Lady everybody was in very festive mood. Not least moved by this memorable occasion was the ex Farrier-Sergeant of the Royal Horse Artillery on the Orwell Park staff who sought the privilege of opening the gates to his Sovereign and who with tears in his eyes bowed low three times to the Royal Visitor, rejoicing in broken speech over this memorable occasion. Sentimental twaddle? May be; but it really happened — and was the world the poorer for this simple gesture of affectionate loyalty?

Harwich itself however, after this burst of enthusiasm was not unduly impressed by the distinction conferred on the harbour by yachting of this — or any other — order. No real effort was made to accommodate the yachts, their owners or the crews. For this reason and possibly also because of the constant traffic of the large steamers of the Continental services, the Club decided to move to Woolverstone on the Orwell where their Club House, which now caters for the owners of more modest craft, overlooks one of the loveliest and most hospitable reaches of this historic river. But this is anticipating the course of history on the Stour.

In spite of all vicissitudes Harwich has been prominent for centuries as a sea-port, naval base and fortress with a harbour unsurpassed on our Eastern seaboard for its size and depth; but it must not be forgotten that its eminence has proceeded directly from that harbour. In itself Harwich would never have had anything to commend it to the attention of its contemporaries or posterity. No home of industry, no market where merchants from beyond the seas would congregate was this little village. Nay! it was not even a village; for Harwich was originally a mere 'place' in the manor of Dovercourt — 'the enclosed place by the water'. Here was the parish church of which St Nicholas' Church of Harwich was a chapel of ease. In the mother church there was a rood, famous as an object of veneration. Maybe because of that very reputation of sanctity four Lollards, three from Dedham and one from East Bergholt, came to Dovercourt on a winter's night in 1532 and having torn the sacred emblem from its beam burnt it on the Green. Lollards were strange folk and whatever may have been the merits or demerits of John Wyclif's views — and even his fellow schoolmen could not always determine what they were — there were among his followers many crackpots and political opportunists. They were in many ways akin to our 'hippies' today and were regarded as disruptive of civil peace as well as theologically dangerous. Of these four who thought to spread the light of the Gospel by making a bonfire of the image of its Author, one escaped and the other three were burnt. Today the importance of the two places is reversed. While Harwich is functionally an important place and a chartered borough, Dovercourt is its residential quarter with some aspirations to be regarded as a watering-place. Here the latter-day vandals have not been idle, as the mutilated statue of Queen Victoria and, when last visited, the gaping window-frames of the cliff top shelter testify.

But to return to Harwich. When at the Restoration the significance of the harbour was appreciated, Lord Howard's commendation of it as a "place to be made much of" was justified over seventy years after his historic letter to Burghley. The threat from Holland was an ever-present menace and the Navy Office was faced with a two-pronged problem. Not only was the maintenance of this hive of naval activity essential to the safety of the realm; for that very same reason the harbour itself must be protected from attack. Both Charles and James were constantly looking-in on the shipbuilding and fortification and their indefatigable Clerk of the Acts was equally preoccupied with this matter which was of prime concern to all who were sufficiently clear-sighted to set the welfare of England before ephemeral matters of internal and party politics.

It is true that even those who had at heart the well-being of the kingdom were sometimes limited in their appreciation of day-to-day matters of practical importance; as for example when Pepys himself, faced with a proposition to erect a lighthouse at Harwich, assured the Duke of York that in his opinion all lighthouses were useless and a burden upon trade!

There were times however when Pepys proved himself a practical and perspicacious man of affairs, as for example when in 1686 an 'Algerine' ship had the audacity to put into Harwich for supplies and a re-fit. For a century or more shipping on the East Coast had been harassed by these pirates from North Africa who did not hesitate to venture outside their Mediterranean hunting-ground to prey upon the rich merchandise of the European merchants. The Mayor of Harwich was a man of deeds. Without further ado he consigned these sons of Islam to the town gaol, confiscated their ship and only then reported the matter to London. This posed a difficult diplomatic problem; for at that time England had for very sufficient reasons, a treaty of peace with the Bey of Algiers. In the circumstances Pepys could see no alternative but to instruct the Mayor to release the Moors and to supply them with stores — at a proper and reasonable price — while at the same time ensuring that any English slaves aboard should be released.

In 1688 the country had to face a fresh Dutch menace, this time of a different order. It was no secret that William of Orange was planning a descent upon England following long and murky intrigues with certain members of the Whig aristocracy. So determined were these patriots to oust their lawful sovereign that they did not scruple to plot with his unsavoury son-in-law. With this in mind the Navy, who were in general loyal to James, whom they respected as a brave and naval-minded man, whatever his religion, took what precautions they could to close the East Coast ports to their traditional foe. To this end, all buoys and navigation marks which could help an invader were removed both at Harwich and in the Thames. Nevertheless William eventually set sail in a fleet the van of which was commanded by the faithless Vice-Admiral Arthur Herbert who was probably aware of the preparations for defence on the East Coast. Eventually the usurper landed at Torbay in Devon. How far that issue might have been brought to naught had the English admiral lived up to the name of his flagship, *Resolution* — herself built at Harwich — is another story, not to be told here.

The arms now used by the borough, 'gules a portcullis or' have been confirmed by a Grant in only relatively recent times; but they seem to have been used for the past three or four centuries. Nowadays the portcullis seems very apt for a mercantile port because this Tudor badge is the official device of the Customs service besides being in common use as a State emblem. In the case of Harwich is it presumably no more than a coincidence that the town should bear such a simple and pleasing heraldic design? In 1565 Harwich lay within the Ipswich Customs area which then extended as far as Tilbury; but the Commissioners who were charged to go into the matter considered that the town should have a Customs House here because large ships frequently could not get up the Orwell as far as Ipswich and in consequence often had to sail away again with their cargoes uncleared — and undischarged. The traffic at Harwich itself must also have fallen off as the harbour silted up and of the nine quays working in 1577 few were practicable for ships of greater draught, by the standards of those days, until the ban on tipping ballast and rubbish brought about a great improvement.

Even with these improvements the approaches were by no means easy and there was always a menacing group of sandbanks in the approach to the haven between Harwich and the Suffolk shore. Like the sands in the Wash even their names were, and still are, gruesome and unfriendly: the Altar, Glutton, Gristle and Bone. One channel keeps for ever the imperishable memory of Nelson. In 1801 he found himself in Harwich Harbour in *Medusa* with a foul wind and an urgent need to get quickly back to the Nore. He knew of a passage across the Naze Flats into the Wallet and Goldmer Gat; but no one would believe that anyone could find there water enough for a frigate. Nelson, being Nelson, was not going to be beaten and with Graeme Spence, the famous hydrographer, by his side took his ship safely through; hence the channel has been known as Medusa Channel to this day.

There must be many people who from their earliest days can remember the caption 'Harwich to the Hook of Holland' which crowned many a poster on railway stations throughout the land; but few will see in this any link with the mediaeval pilgrim ships. It was natural for Harwich to be a port of passage to the European mainland and the regular voyages of vessels carrying passengers or mails had been going on from the early seventeenth century. Even during the Dutch wars these sturdy vessels ran together with their Dutch rivals despite the presence of hostile men-of-war, who, by and large, tolerated this traffic. The packet boats were fast and well-armed and for those reasons generally scorned a naval escort. They were not above a considerable amount of 'free-trade' as well and it may be that a certain amount of treasonable correspondence jostled alongside the legitimate mails. That the Harwich packets may not have always been all that they could be in other respects is evident from an official letter addressed to the Harwich agent complaining that our ships were,

> "so nasty, ill-provided and out of order that we do not only lose many passengers that will not venture with them but it is a reproach to our nation to have such bad accommodation when our neighbours are so neat and exact in theirs."

Whether these shortcomings were peculiar to the Harwich packets is not certain; but Defoe has this to say:

> "Harwich is known for being the port where Packet Boats between England and Holland go out and come in. The inhabitants are far from being famed for good usage to strangers but on the contrary are blamed for being extravagant in their reckonings in the public houses which has not a little encouraged the setting up of sloops which they now call Passage Boats, to Holland to go directly from the river of the Thames, this, though it may be the longer passage, yet as they are laid to be more obliging to passengers and more reasonable in the expense, and as some say also the vessels are better seaboats, has been the reason why so many passengers do not go or come by the way of Harwich, as formerly were wont to do, insomuch that the stage coaches between this place and London, which ordinarily went twice or three times a week, are now entirely laid down and the passengers are left to hire coaches on purpose, take post horses or hire horses to Colchester, as they find most convenient."

The abandon with which public transport undertakings have allowed themselves to be priced out of existence in our own day seems to have had its precedent over two centuries ago.

During the French wars of the late eighteenth century the passage was more hazardous, especially in the post-revolutionary period. The high-sounding formula 'Liberté, Egalité, Fraternité' did not have much application so far as packets and fishing boats were concerned; nor were the Dutch so tolerant as of yore but were always ready to snap up any odd maritime prizes on the side. Even before the fall of the French monarchy they had not always been conspicuously helpful — as at Fontenoy, for example!

The coming of steam was slow to produce any material results, in fact it seemed to a reluctant Harwich still holding on to her erstwhile glories that this was an eccentricity to be left to others. However the Post Office did not believe that it would be impracticable and so it befell that the first steam crossing was accomplished by the General Steam Navigation Company from the Thames in 1832 and it was to their boats that the Post Office mails were entrusted. This was the beginning of the end for Harwich as a regular port of passage.

Strangely enough, steam ships were being built at Harwich as early as 1826, but not to trade locally. In that and the following year ten steamers were built at the old Navy Yard; but they were for service on the Dover-Calais crossing and Harwich was left a mere shadow of her former glory, used only by a few coastal craft and fishermen until the coming of the railway in the late forties of last century. Twenty years later the Great Eastern Railway introduced their service of steamers to Rotterdam and traffic began to return, but only to a limited degree, because the approaches were inadequate to vessels drawing fifteen feet or more. Conscious of the urgent need to cope with this problem the town sought Parliamentary powers to place the whole Haven under one Conservancy Board and employed Peter Bruff as their Engineer. The story of the brilliant work of this great man in arresting the creeping extension of the Landguard shingle spit before it had nipped the haven entrance to an impossible passage and the opposition of the Naval authorities, combined with the reluctance of the Board of Trade to give any assistance to the scheme is a sad saga of muddle and stupidity in high places.

Meanwhile the Great Eastern Railway finding that the facilities for handling their steamers at Harwich itself were inadequate, decided to develop their own quay at Ray Island, a couple of miles up stream. Harwich was not particularly pleased and watched every move of the Railway with a jealous eye; but there was not much to be done about the operations of such a powerful undertaking. As Parkeston Quay — as we now know it — grew, Harwich was left like an unfruitful branch with little or no fruit at its extremity and no passage of sap to maintain its life. There was still the Navy Yard and the fact that Trinity House still maintained a depot there gave a certain semblance of importance and dignity. In times of war Harwich has always re-assumed its ancient pride as a naval base and the old phrase for muddle and inefficiency — "All up at Harwich" is patently seen to be both untrue and unkind. Of more recent years the Navy Yard Quay, now freed for commercial uses has developed wonderfully to accommodate the 'roll-on-roll-off' traffic and as one watches the huge articulated lorries from all over Europe rumbling away through the narrow streets of this ancient and honourable town it seems that the ghosts of old Harwich men must smile benignly on their home-port which, despite the vicissitudes of its history, is still alive and indeed grown to a new stature.

The Train Ferry still goes through to Harwich Town, but this brings no profit to the local traders and if any of them look over their shoulders in historical retrospect they might regard with envy the fine ships which take passengers and goods between Parkeston Quay and Holland, Germany and Denmark quickly and comfortably right past the reduced quayside of the ancient port.

This however like any of the developments of our age, is not without an advantageous side to those whose nostalgic yearnings are tempered by more practical considerations. While our grand-parents, if they were sufficiently sea-minded, may have enjoyed the experience of a leisurely passage to some pleasantly picturesque European port they must have been prepared for the vagaries of wind and tide to waft them on their way in due course. Today the fast steam or diesel-powered vessels make the crossing irrespective of natural weather conditions and the passengers can be assured that, come hell or high water, they can rely on keeping that business appointment or continental train-connection with all the certainty that modern expertise can achieve.

The two lighthouses, the lofty High Light and the more modest Low Light still stand, albeit the former is no longer dependent on a coal fire nor the latter on candles. Once their doubtful validity as 'leading lights' was impugned by the wits who referred to them as 'misleading lights'.

Between these revered veterans there stands on the Green the old Crane set up in the Navy Yard in 1667 and re-erected here. It was operated by a treadmill and is the only one of its kind still surviving in England.

Just as, by a quirk of history, Harwich grew in importance to dwarf its mother parish of Dovercourt, so did Manningtree out-strip Mistley. At the time of the Domesday survey the place was not deemed worthy of mention — if indeed it existed at all as a recognisable community. The etymologists are divided in their opinions as to the origin of the name — 'many trees' sounds altogether too plausible; but that it is evolved from the 'tree of the Mannings', i.e. the folk of Mann or Manna seems much more likely. This provides yet another example of the uncertainty of this unsure science. Surely the possibility that this hypothetical tree marked the place were the local *ting,* or council of elders, met seems to be as fair a guess as any other.

Manningtree speedily became a place of importance. Placed as it was at the head of the Stour estuary, it took a good share of the seabound trade from the nearby 'cloth' towns of Dedham and Sudbury. The importance of the products of the English looms must not be under-estimated; as our excellent wool was no longer sent abroad to be woven into cloth so did the improved standard of our own cloth command the serious attention of European buyers. The only real rival to Manningtree in this respect was Ipswich which offered equal facilities for cloth taken by pack-animals or in later times by waggon. The Whitsun fair or 'ale' was famous and among its attractions was the roasting of an ox whole. Did not Prince Henry in *Henry IV* call Falstaff a "roasted Manningtree ox, with the pudding in his belly." We do not know what the pudding itself contained; but students of mediaeval cuisine could probably tell us.

Here as at Ipswich, Harwich and countless other places near the sea there were salt pans; for before the days of artificial refrigeration the demand for this basic commodity was insatiable. In spite of the refining it subsequently underwent it is unlikely that the final product would satisfy our modern standards of hygiene; but it is also possible that it retained some natural properties which went far to compensate for a trifle of honest dirt.

Today Manningtree is a mere shadow of its former self; but it is pleasant and gracious with some mellow eighteenth century houses. There is still a quay where timber is unloaded and nearby there is the headquarters of a small yacht club.

Mistley — the wood where mistletoe grows say the pundits, ignoring the more obvious meaning of *ley,* a meadow, remained for centuries the poor relation until it was 'taken up' by one Richard Rigby who seems to have been a parvenu with great ideas. The source of his wealth is somewhat obscure; some of it was certainly inherited from his father who had made it in connection with the South Sea Company. It was also whispered that the son's office as Paymaster-General of the Forces had not been entirely without opportunities. He set out to create a port of his own devising not entirely without success, and besides the transmogrification of his own mansion — also to found a spa. No less an architect than Robert Adam would satisfy this eighteenth century 'tycoon'; but little of his work remains today except the twin towers of the church. These are in the typical Adam tradition which is, on the whole, less happy in the result with ecclesiastical architecture than in the domestic field. The towers with their 'anglo-classical' columns and cupolas stood at each end of a disproportionately short church which succumbed to dry-rot within a century of its erection. Today they stand as a melancholy reminder of the social aspirations of Richard Rigby. It is popularly believed that they were preserved as a sailing-mark for mariners on the Stour; in any event they are now protected by the Ministry of Works as an ancient monument.

Of Rigby's ambition to establish a spa at Mistley nothing came; but the pavilion still stands, set off by a pool into which a somewhat unrealistic swan constantly regurgitates a pathetic dribble of water. Live swans are very much a feature of Mistley for here they congregate in numbers sufficient to be reckoned as a natural swannery. Whether at full-breasted high tide or over the bird-haunted saltings at the ebb the prospect is serene viewed from the pleasant riverside grass plot in spite of the demonaic wrecking of the shelter erected for those whose lives and work will be remembered when the antics of the immature are forgotten like a bad dream.

During the Napoleonic period Mistley became known as a ship-building centre; for no place where even a fifth-rater could be launched would be neglected at that time of crises.

Today the place is dominated by maltings where the God-given barley is turned into the good stuff that goes to gladden the hearts of proper Englishmen. As for the unconsidered waste products of this process the swans at least appreciate them and are no doubt duly grateful.

It is impossible to write of Harwich without mention of the *Mayflower* and Christopher Jones: but so much ink has already been spilt on this 'hotly controverted' subject that it has become, to use a modern phrase, a 'hot potato'.

The name *Mayflower* was not an unusual one and at times there may even have been more than one ship of that name or variant thereof in the same port. On balance there seems some ground for accepting the claim that the vessel which carried the early emigrant Pilgrim Fathers may have been laid down at Harwich and that she may have been skippered by one Christopher Jones is equally probable. There can however be no doubt that if she was chartered for this hazardous venture it was not at Harwich but more likely London. An added difficulty in identifying vessels of that period is caused by the fact that precise and compulsory registration of ships on a central basis had not yet come into being.

There was however a *Mayflower* of Harwich whose captain was Christopher Jones, the son of Christopher Jones and born at Harwich. The house which is pointed out today as the birth place of the younger Christopher is in King's Head Street, formerly known as the High Street; but it has been subject to the vicissitudes of nearly four centuries and the precise identity of the actual building is in any event not of vital significance. Whenever and wherever the *Mayflower* was built, there was certainly a ship of that name recorded in the London Port Books as actively engaged in the French wine trade and this seems to be the vessel chartered to take the emigrants to America in 1620. Christopher Jones returned safely to Harwich where his son was born and baptised in 1621.

The recent contest between Harwich and Plymouth for the honour of celebrating the three hundred and fiftieth anniversary of the sailing of the Pilgrim Fathers proved inconclusive. Harwich would seem to have been somewhat tardy in staking their claim; on the other hand Plymouth could only say that the *Mayflower* put back into Plymouth after the first leg of the voyage out of Southampton had proved that her smaller consort the *Speedwell* was not fit to make the passage. This is no place to unravel the tangled skein of defective records, but one may hope that one day the rival claims to fame — albeit reflected in a somewhat murky mirror — will be resolved to the satisfaction of posterity.

Across the river today there stands the impressive facade of the Royal Hospital School at Holbrook, like so many Naval shore establishments having a dignity worthy in its modern idiom to compare with the more traditional river frontage of Greenwich; and hard by at Shotley is *H.M.S. Ganges,* no longer the gallant old flagship built of teak at Bombay in 1821 and the last sailing ship to wear an Admiral's flag before she became a training ship and was towed round here in 1899. Nowadays *Ganges* is a shore station, a 'Stone Frigate', but her name lives proudly on in her present role, training young men for the Royal Navy.

In 1875 Harwich was involved to some extent in a sea-tragedy which resulted in the deaths of many innocent people and brought little credit to this part of the English Coast. For many years Harwich had firmly resisted having a lifeboat stationed there. In fact for thirty years there was not a single lifeboat in Essex although

Suffolk had pushed forward ever since the early years of the nineteenth century in spite of the obstinate objections of the local Beach Companies. These well-knit groups saw their profitable business of salvage threatened if officious do-gooders insisted on wasting valuable time snatching mere humans from a watery grave.

Harwich did not even try to move in this direction; as is testified by an inglorious 'nil' record of rescues by the one life-boat stationed between 1845 and 1851.

However in 1875 a German emigrant ship the *Deutschland* with nearly 250 people on board was wrecked on the Kentish Knock. It may well be that they were unwilling emigrants because some, at least, were nuns exiled from the Fatherland under the notorious anti-Catholic Falk Laws, soon afterwards repealed.

For fourteen hours after the *Deutschland* had struck the news had not reached Harwich and even then the salvage paddle tug *Liverpool* did not put out until the following morning. Admittedly when she did reach the wreck she took off a hundred and seventy-three survivors; but the howl which went up from the German newspapers was anything but complimentary to the English in general and East Anglians in particular. After the tragedy Harwich bestirred itself to have the lifeboat brought back; but even then there were grumbles from those who stood to gain by recovering more inanimate salvage from a wreck. To them the effort by the master and crew of the *Liverpool* was a dastardly piece of interference and they hated them for it with a bitter hate which knew no bounds.

On decent folk the disaster made a profound impression and it did much to stimulate and expedite the provision of more lifeboats and especially in those parts which had lagged behind the remainder of the country. Gerard Manley Hopkins wrote a poem on the wreck of the *Deutschland* of which one stanza paints a vivid picture of the drama and horror of the occasion:

> "She drove in the dark to leeward
> She struck not a reef nor a rock
> But the combs of a smother of sand: night drew her
> Dead to the Kentish Knock;
> And she beat the bank with her bows and her keel
> The breakers rolled on her beam with ruinous shock
> The canvas and compass, the whorl and the wheel
> Idle for ever to waft her or wind her, with these she endured."

IPSWICH today is a place of contrast and paradox. For centuries no town could more fittingly have rejoiced with the psalmist: "The lines are fallen to me in pleasant places". Nestling snugly below the rising ground on the north and east with at her feet the maiden Gipping blossoming into the full-breasted Orwell and facing the swelling slopes of Stoke, Ipswich was indeed a fair town. The lovely and serene panorama painted in 1753 by John Clevely the Elder and now hanging in Christ Church Mansion may be thought a romantic dream; but there is good reason to believe that it is substantially what the artist saw two centuries ago. Why has so much of this gracious charm departed from the Ipswich scene today? We may well sigh in sad nostalgia; but, "tho' much is taken, much abides", and it is easier to find a great deal of what was the glory of this ancient town if we go back in time to the earliest days of its history.

As Ipswich grew, more especially during the urban and industrial development of the last century, much has been overlaid which might have yielded fruitful knowledge of past ages and it is not surprising that archaeological discoveries have been sparse. Nevertheless enough has been uncovered for us to know that man was hereabouts as far back as the Old Stone Age and evidence of Bronze Age culture is not lacking. Later came the Romans who left the remains of a villa on what is now the north western outskirts of the present town. It may have belonged to a prominent official and would have been easily accessible from the road which ran from Camulodunum, Colchester, to Venta Icenorum, Caistor St Edmund. It is possible that use was made of the Orwell; but the Romans would probably have used their own good road with its military security as a safer and more direct link with the seat of government as well as for supplies.

Towards the later stages of the Roman occupation there was certainly an important military station at Walton, the drowned remains of which are receiving renewed and more informed attention from archaeologists today. There was probably also another fort at Walton in Essex which is now so completely submerged by the sea as to be beyond any practicable exploration. It must be remembered however that the main purpose of these defences of the 'Saxon Shore' was not so much the policing of the East coast estuaries for Roman cargo ships as to deny these tempting lines of attack to raiders from beyond the seas.

When the Eagles finally withdrew from Britain to strengthen the hard-pressed defences of the Empire nearer home the Romano-Britons had to cope as best they could with the threat of the barbarians from the Elbe and the Weser. No help could be looked for from the capital city of Camulodunum; for that had fallen to the Saxon invaders a year before the Angles began to feel their way into the heart of that part of Britain to which they were one day to give their name. A century later this was to become that kingdom of the East Angles of which we have already told.

The Angles in their basic motive for coming here were land-hungry and although their treatment of the Romano-Britons was anything but polite, they speedily settled into this new land which was so much more fertile than that which they had left. Unfortunately, they were not allowed to get on with these pastoral pursuits without a deal of gratuitous interference from their kinsmen in those parts which were to be known as Mercia and Northumbria. The next three hundred years were to be taken up with internecine strife and the rise and fall of one kingdom or another as each struggled for dominance. Whether this was achieved by battle or guile, by dynastic marriage or by assassination was of small account. Nevertheless it was as true then as in our own immediate past that trade follows the flag and steadily the ships of the Angles and Saxons and of other merchants from farther afield crept up the Orwell to the town which had begun to spring up as a centre for bargaining.

It is from about this time that it came to be known as *Gipes Wic* — the town or settlement of Gipi. Who Gipi was we know not; but the pundits assure us that the pronunciation of the initial 'G' was such that this gentleman would be addressed by the convivial-sounding name 'Yipi'. The Normans in their turn rejected the 'Y' and so we get 'Ippeswiche'. The river which joined the estuarine Orwell at this point took its name from the town and is still known as the Gipping — call it how you please.

But we anticipate the measured pace of history. Hardly had this settlement found its feet before other visitors began to arrive, unasked, those 'loathly guests' of whom we read in the Song of the Battle of Maldon. The first raiding party of Danes who had descended upon the Wessex coast in 787 were but a trickle which was soon to become a flood. All along the coast of what came to be 'Angle land' the sea-wolves from Jutland grew bolder and raids became even more frequent. These were no would-be settlers seeking 'lebensraum' but a human scourge as merciless as tigers, practising an old dark faith of rapine and slaughter and loot. The East Angles in their settled homesteads, the Christian shrines with their treasures offered a constant invitation to the raiders who would strike without notice. Unlike the Angles and Saxons in their day whose ships had been slow moving and oar-propelled, the Danes had faster sailing ships and when they had done their worst would pass on leaving a wrack of smoking ruins and mangled bodies.

In 991 Ipswich was attacked and sacked, although this was a century after the establishment of the Kingdom of Guthrum within the Danelaw. The invaders were a mixed force of Danes and Norsemen who then went on to meet the Anglo-Saxon defenders at Maldon.

In 1010 the town was seized by one Thurkill who made a regular habit of backing either side, according as luck or lucre offered; but six years later the ships of Cnut sailed up the Orwell as a prelude to his occupying the English throne and bringing peace to Englishman and Dane alike. At that time Ipswich had become a town of importance with five hundred houses and a population of between two and three thousand.

Lastly in 1069 Swein Estridsson of Denmark rashly sought to grab a morsel for himself from the Norman conquerors, but he got short shrift from the forces of three of William's feudatories, Roger Bigod, Robert Malet and Ralph Guader — who were probably not much better than the Danish opportunists they so virtuously repelled.

From all this it may appear that the River Orwell provided a tempting approach to an invader leading right to the heart of the town; but even in those days and with the relatively shallow draught of the Danish longships there is reason to believe that the sandbanks and shingle bar at what was later known as Downham Bridge offered an obstacle which was of substantial advantage to the inhabitants with their more intimate local knowledge of these hazards.

Many have been misled by the frequent occurrence of these 'bridges' where it was manifest that there was not, never had been and never could have been a bridge in the modern sense of an architectural span of timber or stone. In these cases it will usually be found that the word is applicable to a cansey, causeway or ford whereby men, animals and sometimes vehicles could cross; this as well as the man-made contrivance is what the Anglo-Saxon word *brycg* meant. There are several examples in East Anglia of this use of the word, although it is also found in other parts of England.

At the Conquest William held Ipswich in direct fief to the Crown and therefore put his Sheriff Roger Bigod in charge. The Bigods were quick to assume the role of local war-lords which they were to wield to their own advantage for another two centuries. Roger upheld the dignity of the king whom he was appointed to represent by making substantial increases in the farm-rent paid by the burgesses of the town for their privileges. It was not long before Bigod was enjoying a third of these revenues for his own benefit.

Although both Henry I and Henry II had recognised the status of Ipswich, the first effective charter was granted by John in 1200 and from this time onwards must be dated the life of the town as a borough corporate governed by its own bailiffs, twelve portmen and twenty-four headboroughs. There is a distinction between these portmen and the 'portsmen' who represented the Cinque Ports in the more contentious occasions at Great Yarmouth and King's Lynn over which the Ports claimed certain hotly-disputed rights of suzerainty. The twelve portmen of Ipswich seem to have constituted a town council with powers and duties not limited to maritime affairs. Nevertheless one of their responsibilities was to meet and assist those coming into the port on their lawful occasions. In their hands resided the chief executive power of government and they were under oath to administer justice impartially. In the main these laudable offices were duly performed, although there were to be times when this admirable arrangement was less than admirable in action.

All now would have seemed fair for the steady growth of Ipswich, already a flourishing port for ships which in those days with their shallower draught had no difficulty in reaching the Common Quay. Henry III in his turn granted the town another charter giving the local courts greater status and the King acquired land for the Black Friars whom he established in 1263. It seems apparent that all was not well, and from time to time there were some strange goings-on. In 1271 the Common Clerk — or as we should say, Town Clerk — disappeared, taking with him the first Domesday Book for the town as well as many other important legal records. In 1283 a mob of the lewd or baser sort assaulted no less a person than the Sheriff while he was presiding in the County Court and held him until he ransomed himself with two tuns of wine. This sort of thing was not to be endured and a very righteously angry Edward I abrogated the town's charter, putting in his own stewards to administer the borough and sequestering all the customs tolls and fees payable into the courts. In 1344 Edward III was affronted by a similar outbreak of mob violence when no less a person than his Justice of Assize was insulted in his own court. The chief offenders were sailors who seem to have been acting in sympathy with the accused and having put one of their number in the judicial chair held a mock trial of the judge and his officers. The significant factor in this scandalous affair is that the defendant had been charged with smuggling wool to Flanders and Gascony for some years. It is not expected that Edward who had established the Staple strictly to control the trade in wool for his own profit would take this kind of behaviour kindly; and Edward had a nasty temper. Holding these riotous happenings to be due to the inability of the portmen to keep order in their own house, the King suspended the corporate body and put the town in charge of the sheriff.

At this time Edward had a French war on his hands. He had set forth from the Port of Orwell on that expedition which was to bring about our first successful naval engagement at Sluys. The letter written to his son, afterwards to achieve military fame as the Black Prince, is still in existence and is one of the treasured archives of the City of London. Written in the French of the period it gives a vivid personal account of the battle which has lost nothing of its drama over the centuries and little in the translation.

"Dearest son, we are certain that you are desirous of knowing good news of us and what has happened to us since our departure from England, so we inform you that on the Thursday after the day on which we set out from the port of Orewell, we sailed all day and the following night and on the Friday at about the hour of noon, we came to the coast of Flanders before Blankenburgh, where we had the sight of our enemies fleet, which was all massed together in Swyne harbour and because the tide was not then favourable for us to draw in on them, we lay to all that night. On the Saturday, St John's Day, soon after the hour of noon, in the name of God and trusting in our just quarrel, we entered the said harbour and with the tide (to attack) our said enemies who had assembled their ships in a very strong array and offered a very noble defence all that day and the following night, but God with His power and miracle granted us the victory over our enemies, for which we thank Him as devoutly as we can. Moreover, we inform you that the number of the ships, galleys, and large barges of our enemies amounts to 180 and 10 which were all taken save 24 in all, which.fled and some are since taken at sea. The number of men-at-arms and other armed people amounts to 35 thousand, of which number by estimate five thousand have escaped and the remnant, as we have been given to understand by certain men taken alive, are lying dead in a great many places on the coasts of Flanders. On the other hand all our ships, that is to say the *Christofre* and the others which were lost at Middleburgh are now regained and there are gained in this fleet three or four as big as the *Christofre*. The Flemings willingly came over to us as well at the beginning of this battle as at the end. Thus God our Lord has shewn us sufficient grace, for which we and all our friends must rightly render him thanks. Our intention is to remain in peace on the water until we have come to a certain decision with our allies and other friends in Flanders about what is to be done. Dearest son may God keep you. Given under our secret seal in our ship *Cogge Thomas*, on Wednesday the eve of S. Peter and S. Paul."

Preoccupied as he was with the waging of a successful campaign, to say nothing of finding the wherewithal to pay for it — Edward was probably only too happy to grant to the men of Ipswich his royal licence to strengthen the town wall with one of stone. He could at least be fairly sure that with this task in hand they would not have much time for further mischief.

Twenty-five years later, with Edward dead and his young grandson, Richard, on the throne, the town received a fresh charter and again, two years after, yet another one. This did not prevent various bands of insurgents in the Peasants Revolt attacking houses, the occupants of which had incurred the odium of the rebel leaders, many of whom were anything but of peasant stock.

During all this time the maritime activity of Ipswich was steadily growing and the export of wool which had been such a rich source of England's wealth since before the Conquest was reaching the zenith of its prosperity. Although Ipswich was not one of the original Staple Towns like Norwich or Lincoln there is reason to believe that the Staple had a local 'mayoralty' entirely independent of the town council for the collecting of wool and despatching it to the Calais Staple. Moreover until the English weavers learnt how to make better use of English wool it was to Ipswich that the Flemish cloth returned, so that the port was handling this valuable traffic both ways. Besides this, the ships tying up at the Common Quay were discharging wines from France, silks and spices from the near East, furs from Scandinavia, bow-staves from Italy and Spain.

Nor was the traffic only in goods. More than once the townsfolk of Ipswich witnessed the departure of a princess to her nuptials in foreign parts. Blanche, daughter of Henry IV, to be married to Ludwig of Bavaria, and her sister Philippa to Eric IX of Denmark, each set sail from Ipswich. Indeed one royal marriage took place in the town in 1297 when Edward I's daughter Elizabeth was wed to John, Count of Holland.

This rise in the importance of Ipswich had its repercussions in the town's relations with Harwich. In the days when the Bigods were a power in the land they had conferred many privileges upon Harwich which Ipswich watched with jealous apprehension. The sharing of a common outlet to the sea was bound to bring its own complications, especially as Harwich, originally a mere hamlet of Dovercourt and without the wealth and civic status of Ipswich, was seated on a large and inviting spread of sheltered water. This it was which attracted ships which Ipswich regarded as the bearers of commerce and as such her just concern. The situation between the two towns was not improved when Richard III in 1485 confirmed Admiralty jurisdiction to the older town, a privilege which was renewed and amplified by Henry VIII. This meant that matters concerning ships and merchandise which would otherwise need to be referred to the Court of Admiralty in London with great expenditure of time and money could be heard on the spot with expedition and in the light of local knowledge. It was a privilege not unusually enjoyed by maritime towns and it would seem reasonable enough for the status to be conferred upon Ipswich. Alas! it seems to have gone rather to the heads of the

Borough Fathers and nothing would serve their just pride but that they must send their water-bailiffs to sail over the Liberties and so define the boundaries of their jurisdiction. Taking boat at Shotley they landed at Harwich, marched through the north-eastern corner of the town and then re-embarked to go back to Polleshead which was the limit of the port for Admiralty purposes.

The men of Harwich were justifiably affronted and buzzed like a hive of angry bees. On more than one occasion the stately expedition returned in somewhat less stately fashion, their plumage distinctly ruffled by their reception on the Stour. It was the kind of situation which was not forgotten in after years when with Harwich now a centre of naval activity and Ipswich losing out on her bid to receive ships she found herself left at the post. This turn in fortune's wheel was not entirely due to lack of enterprise on the part of Ipswich but was compounded of several other factors.

Like most ports which exercise, or ever have exercised, Admiralty jurisdiction, Ipswich includes among the civic insignia a silver oar which was the badge of the water-bailiff. It is a very modest example being only 10½ inches long and is hall-marked 1811, the year when it was 'acquired'. On one side it is engraved with the borough arms; perhaps the other might fitly have been inscribed 'Ichabod'.*

It is difficult to read or write or even to walk about Ipswich, even in the most desultory manner, without continually coming up against some mention of her best-known son, Thomas, Cardinal Wolsey. This is not the place to digress at length upon the rise and fall of this enigmatic figure of an enigmatic age. Was he indeed the "great child of honour" so acclaimed by generations of local chroniclers that one might be tempted to think that Ipswich had never had any other famous men? Or was he the living apotheosis of opportunism in a parvenu Tudor society? Like many self-made men he yearned to be a public benefactor and showed great ingenuity in providing himself with the wherewithal to finance his benefactions. His climb to power was ruthless and the path of his progress was bestrewn with victims and those who had cause to hate him. One of his most ambitious schemes was the foundation

---

*The Borough also uses a sword, which was presented by the Mayor to commemorate Queen Victoria's Jubilee, 1887. As the privilege of bearing a sword before the Mayor is normally granted by the Sovereign, the authenticity of this piece of municipal pomp is a trifle obscure!

of a school which could be linked to the College he had established at Oxford; but barely had the first scholars taken up residence and before the buildings were complete, when he fell from power. A great part of the building material was taken by the king for his new palace at Westminster, and all that remains today is a gateway bearing the weather-worn arms of Henry VIII — which leads nowhere.

> "Had I but served my God with half the zeal
> I served my King, he would not in my age
> Have left me naked to my enemies."

In some ways this failure to bring good plans to their full fruition has been paralleled from time to time in the history of Wolsey's native town.

Nevertheless the period was not without its men of vision and solid prosperity such as the great merchant and benefactor of the town, Henry Tooley, who coming from a family already modestly well-to-do, attained a standard of eminence founded upon enterprise which was outstanding even in that age. There were few trading activities in which he did not take part with profit to himself. His famous ship *Mary Walsingham* seemed always abroad on her master's business — Biscay, Flanders, France as well as the home ports of England. The Icelandic fisheries also brought gain to Tooley.

There were others of Henry Tooley's calibre — Thomas Pownder, John Knapp, Augustin Parker; but in spite of these men of stature there seems to have been a sad lack of enterprise on the part of those in whose hands lay the governance of the town. It would appear that things have not changed much over the past four centuries, so often did there seem every promise of the future for Ipswich in some new enterprise and then for one reason or another the opportunity slipped away. Sometimes it was the result of ill-management by the townsmen or their governors, sometimes through natural causes which, with a little more energy or foresight, might have been countered or turned to good effect.

Nowhere is this illustrated with greater force than in the decay of Ipswich as a port just as all seemed set fair for firmly based prosperity. The river front had three quays in active use, the Common Quay, Bigods Quay and Harney's Quay; but with the passage of the years two factors combined to cast a shadow over the maritime scene.

Gradually the river was silting up especially above Downham Bridge and indeed it is probable that this shingle bank was largely responsible for causing a pile up in the upper reaches. At the same time the developments in the design of sea-going ships resulted in vessels of greater draught which could only reach the town quays on high tide — and in the case of some craft, not at all. By the same token the shipbuilding which for three centuries or more had flourished on the Orwell languished except for vessels of small burthen. As a result of all these handicaps the building of the more important sea-going ships passed gradually to the hated rival Harwich, and even farther afield.

Henry VII, who when he came to the throne found himself with only four ships, soon showed a lively interest in the need for an effective navy and was prepared to loosen his cautious purse-strings to that end. An important development in his naval policy was that, instead of buying ships, he began to build them. This was continued by his son who moreover realised the prestige value of large and magnificent vessels, over and above their fighting qualities. The result of this demand for bigger shipyards and the depth of water in which to launch the ships built there was that King's ships were built almost exclusively on the Hamble or Southampton Water as in Henry V's days or at the new Thames yards at Woolwich and Deptford. Only these waters could take such monsters as the 1500 tons *Henry Grace A Dieu* which, although perfectly seaworthy, did little of note beyond taking Henry VIII to his meeting with Francis I at the Field of the Cloth of Gold. She ended up like many fine ships in those happy-go-lucky days by being accidentally burnt.

In order to encourage shipbuilders to concentrate on larger ships, the Tudor monarchs offered a bounty on ships with a tonnage of over a hundred, and by Elizabeth's reign this stood at five shillings a ton. This by the contemporary value of money was a great inducement to lay down ships of a size which would be of practical value if and when the Crown needed them.

In spite of the natural handicaps of the Orwell the traditional skill of the Ipswich shipwrights did not falter and many stout ships were built where there was always an abundant supply of Suffolk oak ready to hand.

It is ever the way of sailormen to value a ship for what she is and not for the place of her birth and so it came about that two of Suffolk's best known mariners sailed together in the Harwich *Desire* (120 tons) when Thomas Candish — or Cavendish — of Trimley and Thomas Eldred of Ipswich set off from Plymouth in 1586. Two years later Candish returned to Plymouth, the second Englishman to have circumnavigated the world.

A great deal of attention has been focussed on two panels showing Thomas Eldred "and his ship". In fact there is no very definite evidence that Eldred played any important part in the expedition, although one may suspect that he regaled his Ipswich cronies with a plethora of traveller's tales when he finally settled down in Suffolk. Of the two versions of the similitude of the ship in which he is reputed to have voyaged one is of very eccentric rig and it may well be an amateur and second-hand attempt to represent the *Desire*. The other panel shows a large war ship of a type at least forty or fifty years later than the voyage. The popular picture of the early English navigators is often a highly idealised one and no more to be relied on for detail than the fanciful conceptions of early seal-cutters or the mediaeval heralds of the ships of their days.

> "They that go down to the sea in ships, that do business in great waters; these see the works of the Lord and his wonders in the deep".

Thus the Psalmist; but when we read Hakluyt's accounts of how these rumbustious viewers of divine wonders comported themselves we may take a somewhat less rose-tinted view of their adventures. Thomas Candish is writing to Lord Hunsdon to give a brief account of his voyage:

> "Right honourable, as your favour heretofore hath bene most greatly extended towards me, so I humbly desire a continuance thereof: and though there be no meanes in me to deserve the same, yet the uttermost of my services shall not be wanting, whensoever it shall please your honour to dispose thereof. I am humbly to desire your honour to make knowen unto her Majesty the desire I have had to doe her Majesty service in the performance of this voyage. And as it hath pleased God to give her the victory over part of her enemies, so I trust yer long to see her overthrow them all. For the places of their wealth, whereby they have mainteined and made their warres are now perfectly discovered: and if it please her Majesty, with a very small power she may take the spoile of them all. It hath pleased the Almighty to suffer mee

to circompasse the whole globe of the world, entring in at the Streight of Magellan, and returning by the Cape de Buena Esperanza. In which voyage I have either discovered or brought certeine intelligence of all the rich places of the world that ever were knowen or discovered by any Christian. I navigated alongst the coast of Chili, Peru, and Nueva Espanna, where I made great spoiles: I burnt and sunke 19 sailes of ships, small and great. All the villages and townes that ever I landed at I burnt and spoiled: and had I not been discovered upon the coast, I had taken great quantity of treasure. The matter of most profit unto me was a great ship of the kings which I tooke at California, which ship came from the Philippinas, being one of the richest of merchandize that ever passed those seas, as the kings register and merchants accounts did shew: ...... Which goods (for that my ships were not able the least part of them) I was inforced to set on fire. From the cape of California, being the uppermost part of all Nueva Espanna, I navigated to the Islands of the Philippinas hard upon the coast of China; of which countrey I have brought such intelligence as hath not bene heard of in these parts. The stateliness and riches of which countrey I feare to make report of, lest I should not be credited: for if I had not knowen sufficiently the incomparable wealth of that countrey I should have been as incredulous thereof, as others will be that have not had the like experience. I sailed along the Ilands of the Malucos, where among some of the heathen people I was well intreated, where our countrey men may have trade as freely as the Portugals if they will themselves. From thence I passed by the cape of Buena Esperanza, and found out by the way homeward the iland of St Helena, where the Portugals use to relieve themselves; and from that iland God hath suffered me to return into England. All which services with my selfe I humbly prostrate at her Majesties feet, desiring the Almighty long to continue her reigne among us: for at this day she is the most famous and victorious prince that liveth in the world.

Thus humbly desiring pardon of your honour for my tediousness, I leave your lordship to the tuition of the Almighty. Plimmouth this ninth of September 1588.

Your honours most humble to command.
THOMAS CANDISH.''

However it would be less than fair to these stout-hearted adventurers if we overlooked the meticulous manner in which they logged their voyage and, without our present day aids to navigation and oceanography, gave precise details of depths, currents, prevailing winds, landmarks and all the data which would aid those who followed after.

In 1591, only three years later, Candish set out on his travels again, this time with a fleet of five vessels, including the *Desire*, but himself sailing in the *Galeon* as flagship. He encountered bad weather and was hampered by dissension among some of his crews; after passing through the 'Streight' of Magellan the Admiral became separated from the rest of the fleet and was never heard of again. Despite the shortcomings of these voyagers as apostles of European civilisation, let us salute the memory of a brave man who like the aged Ulysses could have said:

"I am become a name."

Thomas Eldred, after his adventurous first voyage with Candish, turned his attention to the developing trade with the East Indies, wherein he prospered and takes his rightful place in the Ipswich pantheon.

During the Armada affair, which Candish and Eldred missed because they were away on their travels, Ipswich found two ships, *William* (40 tons) and *Katherine* (120 tons), both of which returned safely, as well they might, seeing that the Spanish fleet, storm-buffeted and in confusion, had streamed away on its disastrous flight around the northern isles while Elizabeth, her histrionic Tilbury speech delivered and duly applauded, could return to London amid the plaudits of a credulous plebs.

In 1616 the Ipswich shipbuilders nourished such a fine conceit of themselves that they conceived a project to promote a Private Bill in Parliament to dissolve the Shipwrights Company of London in favour of that of Ipswich — nothing less! This may have been born of an excess of *amour propre;* but there had been a long story of caulkers and other craftsmen being drawn off to the Thames navy yards, either by inducement or impressment and it may well have been a gesture of desperation and defiance. Be that as it may the London guild sought the protection of one of the Secretaries of State and this preposterous proposal was duly scotched. By an irony of timing within a quarter of a century a decline in the Orwell trade had set in and although by the end of the seventeenth century ships of war began once again to be built at Ipswich they were never larger than fifth-raters.

Of these the *Hampshire* (854 tons) was the largest and she was built below Downham Bridge. Of the smaller vessels there was always a steady number coming off the stocks and some of the more prominent Ipswich builders, such as the Bayley family, were building smaller government ships, sloops of three hundred to five hundred tons and the like, up to the early years of the nineteenth century. This business continued with small trading schooners right up to the age of steam. Mention must of course be made of the East Indiaman *Orwell* which in 1817 was launched at the Halifax yard. With a tonnage of 1,400 she was a great achievement and aroused interest and enthusiasm in the county for many miles around.

Nor must the smaller builders of those famous spritties and boomies be forgotten. These solidly built and seemingly ageless craft are distinctive of the East Coast trade in grain. Some are still plying in and out of Ipswich Dock, although their spritsails are laid aside in favour of a thumping diesel.

Despite the long and sad history of missed opportunities Ipswich has somehow adapted itself to changing circumstances, although there have been times when it has taken a long time for the lesson to sink in — at least so far as the Borough Fathers had any concern in what was passing. In 1805 certain business men, impatient with what they deemed to be the ineptitude of the Corporation formed themselves into a body of River Commissioners and in the teeth of official opposition secured an Act of Parliament to deepen, widen and improve that stretch of the river between Stoke Bridge and Levington Creek. In 1837 the part of the river which had flowed past the old Common Quay was enclosed by lock gates and thus became what was at that time the largest wet dock in the country, a fitting enterprise for the year which saw the youthful Victoria come to the throne. Two years previously the borough had been described by the Municipal Reform Commissioner as "an ill-regulated republic" — which of course fell an inevitable victim to the Municipal Reform Act of 1836.

The progress of the new Dock went on from strength to strength and the Commission went on to develop the river bank below the Dock to accommodate larger vessels. Today the spirit of maritime Ipswich lives on, although from time to time it would seem that the spirit of the late Mr Bumble is still not finally laid.

Although in the days of its decline as a major home of ship-building many ancillary trades dwindled, there was always a demand for ropes both for ships and other purposes and the sail-cloth known as 'Ipswich Double' was in general demand far beyond the banks of the Orwell. It had a high reputation and although it was perhaps never the equal of its French counterpart it had the advantage of being cheaper. Moreover owing to our habit of being so often at war with France the higher grade article was often impossible to obtain.

As tastes changed with the years fresh trades sprang up and brought prosperity to the town. Such were snuff and tobacco, paper and patent plough shares and other implements of husbandry. The last commodity, always in high demand in a part of the country where agriculture was an important part of the common life, even by contemporary standards, was equally in demand beyond East Anglia long before the coming of mechanical power. But the days when manufacturers of this kind were to play a critical part in the town's character were yet to come and the basic traffic by water was still predominantly in coal and grain. The traffic from Newcastle in the former commodity and in grain and malt to London kept the port busy even if the ships were only of moderate size.

It seems strange that with all this prosperity at their feet the townsmen still seemed to neglect many of their opportunities. That indefatigable traveller, Celia Fiennes, who visited the town in 1698, has so often been cited as being critical of the enterprise of the men of Ipswich that it is worth quoting exactly what she did write.

> "So I went to Ipswitch. . . . . this is a very clean town and much bigger than Colchester is now, Ipswitch has 12 Churches, their streetes of a good size well pitchid with small stones, a good Market Cross railed in, I was there on Satturday which is their market day and saw they sold their butter by the pinte, 20 ozs. for 6d. and often for 5d. or 4d. they make it up in a mold just in the shape of a pinte pot and so sell it; their Market Cross has good carving, the figure of Justice carv'd and gilt, there is but 3 or 4 good houses in the town, the rest is much more like the Colchester buildings but it seems more shatter'd and indeed the town looks a little disregarded, and by enquiry found it to be thro' pride and sloth, for tho' the sea would bear a ship of 300 tun up quite to the key and the ships of the first rate can ride within two

mile of the town, yet they make no advantage thereof by any sort of manufacture, which they might do as well as Colchester and Norwitch, so that the shipps that brings their coales goes light away, neither do they adress themselves to victual or provide for shipps, they have a little dock where formerly they built shipps of 2 or 300 tun but now little or nothing is minded save a little fishing for the supply of the town".

Mistress Fiennes then goes on to describe Christ Church Mansion which she thought "pretty good." Today this might seem damning with faint praise, but in her day the adverbial use of "pretty" was different to ours and the context shows that this good-natured friend was favourably impressed.

Twenty-five years later Defoe visited Ipswich on his *Tour through the Eastern Counties,* which formed the first part of his *Tour through the Whole Island of Great Britain* and he painted a far more favourable picture. Although he was only a year older than Celia Fiennes he claims to have known the town as far back as 1668 (when he was seven years old!) and on the strength of that he assures us that there were at that time over a hundred Ipswich ships engaged in the coal trade between Newcastle and London and that masters and seamen did so well during the sailing months that they were able to lay the ships up for the winter and to live comfortably on their summer profits. To such an extent was this done that the population of the town increased during this laid-up period by as much as a thousand men. These Ipswich built ships had a high reputation for being strongly built and frequently had a useful life-span of forty or fifty years. This situation seems to have continued for another twenty years; but when at the age of sixty or thereabouts Defoe again visited the town he learned with melancholy that there were scarcely forty Ipswich ships still in commission, most of the trade having passed to Dutch 'fly-boats' which having been taken as prizes-of-war were cheaply acquired and capable of taking large cargoes. He remarks sourly that the principal beneficiaries of this state of affairs were the Yarmouth and London merchants; which goes to show that the stark realities of commercial economics seem not to have changed much in the past two hundred and fifty years.

Defoe was much exercised in his mind as to why the building of larger ships of war should have passed to London, seeing that there was still sufficient depth of water to launch them below Downham

Bridge and concludes that like other maritime towns Ipswich was affected by the indraft of trade to London.

About this time there was a proposal to develop in the direction of the Greenland whaling trade. On this too Defoe had something to say, perhaps with more eloquence than detailed knowledge:

> "I could say much more to this point if it were needful, and a few words could easily prove that Ipswich must have the preference of all the port towns of Britain for being the best centre of the Greenland trade, if ever that trade fall into the management of such a people as perfectly understand and have a due honest regard to its being managed with the best husbandry and to the prosperity of the undertaking in general; but whether we shall ever arrive at so happy a time as to recover so useful a trade to our country which our ancestors had the honour to be the first undertakers of and which has been lost only through the indolence of others and the increasing vigilance of our neighbours, that is not my business here to dispute".

It would seem that Defoe was unaware that King's Lynn had already been very quick off the mark when the Spitzbergen whale 'fisheries' had begun to attract ships from England although it might be difficult to establish from which port the first English whalers had set sail. Certainly Englishmen had been sailing to Greenland for whales a hundred years before Defoe was writing and blubberhouses were set up at King's Lynn for the production of trane oil which England had previously brought from Bayonne. The real pioneers of whaling were the Basques who had been catching whales in the thirteenth century and indeed there is evidence of whale-fishing off the coast of Flanders in the eleventh century. Daniel Defoe wrote — as he always did — like a "true-born Englishman," but alas! he had his facts wrong and it would seem that the men of Ipswich had not done their own homework very well before adventuring their capital in this venture.

In fact, it was nearly forty years after Defoe wrote that a gentleman named Grove had much the same idea — and wrote about it. Ten years later a Mr Nathaniel Spence re-opened the matter and fifteen years after that an advertisement appeared in the Ipswich Journal inviting subscriptions from hardy speculators. The following year in March, 1787, the *Ipswich* (312 tons) and *Orwell* (346 tons) sailed from London and on 30th July of the same year the

Orwell arrived with seven whales and 4 cwt. of whalebone. A month later *Ipswich* returned to Harwich with — nothing! The result was a gross profit of not more than seven or eight hundred pounds. During the winter one of the skippers, Harrison, occupied himself with local 'longshore' whaling and hearing that a whale had been seen in the Wallet, off Great Clacton, he and a local wherry-man, John Woolward, set off in pursuit in a wherry and armed with a 'whale-gun'. Whether this was a harpoon-gun or a kind of glorified punt-gun is not very clear, but the whole operation seems to smack of Tartarin of Tarascon rather than Moby Dick. After three or four days the two Nimrods returned unsuccessful and worn-out with fatigue. They reported that the whale was between fifty and sixty feet long and "in a very wild state". Some days later, with a misplaced sense of humour, Leviathan was seen to be gaily disporting himself in Dunwich Bay!

In the second season four ships set off for the whaling grounds under the auspices of the original company, now working in concert, or rivalry, with another group of optimists. This resulted in a gross loss of £800. A third attempt produced a gross profit of £150 on the *Ipswich* and *Orwell,* and for the rival company a gross loss of two hundred pounds. This dismal situation was not relieved by sundry squabbles between owners, skippers and crews.

Whatever may have seemed to offer good prospects at the outset, it was pretty obvious that perhaps because the enterprise had not been handled by such people "as perfectly understand and have due regard to its being managed with the best husbandry", Ipswich had backed the right horse but the wrong rider. Nevertheless, the idea still simmered in the background and even took on the nature of a myth, for in 1837 the Directory of Suffolk stated categorically that the Greenland industry was being prosecuted at Ipswich "with success".

Of the two sturdy ships which carried the high hopes of the speculators the *Orwell* was used as a collier until 1804 and the *Ipswich* after a final fling in northern waters continued afloat until 1841 when she was crossing the Atlantic in the North American trade.

The Cleveley panel is reasonably good evidence that at about 1753 Ipswich was still active both in building ships and in handling them and their cargoes. The Napoleonic War provided a fresh stimulus to the Ipswich yards, although the size of the vessels was still limited to what the river could take; as we have seen, the *Hampshire*, 1741, was still the only vessel of her size until the building of the East Indiaman *Orwell* in 1817.

In 1798 the town looked forward to welcoming a distinguished newcomer when Vice-Admiral Sir Horatio Nelson bought Roundwood, a house standing near what is now the junction of Woodbridge Road and Rushmere Road. Lady Nelson and the Admiral's aged father took up their residence there and two years later the Corporation did itself the honour to elect the victor of the Nile as High Steward. In November, Nelson and the Hamiltons arrived at the house, but finding that Lady Nelson and her father-in-law were in London they spent the night at the Great White Horse before resuming their journey to the capital, never to return to Ipswich.

The Industrial Revolution resulted in the development of several profitable industries besides giving a new slant to shipbuilding, both as to hull construction and mechanical methods of propulsion. In 1789 Robert Ransome had set up his foundry to develop his invention for tempering cast-iron agricultural implements and as his business grew so did the problem of housing his workpeople. From this time dates the less desirable kind of development which did much to destroy what was left of the mediaeval and Tudor town. From this increase in manufacture there might easily have arisen a state of strangulation where the products of industry could not be transported to the customer as fast as they were made. The development of the dock area did much to avert this aided by the improvements to the Gipping. At a later stage the coming of the railway helped even more materially to the same end. Today the Docks are busier than ever and the ancient port is throbbing with life in a modern idiom.

This chapter began with Ipswich River and it cannot but end on the same note. Let us turn our backs on the warehouses and the 'tower blocks', the chimneys of the power station, the giant dock-side cranes and Scotch derricks used to handle the port's con-siderable container traffic. Hardly are they left behind and long before they are beyond our backward glance we are back on the broad bosom of the river without which Ipswich would never have a yesterday, a today and a morrow. Truly it is fluid history and at the same time pure and utter beauty.

Passing Wherstead to starboard, which according to Skeat denotes an Anglo-Saxon wharf — wharfstead, a notable landmark, on the same bank is Freston Tower about which imagination has run riot. Those who would explain its origin have hazarded guesses that it was an eccentric's folly to humour a daughter, that it was a mere gazebo or that it was an observation tower from which a ship owner could gain 'early warning' of the return of his ships safe home from sea. This could be more probable than it seems, for such towers are not unknown along the lower Thames valley and in some cases this reason is tolerably well authenticated. Still farther down stream there is the Cat House where once a white china cat set in the window was a warning to smugglers that the preventive men were around — or so 'twas said. Here is now the Headquarters of the Royal Harwich Yacht Club. The migration of this long-established Club from its traditional waters in the Stour estuary to the more hospitable valley of the Orwell might seem to be a case of poetic justice. So often Harwich had basked in the effulgence of royal patronage and naval prestige; but when it became evident that the town which owed much to Charles II and James II was slightly bored with the sport which the two royal brothers had brought to the place, then it was time for the R.H.Y.C. to find a more congenial home.

So passing Woolverstone and the Cat House we come to Pin Mill, and here there is little change over the years. The lush, somewhat brashly expensive bungalows which crown the high ground behind the *Butt & Oyster* will mellow with the passage of the years and the caresses of the wind and weather. At the moment they stand out against the native cottages like a sore thumb. Down by the river bank the spritties which have retired from serious work slumber in well-earned ease, rising and settling with each tide. Beside them the trim yachts and dinghies sparkle in the sun. Sometimes the scene is dominated by *Cambria* herself lying in dignified confidence like a grande dame, soignée, conscious of her power to command the hearts of sailormen, ready to move serenely on the swan's path at the touch of her true love's hand.*

And so as the banks open out on either hand beckoning and blessing us as we pass we come to Orwell Haven and the long tongue of Langer Point — or if you must be pedantically erroneous, Landguard Point. But more of that hereafter.

---

*Since this was written *Cambria* has passed into the protective custody of the Maritime Trust and now lies in dignified retirement on the Medway, a lasting and revered memorial to the grace and beauty of the spritsail barges which plied so gallantly between East Anglia and the Wessex ports.

"SPEECH was given to the ordinary sort of men whereby to communicate their mind, but to wise men to conceal it." In spite of a persistent tendency to attribute these words to Voltaire, they were, in fact, uttered by an English clergyman a half-century before Voltaire was born. A valid touchstone to test the reverend gentleman's perspicacity lies ready to our hands, thanks to the inestimable benefits of modern electronics. Let us wait until some political spell-binder is essaying to lure us with honeyed words through the medium of television; then let us switch off the sound and watch his face. The result can be most revealing!

Whatever use Man may make of his power of articulate speech, the word is an essential element in his ability to communicate with his fellow-man: it is, so far as we can judge, a supreme point of difference between him and the animals. It is therefore natural that much time should have been given to the study of words, how they are spoken or written, what they mean and how they have come about. This last aspect is the special business of etymology, a somewhat high-falutin' term for the study of the derivation of words. Notwithstanding its own derivation from the Greek, meaning the true science (or word) it is anything but simple in its application. It has been used in English for longer than might be thought, reaching right back to that 'Morning star of song', Dan Chaucer. As we struggle through the rich but complex jungle of our mother tongue this etymology may seem a tempting path to tread; but like many jungle paths, it is perilously beset with pitfalls and it calls for experience and the caution which comes with experience. Nowhere is this caution called for in greater measure than in approaching the derivation and meaning of place-names.

As we break out into the full breadth of Orwell Haven and bear south for the open sea we pass the busy docks of Felixstowe and round the tip of the long shingle spit marked on the charts as Landguard Point. On that same shingle spit stands Landguard Fort, the history of which is bound up so closely with the story of this part of the coast. At first blush the name 'Landguard' sounds a very natural one for a coastal fort guarding this particular strip of land; but in fact it is a corruption of 'langer' which derives from the Anglo-Saxon *lang gara*. *Gara* or *gore* is a piece of land shaped like a spear — *gar*, a spear. You have the same word 'gore' in tailoring to describe a triangular piece of cloth let into a garment. This is a typical example of the pedantry which so often bedevils the study of place names.

As we passed the entrance to Felixstowe Docks it may have seemed odd that this very discreet watering-place should have a thriving modern port in its own right while we see so many great harbours of the past now in decline or even non-existent today. The Docks are in fact some distance from the centre of what is now Felixstowe and the road connecting docks and town — very properly known as Langer Road — runs parallel to the coast for a full mile before jinking westwards to Landguard Marshes and so for another half mile to the dock area. Here there is a passenger ferry to Harwich which replaces an older ferry nearly a mile farther up the haven. Its Felixstowe end was marked by the *Ferry Boat Inn*, better known as the 'Dooley' a name the origin of which is obscure. One theory is that it was so called by Service-men as a corruption of 'Doolally' which to the older generations of soldiers — and sailors too — meant what we today would call 'bonkers'.* Although the Port of Felixstowe is of very recent growth this is all very historic ground and it seems a good time to consider the shadowy past of Felixstowe itself — as shadowy indeed as the origin of its name, which provides yet another example of muddled etymology.

Despite determined efforts by many writers to identify Felixstowe with St Felix, the apostle of the East Angles in the seventh century, going even so far as to claim that this was where the Saint landed, there is only the faintest connection between the man and the place and even that is entirely fortuitous. The earliest form of the place-name was *Fileth stowe*, which merely means a place where trees have been felled or 'filled' and in the West Country there is a dialectal word 'fellet' which means a piece

---

*'Doolally' is itself a corruption of 'Deolali tap'. Deolali was the name of the fever hospital near Bombay and *tap* is Hindustani for malarial fever.

The prevalence of Hindustani words in service slang is a commonplace; it may not be unduly fanciful to wonder whether a similar habit among Roman soldiers brought many words of Celtic origin into late Latin.

of land cleared by periodical felling of trees — or as we might say, a 'clearing'. The name of this place in Suffolk — for it was not even a village — has some ten other forms; but they all amount to very much the same thing; the name of the manor was Walton and in this same manor Roger Bigod founded a priory dedicated to St Felix about 1105. The nearness of this priory to the adjacent Filethstowe where there was also a religious house caused some confusion in later years, although when the Commissioners of Henry VIII were doing their homework prior to the Dissolution there is no doubt that there was a clearly understood distinction between the two. It was left for the rather hazy antiquarians of succeeding centuries to perpetuate and embroider this confusion — and so another myth was born.

One writer in recent years has even translated the modern place-name as 'Happy Place', thus seeking to sanctify a most irregular marriage of Latin and Anglo-Saxon! That Walton itself had a past which is still not fully explored is beyond dispute. We have already referred to Walton Castle which is itself somewhat of a mystery; for although the fact that the Bigods had a castle here — which castle was very thoroughly and justifiably razed to the ground by Henry II — is a matter of history, the belief that there was once a substantial Roman fort hereabouts is still not finally substantiated. There are still remains of brickwork or stone-work under the sea at the foot of the cliffs and such portions as are recovered from time to time support the belief that it is of Roman origin. Against this it may be argued that there is no mention of any fort here in the description of the Saxon Shore defences contained in the *Notitia Dignitatum*. A certain amount of domestic Roman occupation in the neighbourhood there undoubtedly was and there are good grounds for believing that another Roman station was located at the other Walton across the estuary — Walton-on-the-Naze to us today. Any remains of that fort would probably be well out to sea near the West Rocks and may well be beyond our resources even in these days of submarine exploration. Here at Walton in Suffolk the prospect seems to be brighter. A certain amount of work has already been done and will presumably continue. The chief problem could well be to find a sufficiency of archaeologists who are competent aqua-lung divers or vice versa. I know one young lady who dedicates her vacations to archaeo-logical work abroad and who has taken the trouble to learn to 'skin-dive' to enhance her usefulness in that sphere; to the mere amateur it would seem that to get any tangible results the two skills are well-nigh essential and indivisible. But let us return to Landguard Fort; and for convenience we shall spell it thus, however the traditionalists choose to pronounce it.

In Henry VIII's reign the policy, begun very cautiously by Henry VII, of building up an effective navy had made some atonement for the suicidal folly of the Regency following the death of Henry V. England was acquiring a naval force to be reckoned with; nevertheless the authorities continued to place great reliance upon land defences to deny a landing to an enemy. When we recall Thomas Cromwell's suggestion that the proceeds of Peter's Pence should be diverted to provide fortresses it must be remembered that there was no national treasury in those days and the Sovereign was regarded as a kind of father figure who must always provide from one source or another the sinews of war. In the failure to realise this great difference between those times and ours lies much of the misunderstanding of the political and economic background of the Civil War nearly a century later.

The coastal defences of Suffolk were prominent among those under survey and in 1539 the Earls of Oxford and Essex wrote to Cromwell to voice their opinion that 20,000 men might be put ashore at Landguard to prevent which happening they recommended a strong 'blockhouse' there. Eight years later fortifications of some nature were erected, probably earthen walls and entrenchments which were subsequently reconstructed in some part during the Armada scare. In 1626 a substantial stone-built fortress was built and as a 'flag station' demanded that passing shipping should strike their flags; from this ensued some wordy arguments and much insistence on official dignity.

When in 1653 the two Protestant republics, England and Holland, set about each other over issues of economic prestige and maritime majesty the other nations of Europe must have been highly amused, hoping that the two warring states, like the Kilkenny cats, exterminate each other in the process. This is not the place to recall the doings of Blake and Monk on the English and Van Tromp on the Dutch side nor the battle of Camperdown when Van Tromp was killed and his fleet so battered that the States-General were very glad to make peace in 1654 on humiliating terms.

Ten years later war broke out again; for the Dutch bitterly resented the claims of the English to absolute maritime lordship of the Narrow Seas and as a trading nation they needed something better than the armed merchantmen which formed the greater part of their naval strength. In June 1665 they were soundly defeated by the Duke of York off Lowestoft; but they never lacked the desire to come back for more and a year later the two fleets met off the North Foreland, when again the Dutchmen were defeated and chased back to Holland. The victory was celebrated at Harwich with 'bonfires, guns and bells' but preparations to strengthen Landguard Fort went forward with all despatch. A substantial number of troops, both Regulars and Militia were drafted into the area and seven colliers and a twenty-gun ship, suitably disguised with ensigns as men-of-war were moored across the entrance of Orwell Haven. Their real purpose was not so much to make a show of strength as to be sunk, if need be, to block the channel; they were therefore prepared for immediate scuttling.

The Dutch on their part embarked on a game of bluff and on the 2nd July 1667 they sailed northwards along the coast as far as Aldeburgh where they went about and bore back to the Rolling Grounds where some of them proceeded to 'make smoke' as we should say. The plan seemed to be that while they were disembarking a substantial landing party at Felixstowe cliffs the ships in the Sledway and Rolling Grounds were to make a diversionary attack on the Fort by cannon-fire. What they had not reckoned on was that one of their principal ships carrying a Rear Admiral went aground on the Andrews Sand and this hampered the freedom of the other ships to manoeuvre. Meanwhile the ruse of our own moored ships worked to the extent that it had the enemy guessing, especially when they saw some sunk, as they thought, by their own gunfire.

The landing party, consisting of upwards of two thousand men equipped with ropes and scaling ladders* for climbing Felixstowe cliffs, were engaged by such troops as were on the spot, although because of the nature of the ground the English horse could not be deployed to great advantage. The Dutchmen detached about 400 men who approached the Fort under cover of the smoke which still hung over the spit and the marshes; but the garrison under the newly-appointed Governor, Captain Nathaniel Darell of the Lord High Admiral's Regiment, gave them such a warm wel-

---

*One of the Dutch scaling ladders was in the possession of the Darell family until the turn of the nineteenth century—and may yet be for all I know to the contrary.

114

come that they were not only driven off but departed in haste to re-embark. Few dead were left upon the ground; but it seems that they carried off most of their casualties with them, since according to an informed estimate at the time they lost about 150 men. The garrison lost very few men and Darell himself was wounded in the shoulder. A tall Englishman who led the Dutch to the Fort was discovered to be one Colonel Doleman who was a Republican renegade and not above turning his hand to treachery against his own country.

The story that the attacking party was harassed by the fire of three small English ships which caused the shingle to fly has been discounted by some writers; but there seems no doubt that this kept the enemies' heads down and so prevented them from executing a flanking movement.

Thus ended one of the very few attempts to 'invade' this country since 1066!

Life was not always very comfortable at Landguard. The garrison complained of hard living conditions, poor food, they sometimes had to live on the notoriously hard Suffolk cheese, and long periods without pay. There were times when the Governors had to put their hands into their own pockets to feed and pay their men. One famous character commanded a company of Lord Lucas Regiment, now the Border Regiment, in the person of Captain Richard Steele. He showed at that time an aptitude for the use of the written word which was perhaps a foreshadowing of future literary fame when he wrote in 1702 to complain that the men's barrack rooms were so exposed to the weather that thirteen N.C.O.s and men were too ill to do duty.

In 1717 the building of a new fort was commenced and its claims to fame are anything but warlike, although its armament was increased until in 1752 it mounted ten 32-pounder guns, twenty-five 18-pounders and fifteen 6-pounders with barrack accommodation for two hundred men. The new fort was nearer the estuary than its predecessor, and during the American War of Independence additional works of fortification were undertaken; it is not certain whether the American colonials were expected to invade England — and from the North Sea! At the end of the Napoleonic period the inner area was filled with wooden buildings and there were three powder magazines adjoining the kitchens — a terrifying situation one would think! Certainly the authorities were taking no chances over the defence of the Haven from the sea; for later in the century another fort commanding the Harwich approaches was built at Shotley.

The first Governor after the rebuilding in 1717 was the eccentric Philip Thickness, who spent most of his time quarrelling with all and sundry; but he may be forgiven much by reason of his patronage of Thomas Gainsborough whom he claimed to have 'discovered'. Another stormy character associated with Landguard Fort was the Lord of the Manor of Orwell, Colonel G. Tomline, who in 1867 had bought some thousands of acres when the Duke of Hamilton put this large slice of land on the market. Tomline was an arrogant, forceful individual who laid claim to manorial rights over the use of the foreshore which were of doubtful validity when asserted against the Crown. This brought him into conflict with the Secretary of State for War, who was none other than the famous Cardwell whose name has come down in history as the reputed author of the re-organisation of the British Army in the eighties of last century.

Tomline's grandiose schemes for developing his land admittedly fell short of his ambitions in their realisation; but they played a material part in the development of Felixstowe as a town and as a port. Until he came into the picture the place was a quiet fishing village which, in the 1830s, had offered a quiet, attractive holiday retreat amidst pleasant country with the amenities of sea-air. The worthy Colonel was determined that it should be all that, but more so. The first step was to bring the railway to the town and this he proceeded to do at his own expense; commenced in 1875, the line was opened in 1877 and run as his own private undertaking, the staff being dressed in his own livery. This paid off very well and in the fullness of time the Great Eastern Railway Company was very ready to take it over.

The construction of the railway was however only part of Tomline's scheme, the major part of which was to develop the dock around which he visualised the town would grow. In this respect however his judgment was in error; for those who wanted to live in this attractive seaside resort preferred to live up on the higher ground and to have their shops within convenient distance of their houses. The docks in the lower and more marshy area were commenced in 1881 and completed in 1886. Here the railway provided a convenient and expeditious means of getting the workmen to work every day without the problem of accommodating them locally, which would have resulted in setting up a considerable artisan area. As things have fallen out it has not been a bad arrangement; for the docks have developed mightily, in spite of sundry vicissitudes, and the town is still a very pleasant residential and holiday resort.

The First World War found Felixstowe already known for the activities of a hardy and adventurous band of pioneers in the field of aviation and more especially in the development of seaplanes, or as they were earlier envisaged, flying boats. The establishment which was afterwards to become famous as R.A.F. Felixstowe had opened on 5th August, 1913, and its nursery days were steered to such pioneers as J. C. Porte, E. H. Rathbone, Commander C. R. Samson and John Lankester Parker who having been captivated as a schoolboy by the fascination of this new skill, persisted in spite of his elders' scorn of his youthful enthusiasm, eventually becoming and remaining Horace Short's chief test pilot for thirty years.

One of the early visitors to Felixstowe was the First Lord of the Admiralty, Winston Spencer Churchill, who was readily convinced of the future of flying in its naval and military aspect. Nor was he content to remain on terra firma watching these daring pioneers. With that zest for drinking life to the lees which was ever his wont he had to be taken up as a passenger and one day in 1913 while in a Borel monoplane the future saviour of his country took a sound ducking when the machine side-slipped into Harwich Harbour. The exact details of this mishap were never fully revealed because Authority was more than a little uneasy over the escapades of this irrepressible Minister. Nevertheless events were to prove that none of the varied adventures of "Corporal John's" no less distinguished descendant was to be wasted in the dark days which lay ahead in the course of two bloody wars, the outcome of which was to prove vital to Britain.

The importance of Felixstowe both as a seaplane and Naval base was not to pass unnoticed by the enemy and in the Second War both town and docks suffered from air attack. Felixstowe and Harwich naval establishments were better known by their *nommes-de-guerre* of *H.M.S. Beehive* and *H.M.S. Badger* respectively and in the 1939-45 War these towns were never allowed to forget that each was very much in the fighting forefront of hostilities.

Besides the more obvious and visible activities in the spheres of sea and air warfare much quiet work had been taking place even before the outbreak of the War at Bawdsey Manor on the northern lip of the Deben estuary. Here was established in 1936 the beginnings of the electronic system to be known, first to be hinted at with bated breath and eventually fully and freely recognised as Radar. The effect on our National Defence was during the War incalculable and it has developed and continues to develop today until its eventual limits are more fantastic than can be imagined outside the realms of science-fiction. Here Sir Robert Watson-Watt and his devoted band of fellow-scientists who had been working previously at Orford Ness laboured against the ruthless march of time to perfect the system against the hazards of ever-changing circumstances.

The First World War was a temporary set-back to the docks with the inevitable intrusion of military and naval elements and the Second World War, with these factors much accentuated as well as the incidence of continual enemy air attacks, resulted in the docks being neglected nearly to the point of dereliction. In 1953 considerable damage was done by the 'Great Tide' which swamped the docks and caused considerable damage to property and loss of life, particularly in the Langer Road and Orford Road area. In some ways the town was fortunate that things were not even worse; for the winds at Felixstowe were higher than farther south on the Essex coast where the trail of death and destruction was infinitely greater. The highest wind velocity at Felixstowe was 81 m.p.h.

After the flood, the Felixstowe Dock & Railway Company tackled the task of building up a first-class port in real earnest. Not a little help came in a negative way; for the erratic and strike-ridden conditions at London caused a great deal of traffic to be diverted to Felixstowe where the close relations between management and staff have resulted in a markedly progressive and trouble-free port. Many pioneer developments have had their inception here; palletisation, container traffic, 'roll-on-roll-off' traffic and highly up-to-date methods of handling cargo in the Docks have all kept Felixstowe very much in the forefront. A great deal of major reconstruction and development has also taken place to enable larger and larger vessels to be handled and while a wide range of cargoes pass in and out of the port one notices such goods as cars, machinery, chemicals, glass and china and — by no means least — the whole import of a well-known and excellent Danish Lager beer for the southern half of England. One cannot help feeling that if these happy conditions could be adopted elsewhere in England, our shipping could be in a far better state today.

As regards the town itself it has always maintained a certain atmosphere of quiet and restful enjoyment. For the latter part of last century it had many distinguished visitors, like the German Empress who came here with her children on holiday, exiled monarchs like King Manuel of Portugal who came here to indulge his passion for tennis, and our own Kings in two world wars who came to visit their sailors, soldiers and airmen. One famous soldier, Viscount Allenby, was himself a Felixstowe man and spent his boyhood in the country around the town, keeping his connection up in later life and indeed taking the name of the town as one of his titles.

So here we have a corner of Suffolk steeped in history; Romans, Angles, Normans, all part of a robust and vigorous past yet a thriving port of today with every prospect, if left alone to get on with its business, of continuing to thrive and expand in the future.

WITH a great Benedictine abbey at Bury, the ruins of which furnish such a fruitful subject of controversy today, few people would see any connection between Woodbridge, lying serenely beside the head tidal waters of the Deben, and Ely, Queen of the Fens. To trace the link, one must go back to the latter part of the seventh century when Etheldreda, daughter of Anna, King of the East Angles, founded her monastery for nuns and monks (yes! the ladies were given precedence over the gentlemen) in the Isle of Ely. She endowed her abbey with the lands in the Isle which she had received as a marriage portion from her first husband, Tonbercht, prince of the Gyrwas. At that time, as Anna had been killed fighting the heathen Penda of Mercia, the King of the East Angles was Aldwulf, Etheldreda's first cousin — not her brother as is sometimes stated — and being a determined woman, she knew how to weedle what she wanted out of her kinsmen, whether brothers or cousins it mattered not. Aldwulf was persuaded to give her a sizeable slice of his kingdom in what we now call Suffolk, which, either at the time of gift or by subsequent additions, amounted to five hundreds and a third of a hundred. These two benefactions were eventually apportioned, the former to the benefit of the Abbot and the latter to the Prior and Monks. The Ely portion became known as the Honour of Etheldreda and the Suffolk lands as the Liberty of Etheldreda. It is often stated, and by those who should know better, that these lands were the gift of King Edgar (the Peaceful) at the refounding of the Abbey in 970; but in fact all he did was to confirm the rights and privileges of the original foundation some three centuries earlier. Be that as it may, Woodbridge has always been not only the geographical centre of the Liberty but also where to some extent the stewardship resided. It is many, many years since any financial advantage accrued to Ely from this large area of land; but until fairly recently the Dean and Chapter, as successors of the Prior and Monks, had the right of appointing the Coroner for this part of Suffolk and there are people in Woodbridge who can remember the last holder of that office. After this wholly unnecessary digression into remote history let us look at Woodbridge and its river.

The origin of the name 'Deben' has exercised the ingenuity of many learned men. It is true that the Anglo-Saxons had a word *dēop*, meaning deep; but it is not very appropriate for this river. Skeat is quite positive that the river takes its name from Debenham near where it rises and it is certainly true that there are more examples of this relation between a town and its adjacent river than vice versa. Skeat died over a half-century ago; but his guidance through this morass of etymology is not be scorned.

On the origin of Woodbridge there would seem to be no doubt; surely it is self-evident. But is it? If there was ever a wooden bridge, why should it be necessary so to distinguish it at a time when most bridges would be built of wood? In Domesday Book it is spelt both 'Udebryge' and 'Wudebryge', but that is not significant because the Normans always had difficulty with an initial 'W'. If it was a bridge by a wood, that could be a reasonable guess; but surely there would not be a man-made bridge spanning the main river and if it crossed a tributary like the Finn at Martlesham of what interest would that be to the town a mile or so away? And so we come back to my 'King Charles' Head'. Why not a ford crossing the river by a wood? I am convinced that there are more place-names arising from this perfectly normal meaning of 'brycg' than is generally recognised.

The existence of Woodbridge as a trading port does not go so very far back as ports go. A church was here at the Conquest and in 1193 a priory of Austin Canons was founded near by. In 1224 the place acquired town status by the grant of a market, and from that time it grew steadily until it attained some degree of importance. Shipbuilding began to flourish; but it was not until the fourteenth century that ships began to come and go on regular trade. Previously there was certainly a reasonable flow of trade to the Deben; but much of it was through those amorphous havens of which we hear so much but which signified areas rather than ports. Such were Bawdsey Haven or Goseford Haven. Staithes there must have been and we occasionally find examples of customs being levied by individuals to whom the right had been granted — for a con-sideration. It is to be borne in mind that trade could never develop on any substantial scale until there existed practicable road communications whereby the merchandise could be passed inland;

and this certainly never existed at all the odd places where a ship might shelter in a haven or fishing boats were drawn up on the beach. Moreover the action of the tide and shingle drift was a continual factor of change and the time would come when the haven was a haven no longer, let alone a place for the handling of cargoes of any importance. This all tended to build up the importance of a town such as Woodbridge, up-river and admirably suited to take any ships which were current in those days. By the fifteenth century ships were sailing to Scotland and Iceland with cargoes of corn or butter and this trade lasted and flourished for another three hundred years.

For the products of agriculture at any period Woodbridge was ideally suited; moreover its nearness to a well-wooded countryside ensured a constant and easy supply of some of the finest ship-building timber in England. The bounty of 5s. per ton payable on ships of one hundred tons burthen and over, coupled with the returns of ships and men available for impressment in time of war, has resulted in our being able to gauge both the output of ship-builders' yards and the relative sizes of the ships of the various ports. From these returns we find that of ships of one hundred tons and over Woodbridge came second with two ships as against Ipswich with five and Aldeburgh and Southwold with one each. At about this time Ipswich was profiting more from shipbuilding than from trading and this put Woodbridge in a relatively important position as against other Suffolk ports. At that time there were no Suffolk ships of over 150 tons.

This question of 'tonnage' is often somewhat involved, depending upon the elements of time and place. The standard originally —and indeed up to 1628— was 'tunnage', based upon the number of tuns of wine a ship could load into her hold. The ratio between capacity and weight has varied considerably through the centuries and is further complicated by the varying standards applying in different countries. Today we have even further complications because different commodities have also their own units of measurement.

The 'displacement' of a vessel certainly bears a relevant meaning as related to its 'burthen', but the latter is the better term when assessing the size and capacity of early sailing craft because there are no deductions to be made in respect of engines, bunkers, etc. As regards crews' quarters, that factor in those hardy days can be almost completely ignored! We can broadly assume that a 70-ton vessel was sixty-five feet in length and of fifteen feet beam, and by the same computation a 120-ton ship would have measured eighty-five feet by eighteen feet.

After Wolsey's fall from power and the discontinuance of his grandiose scheme for the establishment of a College at Ipswich the question arose as to what was to be done with the endowments which he had earmarked for this foundation; accordingly in 1529 a commission assembled in Woodbridge which declared that all Wolsey's estates should by reason of his breach of the Statute of Praemunire be forfeited to the King. On this commission sat Sir Humphrey Wingfield and five years later, in 1534, the Priory with its lands at Woodbridge was granted to Sir Anthony Wingfield, Knight of the Garter and Vice-Chamberlain to the King! Later the Priory passed into the hands of the Seckfords, a family of established standing who nevertheless had not disdained to take advantage of those days of change and advancement to improve their position still further. In their successes they were not ungenerous and Thomas Seckford became a most munificent benefactor of the town. To him Woodbridge owes many charitable bequests, the Almshouses bearing his name, and not least the distinguished Shire Hall or Market Hall with its Dutch-looking gables, decorated with the Seckford arms.

Meantime shipbuilding had advanced in no small measure, three King's ships, *Darling, Resolution* and *Protection,* being built about 1630. A great deal of timber had been shipped from Framlingham for Deptford Dockyard and not for the first nor the last time was sound Suffolk oak in high demand. In the days of wooden ships the builders needed not only long straight boards, which could only be got from close-planted trees, but also naturally grown 'knees' for which the trees had to be open planted so that the branches would spread and thus give the massive brackets so much stronger and more stable than those which had to be sawn to shape.

In 1633, there came an important visitor to the town; important in his own right as one of the greatest shipbuilders of his age, and doubly important to the future prosperity of the town in this sphere. Phineas Pett, one of a distinguished family of naval architects of Chatham and creator of the greatest ship in the troublous reign of Charles the First, the *Sovereign Of The Seas,* often came to Woodbridge to buy the finest timber he could procure for the vessels he was building at Chatham and Woolwich.

He usually stayed at the Crown Inn kept by Mistress Cole, then in her widowhood and mother of an eligible daughter, Margaret.

Phineas Pett was not only an outstanding naval architect; he was also a calculating, shrewd and acquisitive citizen of the world and he had no doubt considered the prospects of his fifth and favourite son, Peter, marrying Margaret Cole with all the material advantages which that would bring. He had already managed to have Peter, at the age of twenty, appointed Master Shipwright at Woolwich, thus enabling him to retain the Commissionership at Chatham and so still further strengthen the influence of this amazing dynasty of craftsmen who had been building King's ships since the time of Henry VIII. By a marriage with Margaret Peter would acquire an interest in a quay, a shipyard and a wet dock at Woodbridge with scope for still further development; for the Coles a union with the Petts — Phineas had already become a gentleman of coat-armour — must be equally attractive on social grounds. The parents were at one in this, Peter and Margaret were mutually attracted and the marriage at Woodbridge Church of St Mary's on Sunday, 8th September inevitably followed.

For the historian or genealogist any account of the Pett family is a tangled skein; for apparently they seemed to have such a predilection for the names of Phineas and Peter, even in those branches which did not follow shipbuilding, that it is a puzzle to sort them all out.

Between them, Phineas, the forceful egotist, and Peter, the dedicated artist and craftsman, the *Sovereign Of The Seas* was launched and even now, looking at her drawings, the model in the National Maritime Museum and her portrayal by the artists of the period, we are left breathless at her magnificence of ornament, her lines and sailplan, her armament of a hundred guns, maybe more, and her tonnage which impressed the supersitious who duly noted that it matched the date of her launch, 1637. Even Nelson's *Victory* launched a hundred and twenty years later was no more than 2,162 tons.

All this happened many miles from Woodbridge and may seem immaterial to our story; but the repercussions on the maritime history of the town are highly relevant. Phineas Pett died in 1647 and his son Peter continued to build ships not only for the King but also for the Commonwealth. Above all he was dedicated to his profession without regard to the political scene. It is probable that the fourth-raters which came off the stocks at Woodbridge during the succeeding years were constructed under his aegis, although he himself had many other matters in hand. *Advice* (545 tons) and *Reserve* (533 tons) in 1650, *Maidstone* (556 tons) re-named at the Restoration *Mary Rose;* and *Preston* (516 tons), re-named *Antelope,* in 1654, must have done much to boost the prestige of Woodbridge craftsmen and to witness to the excellence of Suffolk oak.

In spite of Peter's dedication, which proved his undoing at the end, there must have been a strain of his father's opportunism in his make-up; for when the King came back in 1660 he was quick to present himself at Scheveningen to kiss the hand of his lawful sovereign and the naval pageantry of the King's return owed much to his stage-management. He was confirmed in his appointment as Commissioner at Chatham and basked in the royal favour. As the Navy became a prime consideration with Charles, encouraged by his equally naval-minded brother, James it seemed that nothing could go wrong for this prince of shipbuilders.

Alas! the men who mattered then, as in subsequent and indeed more recent times, were themselves short-sighted time-servers who had never served a gun nor rove a rope through a block. The story of how we failed to make sufficient preparations to cope with the Dutch threat is general history and may be read elsewhere. Having laid up our capital ships and left a body of mutinous mariners who had been paid off with valueless paper money, some of whom were driven to sell their local knowledge to the enemy, it was inevitable that the fleet was wide open to attack. As is well-known, the Dutch descended on the Thames and Medway, blockaded London and burnt three of our finest first-raters to the waterline, as well as taking the *Royal Charles* and numerous lesser ships as prizes. It was the most humiliating defeat that the Royal Navy has ever suffered, then or since.

The nation was furious; the public had been terrified and like all people who have done nothing in their own defence, the real culprits looked around for scapegoats. The Privy Council arrested Peter Pett who, as Commissioner at Chatham, seemed marked down for destruction. The account of his examination by as fine a collection of double-faced rogues and time-servers as could be imagined is a sad and sorry story. A significant witness to their ineptitude is that the chief charge laid against Pett was that he had used some of the boats available to remove his ship-models before the Dutch could capture them. Only an architect could know that their value to an enemy would be incalculable. To these miserable, highly-placed nincompoops, they were merely 'toys'.

The Commissioner was dismissed from his office with ignominy. He did not live for more than a year or so after his disgrace and whether he returned to Woodbridge to nurse his private grief we know not. He and his family had brought fame and profit to the town and the river, and his eminence as the greatest shipbuilder of his age, greater even than his great sire, has conferred high honour on the little Suffolk town where his wife was born. Let that be his epitaph.

Woodbridge continued to build ships, although the size and importance of her ships was diminished as more and more were built on the Thames or at Portsmouth. Ipswich turned out ships for the Royal Navy until the Napoleonic War, but they were of insignificant size and with one exception, the *Hampshire* (854 tons) built in 1741, they never matched the Deben ships of the Commonwealth and Restoration period.

Meanwhile trade flourished, and when Defoe visited the town in 1722, he had this to say:

> "Woodbridge has nothing remarkable but that it is a considerable market for butter and corn to be exported to London, for now begins that part which is ordinarily called High Suffolk, which being a rich soil is for a long tract of ground wholly employed in dairies, and they again famous for the best butter, and perhaps the worst cheese, in England. The butter is barrelled or often pickled up in small casks and sold, not in London only, but I have known a firkin of Suffolk butter sent to the West Indies and brought back to England again, and has been perfectly good and sweet as at first.
>
> The port for the shipping off their Suffolk butter is chiefly Woodbridge, which for that reason is full of corn-factors and butter-factors, some of whom are very considerable merchants."

In the Napoleonic War, when the whole East Coast and particularly the inviting estuaries of Suffolk was considered an area vulnerable to invasion, Woodbridge had troops quartered in the town for a number of years. Many of the handsome Georgian houses now standing and highly esteemed by those who can afford to buy them today were built for the accommodation of the officers and the socialites who, for family or other reasons, gravitated to this attractive corner of East Anglia. The troops were housed in barracks, chiefly infantry at Woodbridge, with a regiment of cavalry at Wickham Market. Over the years many famous regiments were stationed here, some of them militia battalions whence drafts proceeded to make up wastage in the Peninsula or elsewhere. It is probable that some of the man may have stayed for many years and died here, as for example Henry Crawford, Drum-Major of the Durham Militia, who was buried in 1808 at the fine fighting age of 74.

A not inconsiderable part of the sea-borne trade was in coal brought here in collier brigs from Newcastle and in the eighteenth and nineteenth centuries there were as many as twelve coal wharves. In the days when water transport was surer, swifter and cheaper than land transport it was obviously of advantage to discharge coals at intermediate points on the river without bringing them up to Woodbridge town; accordingly they were frequently landed at Bawdsey Ferry, Kirton Creek and Waldringfield, and where coals could be discharged it is obvious that corn and other goods could be shipped. An interesting incoming cargo at this period was porter, which is not a beer one would associate with an agricultural area, and it may be that this distinctively London beverage was in demand to slake the never-ending thirst of the 'coalies' who unloaded the colliers. A fascinating outgoing cargo over a long period was Suffolk cheese or 'bang'. In the light of the many un-complimentary comments on this exceedingly hard commodity, it is puzzling that anyone should want to buy it. It is on record that after the battle of Dunbar a ship set out with nearly 44 tons of the stuff for the Army, which would seem to suggest that the Iron-sides had teeth and digestions to match. At twopence ha'penny a pound it cannot have been a very cheap diet.

It was probably in connection with the same battle that the church bell-ringers were paid five shillings for their services in thanksgiving for the defeat of "our brethren, the Scots"; and it seems a little ungracious, if politic, for the bells also to be rung on the death of the Lord Protector in 1658.

Besides coal, there were other commodities which contributed to put Woodbridge very high up on the list of East Coast trading ports. There were four regular ships on the London run, one every week carrying corn, flour and cement to the capital and bringing back, besides the aforesaid porter, sugar, hops, wine and spirits, tea, groceries and the products of the London manufacture markets. As the result of this volume of trade, the town had three timber yards, three lime kilns, a cement factory and a tannery. Later, when the railway came to Woodbridge, much of this was lost to the river traffic, and although shipbuilding and a small amount of foreign trade still lingered on, some local poetaster was moved to write in parody of Goldsmith:

> "There was a time ere Deben's griefs began
> When every river wharf maintained its merchantman
> But times are changed, the locomotive's snort
> Has cast its breath on all and dispossessed the Port."

Although the main bulk of the sea-borne trade suffered here as elsewhere by the competition heralded by the 'locomotive's snort', there still remained a deal of trade from abroad and ship-building went on for another two generations. Indeed, with the emphasis now on yachts rather than larger craft, it flourishes today with undiminished vigour. From the aspect of the river there is always brisk activity in building, refitting, and general maintenance of yachts, and this is mostly for hulls of traditional construction and design. The local craftsmen do not take over-kindly to fibre-glass and other 'benefits' of modern science!

A fascinating survival which stands by the Deben is the old tide mill, one of the very few in existence, and it was still in working order until a very few years ago. The millpool has now been converted into a yacht basin but without destroying its general appearance beyond the widening of its sluices into a practicable entry for vessels. The mill building has perforce been shrouded with corrugated iron to keep it weathertight; but there are plans afoot to rehabilitate it as a monument to its past glory.

The mill dates back to 1170 and belonged to the Priory; but in 1532 at an episcopal visitation, one of the Austin Canons who was curate of the Parish Church, and who seems to have been given to a certain carping criticism, complained sourly that the financial affairs of the Priory had been bedevilled by the expense of repairs to the said mill. In 1953, when it was last possible to work the mill by water power, the pond measured 3,100,000 square feet with a six foot head. The wooden wheel housed in a small wheel-house outside the main structure was renewed in 1932 when the preliminary work of assembling and working the parts was carried out on the Whistocks boatyard which adjoins the mill and their Tidemill Yacht Basins. It is twenty feet in diameter by seventy inches wide, with closed wooden buckets and mounted on a twenty-two inch square shaft of oak. To operate it a rear vertical penstock was first raised and with a full head of water this allowed the water to flow at a height to 'breast shoot' the wheel. When the level of the water dropped, the sluice could be adjusted so that the wheel became undershot. It drove four pairs of stones which were controlled by a single pair of governors, and this was a unique arrangement.

The old building, even in its 'utility' cladding, is a traditional and distinctive part of the Woodbridge river scene, and it is greatly to be hoped that it may be possible to preserve it with the machinery as a precious link with the skill and pride of craftsman-ship of those elder brethren who made Woodbridge great. Indeed a Trust has been officially established for this purpose under distinguished patronage to which the ownership of the Mill has been transferred. The success of the venture depends on the support it receives from those who love and value this unique relic.

Another link with the busy town of yesteryear is to be found in New Street just below Market Hill. Here, jutting out over the roadway, is the old 'Steelyard', still commemorated in name as well as in fact by the name of the inn of which it forms part, the *Bell & Steelyard*. I believe that there is only one other steelyard of this size still in situ, and that is at Soham in Cambridgeshire, also in East Anglia. The principle of the steelyard as a weighing device consisting a lever balancing on a fulcrum and with a sliding counterpoise is very ancient and is still employed in weighing, but not on the scale of the Woodbridge and Soham examples. As to why this apparatus should be called a steelyard, we find ourselves involved again in a generally accepted case of muddled etymology. It is not called by that name because it is a yard long, nor because it is made of steel — indeed many of the earliest examples were made of bronze. In the vernacular it should be more properly spelt and pronounced 'Stilliard'. The earliest use of the word in England is probably in the City of London where the warehouse 'Stalhofes' of the Hanseatic merchants was by 1320 anglicised as 'stilehof' or 'steelyard'. It is sometimes stated that the court or yard — 'hof' — was where they sold steel among other commodities;

but this is improbable and meaningless, since *stall* in German is not the same as *stahl*. The real derivation of 'stallhof' is more likely to be that this name was given to a warehouse or yard in front of which stalls for the sale of merchandise were erected. Hence the corruption and loose translation in London became steelyard or stillyard. This is where the Londoners, from Marlowe to Pepys, used to resort to drink Rhenish wine.

It is also sometimes stated that the existence of a steelyard is evidence that the export trade in wool passed this way; alas! wool was not weighed with a steelyard but on an equal-armed balance using special weights.

Be all this as it may, the Woodbridge steelyard —which was used to weigh waggons laden and unladen—thus giving the weight of their contents— remains a fascinating link with the past and a reminder of the volume and value of the trade which passed through this ancient port and market town.

So, through the centuries, men came and went, were born, married, begat children and died. Kings and Queens came and went, religious beliefs changed, albeit a certain immutable truth remained, ships were built and sailed away and came and went on their lawful occasions — and some there were that came never again. All this time, for thirteen hundred years or more, the Deben valley held in its heart a secret the existence of which was undreamt of. Over on the river opposite Woodbridge lies the little village of Sutton, hardly visited except by an odd visitor of an antiquarian turn of mind who wanted to see the old church with its waggon-roofed ceiling, and fine but damaged font. There were also some barrows on the rising ground which although they must have been clearly visible to the local inhabitants had become masked by the growing belt of woodland. In any case they would have held no interest for most people, unless perchance invested with a faint aura of superstitious awe. At some time the site, sometimes known as Sutton Walks, became the property of Colonel Frank Pretty who, if he did not do much about the barrows, at least prevented one of them being dug out to provide spoil for levelling up a farmyard. One of his predecessors, scenting the possibility of buried treasures, put his gamekeeper on to digging in search of this desirable commodity! Mercifully, nothing was found and it was left for the Colonel's widow, the late Mrs Pretty, to take an intelligent and sympathetic interest in the matter. The result is what is now known as the greatest archaeological discovery of an Anglian ship-burial in the country. Although the ship itself has perished through the chemical action of the soil, the corroded remains of the iron nails indicate with some precision the size and shape of the hull. The 'grave-goods', buckles, brooches of gold, garnets, enamel and millefiori, silver bowls, cups, spoons and other articles are splendid beyond belief. As the treasure was found at the inquest to be not Treasure Trove, it remained the property of Mrs Pretty who with magnificent generosity gave it to the nation and it is now safely housed in the British Museum.

This is not the place to describe in detail the various items comprised in the Sutton Hoo treasure, the beauty and value of which both intrinsic and historical is beyond compare. We may, however, take note of one aspect of the find which is still exercising the minds of scholars both here and abroad. This ship-burial is a cenotaph; that is to say, there was no body, either buried or cremated, in the ship. The probable identity of the king — for he could not have been a lesser person — on behalf of whom this great hoard of treasure was buried is yet to be established. Would it be presumptuous to speculate on the possibility of his being a Christian who, while buried elsewhere according to the rites of his Faith, was commemorated by the observance of this pre-christian ceremony to conform to ancient custom. Time and a great deal of painstaking research by those qualified to go further than mere idle guesswork will one day tell us.

Speculation, aided by latterday progress in methods of archaeological methods of dating based upon radioactive decay and chemical mutation, points to a strong probability that the King commemorated at Sutton Hoo may have been Raedwald, the first King of East Anglia to be acknowledged as Bretwalda, or High King of southern England. It is known that during a visit to Ethelbert of Kent, Raedwald was converted to Christianity; but the story goes that on his return to East Anglia this eccentric behaviour did not commend itself to his wife and like Alexander Severus, he found a certain modus vivendi by setting up in his family shrine images or symbols of Christ, together with those of his former tutelary deities of the Northlands. Such a state of affairs would perhaps have called for a funerary disposition which would be in line with the "cenotaph" theory.

And what of Woodbridge today? Of all the towns of East Anglia there cannot be one which in dignity and serenity can compare with this old port by the Deben. Nowhere can there be such an assembly of Georgian facades with an odd half-timbered dwelling or mellow inn thrown in for good measure. Such a succession of distinguished doorways, each an architectural gem in its own right, creates such an atmosphere of tranquillity and timelessness that one may expect at any moment to see the scarlet coatees and tall shakoes of the George III period as their wearers meet on the street or pay their social calls on the good ladies of Woodbridge. Still the bread dole established by John Sayer, Yeoman, in 1638 to be distributed amongst the Poor of the Parish every Sabbath Day, is honoured and it is still paid for out of the income on the lands which John Sayer charged for the purpose. Still the roads slope down to the riverside where the quays were once so busy, and where the yachting fraternity still disport themselves on Deben's broad bosom.

There are still many dignified cottages, albeit some of them have been spoiled by having their windows with their traditional glazing bars replaced with characterless flush frames or their fielded doors cast aside for monstrosities of glass to keep up with the latest trend in the glossy magazines. The river wall is no better for having its grassbanks replaced by hideous concrete blocks which are themselves already disintegrating in sordid decrepitude; nor are the seats on the promenade improved by being painted in an eye-searing blue which, although gay for a boat, is garish in any other role. The once pleasant spinney on the Melton Road, now used as a dumping ground for all kinds of indescribable rubbish is better passed by on the other side in the hope that one day Bumble will come to his senses. Such a fair heritage as this Woodbridge calls for better treatment by those who have its well-being in their hands.

Shingle Saga

WE HAVE seen how tidal flow and shingle drift have combined to shape our Eastern coastline. What the sea takes away at one point it gives back at another. While it erodes a natural haven which served our ancestors as a shelter for ships it also leaves those long shingle spits which have given our rivers their distinctive southward estuarial pattern. Towns standing well back from the sea have been made, and unmade, by what may seem to our finite minds the mere caprice of nature. From this too proceeds an infinite variety of scenery, now warm and welcoming, now stern and inhospitable, sometimes suave and treacherous.

Thus we have the build-up of Landguard — *langer*, the long spear — which at the same time has been both a threat to the mariner and by its very growth a haven of refuge for ships sheltering behind its protecting arm. To Ipswich which has alternately prospered and languished through the centuries has been added the stripling Felixstowe which with the energy and uninhibited enterprise of youth is thriving and ever growing. Wadgate, Goseford, Bawdsey are become ghost havens, living only in the epics of seagoing Suffolk; but Woodbridge prospered in her day and still sits gracious and serene beside the lovely Deben.

With the next river, the Ore, for so we must call it at its estuarine meeting with the sea, we have a different tale to tell. Here in Hollesley Bay, a mile north of Shingle Street, ends the long spit which has provided the most dramatic example in this part of Eastern England of what the wind and tide can do to our coastline. Orford Haven does not belie its name, once the bar has been safely negotiated; but this river is a very different thing to the fair valleys of the Orwell and the Deben. Viewed on a summer's day under the great bow of the Suffolk sky, Shingle Street presents a perfect picture of sunlight and shingle, beach and sky, with the pleasant stretch to Hollesley and Boyton and Staverton Forest away on the distant skyline.

But when the wind and the tide make wild sport the place can be full of a bleak and implacable menace. Let Hilaire Belloc tell of how he set out to sail his century-old boat from Lowestoft to Harwich; but when he got as far as Aldeburgh he decided that he must take shelter in Orford Haven:

"As Orfordness came near, the seas that had hitherto followed like giants in battle now took to a mad scrimage. They leapt pyramidically, they heaved up horribly under her; she hardly obeyed her helm, and even in that gale her canvas flapped in the troughs. Then in despair I prayed to the boat itself (since nothing else could hear me), 'Oh, Boat,' for so I was taught the vocative, 'bear me safe round this corner, and I will scatter wine over your decks'. She heard me and rounded the point and so terrified was I that (believe me if you will) I had not even the soul to remember how ridiculous and laughable it was that sailors should call this Cape of Storms 'the Onion'.

Once round it, for some reason I will not explain but that I believe connected with my prayer, the sea grew tolerable. It still came on to the land (we could sail with the wind, starboard), and the wind blew harder yet; but we ran before it more easily, because the water was less steep. We were racing down the long drear shingle bank of Orford, past what they call 'the life-boat house' on the chart (there is no life-boat there, nor ever was), past the look-out of the coastguard, till we saw white water breaking on the bar of the Alde.

Then I said to my companion, 'There are, I know, two mouths to this harbour, a northern and a southern; which shall we take?' But he said, 'Take the nearest'. I then, reciting my firm beliefs and remembering my religion, ran for the white water. Before I knew well that she was round, the sea was yellow like a pond, the waves no longer heaved, but raced and broke as they do upon a beach. One greener, kindly and roaring, a messenger of the gale grown friendly after its play with us, took us up on its crest and ran us into the deep and calm beyond the bar, but as we crossed, the gravel ground beneath our keel. So the boat made harbour. Then without hesitation, she cast herself upon the mud, and I sitting at the tiller, my companion ashore, and pushing at her inordinate sprit, but both revelling in safely, we gave thanks and praise. That night we scattered her decks with wine as I had promised, and lay easy in deep water within."*

---

* *Hills and the Sea,* by kind permission of Methuen and Co. Ltd.

It is very evident that Belloc, running for safety in this shoal-beset water, found as so many do, that to gain that safety he was in yet further hazard from the bar. However here he was, safe and sound, and like us he could take a good look at this strange, lonely estuary.

The story of this long shingle spit is a strange one; for the sea has been most capricious in its give and take. Although from time to time there has been a tendency to believe that once the Alde came out to sea at Slaughden there is no doubt that if this were ever so, it would be at some period so remote that it is of little consequence to this present story. Some of the sixteenth century maps are so difficult to reconcile with the scale and shape of the coastline as to be of doubtful value; but there is a chart in the British Museum usually dated at about 1530 which shows the estuary as entering the sea approximately south-east of the castle which would seem to be roughly in accordance with the facts at that time, assuming that it is not itself a copy of an earlier map. There are two other maps also in the British Museum, one the date of which is believed to be between 1570 and 1580, and the other "made in Aldeboroughe by Ananias Appleton Aō Dni 1588". In spite of the unpromising associations of this gentleman's forename, there would seem to be no good reason to doubt his veracity, although it is obvious that the scale of his map is so variable as to invalidate its testimony. Moreover, the only copy of this map known to exist is inscribed, "The original of this map I saw at the house of the late Leveson Vernon Esq., at Aldborough in 1830". This statement is unsigned and the original map has never been found.

In 1593 John Norden, then 45, was "authorised and appointed by Her Majesty to travil through England and Wales to make more perfect descriptions, charts and maps" and in 1600-01 he surveyed the lands of Sir Michael Stanhope in Suffolk which includes the area of Orford. We are now on much more reliable ground and Norden's maps are fairly trustworthy on detail, orientation and scale. From his map we now get a fairly good idea of the extent to which the shingle spit had lengthened during the preceding seventy years, something of the order of three miles. This distance was going to increase still farther in the next three centuries; not at a constant rate of growth, but attaining in 1897 its maximum length of nearly five miles. A large part of the shingle drift was undoubtedly derived from that eroded from Orford

Ness itself and swept in a south-westerly direction. By the same token the channel of the Ore narrowed until the eventual opening to the sea at North Weir Point became a hazardous bar. Since 1897 there has been some recession to the extent of a half-mile or more. It may well be that the 1530 map, which is very pictorial, represents the river-mouth as it was a century or so earlier; or again it may well be that the shingle drift had not attained such magnitude in those far-off days when the Ness gave more protection from the restless, swirling movement of wind and tide.

One effect of this build-up of the spit over the centuries is that the Butley River which formerly emptied itself into the sea has become a tributary of the Ore which, divided into two channels, the Gull and the Narrows, thus encircles the desolate waste of Havergate Island. Once the scene of bloody crime and dark deeds never fully known, this now affords a sanctuary where the lovely avocets, once thought to have left this country for good, have returned to breed under the watchful guard of the Royal Society for the Protection of Birds.

But we must not digress overmuch; the river today is a deserted place except for a few enthusiastic yachtsmen, and indeed, with the hazards of the bar, it is hoped that only the experienced will venture out to sea. For the inexperienced such waters are best shunned; the lifeboat service has plenty of worthwhile tasks on its hands without wasting time and dissipating its energies in pulling half-wits from a well-deserved watery grave.

When Henry II decided in or about 1165 to build a castle at Orford he was undoubtedly influenced by two considerations. In the first place the estuary offered a tempting and practicable point of entry to any force, whether friendly or hostile, seeking to make a landfall. There was already a settlement at what later became a substantial borough and we know that there had been early water-borne traffic, whether by Angles or Danes, as far as Snape or beyond. It was therefore a matter of the utmost importance that the King should have a strong-point here which should at one and the same time protect the coming and going of lawful traffic and deny the same facilities to unwelcome visitors.

There was also another political factor which must have weighed heavily with Henry. Ever since the rise of the Bigods, the King's writ had run uneasily in East Anglia and as we have already seen, these opportunists could never be trusted. In 1154 there were no royal castles at all in Norfolk or Suffolk; but Hugh Bigod, Earl of Norfolk by good grace of Stephen, held four: Bungay, Framlingham, Walton and Thetford. It is of course impossible to control one castle from another; but a strong garrison constitutes a base from which the movement of other forces can be held in check. Henry knew well the importance of having such a base which could give him an armoured foothold, so to say, with the object of watching the activities of the irrepressible Hugh. Probably for this reason he put into this castle all that the castle-builders of the period knew of fortification and there was no fortress in the whole country, except Dover, which cost so much to build; more-over the massive keep, which still stands today, was completed in two years, which would suggest that the King regarded it as a matter of urgency. As it fell out Henry, whose judgment was often warped by his own impulsive nature, was in this case justified in the result. In 1173, which saw the completion of the castle, the rebellion, in which the King's three sons were involved, broke out and a force of Flemish mercenaries landed near Ipswich under the leadership of the Earl of Leicester. Here again Hugh Bigod with his usual opportunism cast his lot with the insurgents; but apart from intercepting some supplies for the castle they achieved very little in these parts and were faithfully dealt with by the Royal justiciars. Henry, having reconciled himself with the church for his part in the murder of Becket, now set about cutting the claws of these rumbustious barons for good and all and under his orders the Bigod castles at Walton, Framlingham and Bungay were so 'slighted' as to constitute no further threat to the King's supremacy.

It is often asserted that the town of Orford — the ford by the bank or riverside — was a port of some importance for some time before the castle was built; but if so there remains a mystery which, so far as I know, has never been satisfactorily resolved. The present church stands on the site of a previous one which is believed to have been built at about the same date as the castle; it is quite likely that the presence of skilled craftsmen and available stocks of building material made this a propitious time to build a church; and it may be that 'Wimar the Chaplain' who was one of the King's agents for the construction of the castle, used his good offices to this end. It is however incredible that if Orford had been of any previous importance it would not have had some kind of church instead of relying upon Sudbourne, two miles away, for the religious observances which the mediaeval merchants regarded as essential to ensure their material prosperity. Some have even dated Orford back to the ninth century; but in those days the whole countryside was being harried by the Danes. It seems more likely that Orford itself was not much more than a 'place' where a few fishermen and coastwise mariners could shelter and draw their boats up on the strand.

Be that as it may, Orford rapidly grew with the passage of the years to be an important maritime town. To what extent this was was due to the growing export trade in wool and other native products and how far the presence of a castle garrison, with its political and social implications, made for a greater security is neither here nor there. The size of the craft which thronged Orford Haven was of course slight by our modern standards; but the port was of sufficient size and importance by 1205 for the King to station two galleys to guard the coast from Orford to Yarmouth.

Henry III conferred a charter upon the town establishing a merchant gild and other privileges and subsequent charters were granted by succeeding monarchs, although it was not until 1579 that the town was incorporated by Elizabeth I who granted it a 'mayor and commonalty' consisting of eight portmen and twelve capital burgesses together with nine officers including a recorder, town clerk, coroner, chamberlain, claviger, water bailiffs and sergeants-at-mace. Orford claimed to have been a borough 'by prescription'; but this would confer but a doubtful status until such time as there was a formal charter of incorporation. In 1255 there were 'arrests' or impressments of ships large enough to carry sixteen horses and in this category Orford was specified in company with Ipswich and Dunwich. Not long after that Dunwich entered upon its first stage of decline and although there would not seem any direct relation between the two towns, it would seem that Orford's sun ascended as that of Dunwich declined. In 1293 the town had to find four ships for the King's Scotch war.

It is regrettable, but entirely in character with those rather boisterous days, that in 1309 a vessel from Bruges was 'emptied' and sunk at Orford. In that bald statement we may infer that Orford was no better than its neighbours in taking advantage of whatever a beneficent Providence provided for the taking!

The growing importance of the town may be deduced from the fact that in 1344 it had to send a representative to Westminster to consult on matters of defence and to receive the instructions on the part they should play together with Ipswich, Dunwich and Goseford. Of course, this growth in importance carried with it comparable liabilities and in 1360 Orford was included in an order for the 'arrest' of all her ships to serve the King in his French war.

An important factor in the affairs of Orford was the existence not far away at the head of the Butley River of the Priory of that name. Founded in 1171 by Sir Ranulph de Glanville, chief Justiciar of England and later founder of Leiston Abbey, the house was for Austin Canons and by their original foundation and subsequent benefactions they eventually became one of the wealthiest religious houses in the kingdom — not taking into account the great Benedictine abbeys. Most of Butley's income came from the many benefices of which they had the advowson and in consequence the Priory had much business to transact; therefore their influence in the affairs of Orford was considerable and the coming and going of important visitors must have brought much business to the town. There was also a house of Austin Friars founded in 1295 in Orford itself, although they do not seem to have been very numerous; as friars they would not have had need for extensive buildings. There were also two Hospitals, one of which was probably for lepers. From this, as well as from the increased flow of shipping, can be gauged the evergrowing size and importance of the town. That the town claimed Admiralty jurisdiction was recorded by the two silver oars which were the insignia of the water bailiffs until the demise of the borough. Although they are hall-marked 1812-13, the Tudor royal arms suggest that they may be replacements of earlier ones.

No story of mediaeval Orford would be complete without some mention of the 'Wild Man' who in 1180 is said to have been taken by certain fishermen in their nets. He was covered with hair and had a long and shaggy beard, but could not be persuaded to talk although he was harshly tortured, nor would he show any conventional sign of reverence when taken into the Castle chapel. At first he seemed to have no desire to escape when taken into the sea; but eventually he escaped and was never again seen. It seems unlikely that the fishermen would have failed to recognise a seal; or could it have been a small walrus a bit off course? The suggestion has been made — perish the thought! — that he could have been fobbed off by the fishermen to make monkeys of the castle garrison, who would presumably be unlearned in marine zoology!

It is believed that in the thirteenth century there was considerable traffic in wool between the farmers and religious houses in this part of Suffolk and the continent. This may well have been so; but as the whole export trade in wool came under the strict and over-riding control of the Staple it seems likely that Orford, like Ipswich, was merely a port of lading and that beyond the freightage little profit would have accrued to the town. When under Edward III more and more English wool was woven into English cloth the whole pattern of the traffic would have changed. Nevertheless Orford continued to flourish and its importance can still be judged from the demands for ships for the King's service which went on until the Tudor monarchs set about making their own provisions for naval requirements. Even then in times of emergency there would come orders for impressment of vessels to meet the sovereign's demands and for the defence of the realm.

Meanwhile the shingle spit was constantly though not consistently extending southwards. It does not seem to have obstructed the channel to the town overmuch; but with the passage of time the importance of Orford's nearest neighbour was increasing and it may well be that the eventual decay of the town was due not entirely to the action of the sea but also to competition. Nevertheless there is no doubt that the navigation of the ever-lengthening channel of the Ore was to the disadvantage of shipping and in 1813 some speculators proposed to cut an opening to the sea opposite Orford which would had the effect of restoring the original estuary. At the same time a wet-dock was to be constructed behind Havergate Island by erecting lock-gates in the Lower Gull, presumably above its confluence with the Butley River. A similar scheme was revived at the end of the century in the hope of providing a haven for coastal and Baltic ships. However nothing came of either scheme and Orford was left to the peaceful, if unambitious life which she enjoys today. The town lost its two members of Parliament by the Reform Act of 1832 and its corporate status as a borough by the Municipal Corporations Act, 1835.

The ancient traditions of the town are now preserved, in memory, by the Orford Town Trust in which is vested the custody of the former municipal insignia. The gracious peace remains inviolate, albeit the place is in appearance little more than a large village, although much valuabie and effective work has been done of late to restore the tower of the church to a state worthy of the dignity of the surviving portion of the original nave.

How long the peace of Orford will endure the traffic which is an inevitable consequence of the completion of the Orfordness 'project' is a matter of uneasy conjecture, as conjectural in fact as the various speculations concerning the exact nature and extent of all the mysterious operations upon which this essential factor in the defence and welfare of the realm would seem to depend. A beneficial by-product of the 'project' which will be appreciated by the yachting fraternity is an improved quay and a practicable slipway.

At the present time there is a small but flourishing trade in oysters which is a revival of a form of fishing once very active and indeed a great cause of contentions between Orford and her neighbours. As if the fame and prolificacy of the Essex and Kentish oyster-beds were not sufficient, the men of Brightlingsea and Colchester yearned to hire Orford's river to take their oysters too. When this proposition was rejected the strangers were not above creeping in at night to take by stealth what they could not obtain by fair dealing — and moreover were disposed to fight it out. This was in 1790 and eventually the matter went to the Court of King's Bench at the Bury Assizes, which resulted in a verdict with costs for Orford. It is worth reflecting that all this pother was about a succulent mollusc which the Romans had esteemed as a delicacy but which in the eighteen-fifties was sold in London by the million at a farthing each; which may account for the virility of the Victorians!

One of the hazards of Orfordness to passing shipping was recognised in the early seventeenth century when a lighthouse was erected on the Ness, or rather a little back towards the river where the standing was more stable. Originally it had been hoped that this would have been erected at Aldeburgh, the bailiffs of which town asked for one in 1627; but in those days the material factor was not so much where a lighthouse should be erected for the benefit of shipping as where a speculator could secure a site which would be to his advantage. We shall be considering the story of the High Light at Lowestoft in due course; this was built by Trinity House, but the Corporation at its inception was more concerned with pilotage rather than lighthouses. The result of this state of affairs was that most of the early lights were put up by private speculators who, having built the lighthouse by Royal Patent, enjoyed the tolls levied for their upkeep on passing ships. These were collected at customs ports where the ships called, often not without some amount of tendentious argument. It is not certain exactly when the Orfordness light was installed; but it was probably before 1637 in which year a patent was issued in favour of Sir John Meldrum, who together with Sir William Erskine had erected lighthouses at Winterton under a patent of James I. Erskine's interest had passed to one Gerald Gore and it seems that Meldrum had already put up two lights at Orfordness, presumably a high light and a low light. Between them Meldrum and Gore had established quite a nice little empire, combining both Winterton and Orfordness, and from thenceforward the interests were bandied about along a whole chain of speculators, none of whom was particularly concerned about maintaining the efficiency of the lights but drew an enormous income from the concession. Lease followed lease and in 1823 when Parliament began to give attention to this bonanza of speculation the net profit on the two lighthouses at Winterton and Orfordness, which together were then held by Lord Braybrooke, amounted to £13,414 a year. As a further example of the dimensions which this private monopoly had attained throughout the country it is significant that in 1834 there were still fourteen lights in private hands and the speculators received from them nearly as much as Trinity House received from the fifty-five under its control!

Apart from the few vessels which passed farther up the river to the small quay at Slaughden near Aldeburgh, there had been from early times a certain traffic in ships of limited burthen as far as Snape and a few probably got as far as Framlingham; but these would not be of any size and were probably comparable to relatively small wherries. As regards Snape however there was still barge traffic as far as the bridge, and even up to 1826 ships of up to ten feet draught could make this passage to the Garrett Maltings.

That Snape had had much earlier visitors was made evident in 1862 when an Anglian ship-burial was discovered. Various guesses have been made as to the identity and status of the warrior thus interred; but there is little to go on because the discovery was lamentably mishandled by those concerned. What might have been a valuable link in the chain of Anglo-Saxon archaeology was lost for ever with nothing to show but a few bones and an intaglio ring of mediterranean origin of about A.D.630. It may have been of the same period as the Sutton Hoo burials; but neither the ship nor the 'grave goods' are comparable in size or magnificence with the Deben remains. What is very certain is that it was not a 'Viking' ship as some writers have fancifully described it.

Although the tempting stretch of Orfordness has never suffered the indignity of invasion from the sea it has not entirely escaped the noise of battle. On 6th July, 1543 a sea battle was fought off-shore between an English squadron under Sir Rice Mansel and a French force of fifteen ships returning from carrying troops to Scotland. Honours were fairly even, two French ships and one English ship being captured; but Sir Rice persuaded the French to return to the Forth with more haste than credit.

It is now time to take a look at what had been happening a few miles farther up the coast, and also a like distance up the river. A certain amount of traffic had always passed through Orford into the upper waters of the river which had been known for centuries as the Alde from the ancient town of Aldeburgh — the old borough. The circumstances in which Aldeburgh on the seaboard and Orford on her river should find themselves at variance are tied up so much with Aldeburgh's own complex story that it will be best to look at Aldeburgh as a coastal town, an ancient borough and a port.

For the past century and a half the name Aldeburgh has con-jured up in the minds of most people a genial picture of a town by the sea which is yet not a 'seaside' town. A place for middle-class folk and those who have withdrawn from the hurly-burly of business or lives spent in their country's service to enjoy their latter days in peace; a town which welcomes visitors, but does not need to attract them by the meretricious glamour of the 'holiday resort'; a borough which is quietly proud of its antiquity as an historic sea-port and is tolerantly pleased to watch the occasional pomps of municipal pageantry. Modern activities such as golf and dinghy-sailing rub alongside the traditional fishing by the men whose ancestors made Aldeburgh in the past and are the very salt of the earth today. If the noise of their winches in the early morning jars on the ears of those who would slumber on, one does not notice any reluctance to enjoy the fresh-caught fish on the breakfast table. For the past few years Aldeburgh has been identified with the Festival which brings the most distinguished in music and her sister arts to this quiet town by the eastern sea.

All this aura of civilisation and urbanity is sometimes apt to obscure the long-time vista of a town which, while never great among our Eastern sea-ports, has been active and flourishing; able not only to stand upon its own feet but to recover from a natural set-back which could have ended it as a maritime community; a recovery which turned its face from calamity to fresh prosperity.

The Anglo-Saxon *burh* can mean either a town or a fort; but although there is evidence of some Roman occupation hereabouts, it does not necessarily follow that this was a considerable military station. It seems likely however that it had some maritime significance as a port and as such would not have lacked some defences. But where was this port which in those days would have called for a secure haven for vessels? A glance at any map of Tudor date shows that in those days Aldeburgh extended not only farther out to sea but also considerably more to the north. Today the sixteenth century Moot Hall is the proverbial biscuit-toss from the beach and nearly at the northern limit of the town's built-up area; but in these earlier maps it is almost exactly in the centre of the town as there portrayed. This brings the northern boundary of the town to the large near land-locked inlet then known as the Haven, the remains of which is seen as Thorpeness Mere today. This was the original port of Aldeburgh, large enough and deep enough to afford moorings to any craft which in those days sailed the seas. The sad and sorry little stream still known as the Hundred River which after flowing through Knodishall and Aldringham enters the sea ignominiously through a concrete pipe at the sluice between Aldeburgh and Thorpeness, once had a wide and spacious estuary upon which rode the ships which brought trade and prosperity to the mediaeval 'old borough'. Indeed it is probable that some of these ships may have been able to find their way up the river itself to where it now sneaks beneath the main road at Aldringham near the famous *Parrot and Punch Bowl Inn*. Today the water of the Hundred River is called upon from time to time to maintain the level of Thorpeness Mere which is now a lake for the delectation of the young, of all ages, who enjoy messing about in boats. Of course, the Haven was of far greater extent than the present Mere, and certainly extended southwards as far as where the sluice is now. The exact position of Aldeburgh's waterfront must be a matter of conjecture until some fortuitous find which may add to our knowledge on this; but in any event it has little bearing on the Aldeburgh story. Whether at some remote time the Alde, as we must now call it, ever had any common estuary with the Hundred is entirely open to speculation. It may or may not be significant that the Haven was sometimes known as Almouth. But yet again let us not forget that the Alde is held to have derived its name from Aldeburgh and not vice-versa.

That Aldeburgh had a corporate existence in Anglo-Saxon times is self-evident from its name and lying in Plomesgate Hundred, it fell just within the Liberty of Etheldreda. It is therefore natural that from time to time one comes upon the Prior and Monks of Ely as having some slight interest in the place; but it is in another connection that we find a certain maritime interest recorded when in 1155 the manors of Snape and Aldeburgh were bequeathed to the Benedictines of Colchester with the right to flotsam and jetsam between Thorpeness and Orford. From that time forward it is evident that the men of Aldeburgh were vitally interested in the sea, not only for what they could draw from it in their nets but also for what the sea-god in his bounty cast upon their shores; and if perchance some of that flotsam and jetsam failed to reach its lawful owners, no doubt these beachcombers could have told a tale of that too.

In the earliest days the maritime activities of Aldeburgh centred chiefly around fishing. The task of supplying the whole country with fish in pre-Reformation days was an enormous one. While coarse freshwater fish was eaten to a far greater extent in those days than today, undoubtedly those who were near enough to the coast to get sea-fish would prefer it, and, as we shall see in the case of Lowestoft, what could not be caught would be bought from others for re-sale. As regards herring dealings in this fish were strictly controlled; but Aldeburgh was sufficiently far from Yarmouth to be fairly free in what they caught and where they sold it, subject always to local provisions as to the distribution of the various 'doles' between the Town, the Church and the various members of the crew. It is important to remember that the demand for fish did not fall off to any marked degree during the Reformation period — itself of far longer duration than is commonly supposed — and indeed in Elizabethan days it was regarded as essential and of obligation that the days of abstinence be observed, not only for reasons of ecclesiastical discipline but even more for the economic needs of the nation.

As with other places the size and importance of the port can, to some extent, be judged by the number of ships found for the king's service from time to time and although Aldeburgh does not figure in this way so early as other Suffolk ports, there must have been ships using Thorpe Haven, if only as a harbour of refuge in bad weather. In 1497 we find Aldeburgh and Dunwich each finding two ships for the Earl of Surrey's invasion of Scotland. These compare well with three from Walberswick and one each from Southwold, Orford, Easton on the coast and Sizewell. Thirty years later there were Aldeburgh ships involved in the Iceland fishing trade so they must have been stout enough to undertake that hazardous voyage.

Aldeburgh ships, whatever their tonnage or function, were among those which suffered from the depredations of the Dunkirk pirates and we find moreover that even the townsmen were put in hazard by the presence off-shore of these unwelcome strangers. From this it was logical to think of the possibility of a descent upon the coast by the King's enemies and the Eastern seaboard has ever been regarded as our Achilles heel. It was therefore natural for Henry VIII to embark upon a survey of the country's land-based defences in these parts of his realm, and as we have seen, Cromwell suggested that the proceeds of a small tax formerly paid to Rome might well be diverted to national defence. We may think that this would be a better purpose than lining the pockets of the King's sycophants. In 1539 Aldeburgh together with Lowestoft and Landguard was suggested as an appropriate place for defences.

The difference between piracy and privateering in those days seemed a fine point of distinction and if the East coast ports suffered from the Dunkirkers, some of our own men were not above doing a bit of business in that sphere on their own account. In 1569 no less notorious a character than Martin Frobisher was involved concerning a prize which he had brought into Aldeburgh, wherefore he was committed to the Marshalsea prison; but eight years later we find the pirates are busy again —on which side is highly doubtful. What is a regrettable fact is that there were many receivers of pirated goods and a number of Aldeburgh burgesses were fined for dealing with pirates, at least one of whom was a local man, John Flicke of Woodbridge. An interesting sidelight on this activity is that many of these receivers were people of some degree of wealth; perhaps this propounds a fascinating exercise in the allocation of cause and effect. Two years later a search of the town revealed fresh hoards of booty— which argues that the men of Aldeburgh were good triers!

Meantime there is abundant evidence that the size of ships based on Aldeburgh was increasing, and indeed the large ships seem to have run out of trade. At least two of Aldeburgh's ships of 200 tons are said to have 'decayed' presumably for lack of use. A further indication of the size of the port may be found in the figures of the seamen returned as available for service in case of emergency, which in 1566 amounted to one hundred and fifty-five men. This number is not exhaustive because it would not take account of those actually at sea, and it may not include fishermen. At Aldeburgh the fishing boats totalled eighty-nine, which seems high as compared with the men; but it could be that these were manned by men and boys unfit for the Queen's service. In 1582 Aldeburgh had fifteen ships of 100 tons or more of which two were of 200 tons.

In 1588, with the menace of the Armada looming large over every other consideration, the deputy-lieutenants and Captain Turner, who had been sent into Suffolk to survey the defences, reported that Aldeburgh 'being now a town rich in shipping and otherwise' required a fort for which the burgesses would contribute and added that the people,

> "from the best to the meanest are ready, according to their own most bounden duties, to bestow their lives in the service for God, her Majesty and country. And if these necessary defences and succours may be had we shall no doubt fight with the better courage; if not we shall yet, notwithstanding, do the duties of loyal and truehearted subject, but with greater hazard".

Brave words and worthier than deserved by a sovereign who waited until the gravest danger was passed before leaving the safety of London to deliver her vainglorious speech from the back of a white horse at Tilbury!

Aldeburgh got its defences; three batteries carrying twenty guns; but these were never needed for serious use and some must have been removed or deteriorated over the years, for in 1625 the defences were described as eight 'old honeycombed iron pieces'. Let us hope that no one had the temerity to fire them!

Meantime Aldeburgh had for the previous century a problem which threatened her very life as a seaport. The haven at the Thorpe end of the town had been silting up. How much this was due to a reduced rate of flow in the Hundred River, how much a complex of currents and shingle drift around the Ness it may be difficult to establish. A very curious development was that the outlet from the haven to the sea had shrunk to a narrow passage which flowed not in a southerly direction like most East coast estuaries but northwards under the lee of the Ness. The reason for this divergence from the general pattern may have lain in the general tidal flow sweeping around the Ness and so forming an eddy which swirled the shingle round into this curious formation. Be this as it may, the neck gradually filled up so that with the years this wonderful haven became ever less and less accessible to ships of any normal burthen — and with those years ships were getting larger and larger. It behoved Aldeburgh to look elsewhere unless she wanted to go the way of other ports whose front door to the sea had become impassable. Fortunately the Providence which had placed Aldeburgh where she was had provided her with a back-door at Slaughden where the Alde in its seaward journey took a sharp turn southwards before wending its long way parallel to the sea to which it was finally united beyond Orford. In this elbow there had been for a century or so a small quay and a hamlet chiefly for fishermen and the smaller coastal craft, many of which could be hauled out on the shingle and it had formed a convenient place for building boats of these dimensions. There had been for some time a certain number of vessels finding their way up from Orford either to lie here or on their way farther up the river to Snape or beyond. Their passage by Orford was not always without difficulty; for the town under the castle was jealous of its rights and like others in similar case was quick to exploit its position at the river's mouth to interfere with passing craft by the imposition of petty dues and restrictions.

As a result of this turnabout Aldeburgh worried less and less about its shrinking haven at Thorpe and so it came about that Slaughden became in fact the port and gradually the town spread out to link the town centre with the quay. At the same time the voracious sea began to encroach on the town and the time was not far distant when two whole streets would be swallowed up, leaving the borough in a shape approximating to its drawnout plan today.

After the suppression of Snape Priory, Wolsey had appropriated its manorial interest in Aldeburgh to his new college at Oxford and as the result of his fall from Royal favour it was granted by the King to the Duke of Norfolk. On the accession of Edward VI the young

King granted a charter of incorporation providing for the government of the town by two bailiffs, twelve capital and twenty-four inferior burgesses. Charles I authorised the appointment of a Recorder and other officers and in 1885 a new charter established a Mayor, four aldermen and nine councillors. Until the Reform Act, 1832, Aldeburgh retained two Members of Parliament; but this alone is not any indication of the town's importance, the practice of granting charters involving parliamentary representation and other privileges being a fixed policy of some sovereigns and notably the later Tudors. From the Crown's point of view this had the double advantage of raising revenue, since the borough had to pay for this status-symbol, and also ensuring that there should be a sufficiency of members in the Commons with a sense of obligation to the Sovereign. Aldeburgh, like many other similar small towns, was in fact a 'pocket-borough' and the manner in which 'elections' to Parliament were conducted is fully in character. It does not however seem to have descended to the inglorious level of a 'rotten borough' and such bribery as occurred seems to have been in the main limited to lavish entertainment at election time. In 1669 Samuel Pepys contested one of the seats, but the town would have none of him; some even accused him of being a Papist and in those days no more heinous accusation could be levelled at anyone. This could have arisen because of his close association with the Duke of York, or perhaps the men of Aldeburgh feared lest the Secretary to the Navy Office should pry overmuch into their maritime affairs!

That the men of Aldeburgh never lacked an eye to the main chance is constantly evident. During the Dutch war in 1652 they hastened to join as volunteers in such numbers that there were barely enough left to man the merchant ships and fishing boats; but the attraction of this wore off as they realised that better pay was to be earned in privateers and with a share of prize money to boot. As a result the pay in government ships was raised and off went our heroes to serve the Commonwealth. This was only a temporary enthusiasm; for that same Commonwealth was running into serious financial trouble and the men were soon not only in arrears for their pay but the food and living conditions were growing progressively poorer.

The growing shipbuilding trade at Aldeburgh provided a small empire for the builders and for none more than Henry Johnson who, springing from a local family of note, left Aldeburgh in 1650 to found a shipyard on the Thames at Blackwall where he built tall ships of battle for Charles II. He also had the honour to dine the King at the shipyard which seems to have earned him not only the royal approbation but also a knighthood. His yard continued to be famous for many generations and eventually became the celebrated Thames Ironworks Company, famous for ships of timber as well as metal construction up to our own time and builders of many fine lifeboats for the Royal National Life-boat Institution.

The departure of Sir Henry Johnson undoubtedly led to some falling off in shipbuilding on the grander scale; but it never languished to the point of extinction and there were always builders of working ships of quality at Slaughden. Here as at Woodbridge a prime factor was the supply of first-class Suffolk oak from Framlingham and thereabouts. Besides those who sailed the sea there were always others who profited in one way or another from what the ships brought and just as in the sixteenth century some did not disdain to handle pirated goods so in the eighteenth and nineteenth centuries smuggling provided a fruitful field of interest and a substantial source of income.

At one time it was said that the only man in Aldeburgh who was not involved in smuggling was the parson! Whether this was a true indictment or not it was a graceful reversal of the usual situation where the reverend gentleman was the keystone of the 'free-trade' in many coastal parishes. Certainly the 'old borough' had got the whole affair pretty well organised as on one occasion when it is said that three hundred men were engaged on a single 'landing'. This may well be not such an exaggerated story as it seems at first telling; for so far as the East coast is concerned, smuggling was probably more prevalent in Suffolk than anywhere else. The coastline abounded in lonely stretches, gently shelving beaches and roads leading inland to a convenient point not more than two miles from the sea whither cargoes could be speedily conveyed and hidden-up while they were allocated to various places of further distribution.

With the threat of invasion during the Napoleonic period the subject of coastal defences was a matter of renewed attention and activity. The bulwarks and batteries of two centuries earlier would afford little or no resistance to the more sophisticated weapons of attack in terms of ships and guns. A plan of Aldeburgh in 1779 showed four batteries and a redoubt. How far these were related to the earlier Elizabethan batteries is not very clear but London did not assess then very high; for two years later their condition was reported upon as falling below a practicable standard of efficiency and more reliance seems to have been placed on the presence of militia and cavalry patrols who were on duty by night and day.

In 1798 the freedom of fishermen from impressment for the Navy was suspended and a new force intended to be raised from volunteers was raised to be known as the Sea Fencibles. Their duty was to supplement the existing coastal defences by both land and sea. The value of this defensive endeavour was doubtful. By 1801 the strength for Suffolk was only a little over a thousand men of which Aldeburgh had found eighty-nine. Nelson never thought much of the force as a whole and at least one officer commanding in Hollesley Bay wrote, "They are a set of drunken, good-for-nothing fellows, and I beg that none of them be sent to my ship."

About this time the military strategists were greatly absorbed in a new device, the Martello tower, an elliptical strong-point which derived its name from Mortella in Corsica where a structure of this design had proved a hard nut for our naval guns to crack. Although the erection of a chain of these towers was recommended by Lord St Vincent in 1796 nothing was done until the renewal of hostilities in 1803 and none was commenced in Suffolk until 1808. By this time Trafalgar had been fought and won, and Napoleon's invasion plans were no longer a serious threat to the sleep of English children. Military and naval preparations moved with the same stately deliberation then as they have done ever since. Each tower might use nearly three-quarters of a million bricks in the building and as these were of a specially hard yellow variety which had to be brought by sea from London, it was a long-winded process. The whole system when complete extended from Aldeburgh through Essex and Kent to Sussex. Most of them have become 'white elephants' for they are enormously expensive to demolish; although a few have become coastguard stations, stores, local museums and private houses. The tower at Slaughden is larger than most and is quatrefoil in plan. The armament was substantial, consisting chiefly of 24-pdrs. with supporting batteries of the same calibre.

Much play has been made of the lines of George Crabbe, whose long and somewhat wearisome poem, *The Borough* is quoted on every possible occasion as if Aldeburgh had never produced any other literate character. Crabbe himself was the son of a village schoolmaster turned Collector of Salt Dues at Slaughden. He did not have a very happy boyhood; for Crabbe Senior was a harsh overbearing man, especially when the drink was in him. Having failed to make a success of doctoring to which he had been apprenticed, George borrowed five pounds from a friend and sailed for London where after suffering the usual vicissitudes of the would-be writer, he managed to bring himself to the notice of Edmund Burke, who not only helped him to get his first manuscript published but suggested that he took Holy Orders. With a little help he secured a Lambeth Degree and was duly ordained, after which he returned to his native town as curate. Here he was regarded as a local boy barely made good and although he seems to have attended to his pastoral duties — he was once described as "the gentleman with the sour name and the sweet countenance" — he was never really popular and it must have been a relief to leave to become domestic chaplain to the Duke of Rutland. Eventually, he was presented to the rich living of Trowbridge in Wiltshire where he died in 1832. It may be that Aldeburgh was not over-happy about the picture of the town that Crabbe painted in *The Borough*. In those days of a recession from its former prosperity there was certainly great poverty among the poor and Crabbe did not mince his words. Yet reading through the poem one is brought to realise with a jolt that in those days the small country town was a real and vital social unit. Indeed even today those of us who can cast our memories back fifty years can recall more spontaneous, if modest, culture in a town of less than three thousand inhabitants than is found in many a select community indulging sophisticated but prefabricated interests chiefly on the strength of a handful of socialite 'incomers'. In Crabbe's day, there were clubs and coteries which were lively in their interest, if not fully-informed, and indeed perhaps all the more vital by reason of that alone.

Besides the native population of Aldeburgh, the town soon began to receive a new type of resident as the people of the Metropolis discovered this delightful coastal town, which offered so many of the social amenities of Weymouth or Brighton without their high life. Many men of social eminence had houses here and gradually the place began to attract others, such as retired service officers to whom the quiet atmosphere of the borough offered a pleasant milieu for those of modest means. Later in the century

Edward Fitzgerald spent almost as much time here as at Woodbridge and his yacht *Scandal* was often seen. Of Aldeburgh he wrote:

"It has but little to recommend it, it is so far more agreeable, as it attracts but few, and those very quiet visitors".

An Aldeburgh family a generation or so earlier than Sir Henry Johnson, but co-eval with the Johnsons, was that of Bence. One of them is reputed to have brought those famous guns from London in Armada days and another fought hard against a proposal to pan salt from the local sea water. The real grounds of this surprising opposition lay in the fact that when his ships returned from France they avoided making the passage in ballast by loading up with French salt, which represented a source of further profit.

In 1812 was born at Leiston Newson Garrett, whose grandfather, Richard, had been the founder of the great dynasty of ironmasters whose name and products were to be known throughout the world. As a younger son Newson left Suffolk to make a way of life for himself and after a humble beginning and some vicissitudes he returned to found a malting business at Snape. Here he throve exceedingly and to convey his excellent malt to London, Norwich and elsewhere he began to build his own schooners.

For much of the year Newson lived at Aldeburgh and in spite of his somewhat truculent manner, or perhaps because of it, he was elected a Burgess of the Corporation, holding office later as a Bailiff and Borough Chamberlain. Eventually when in 1885 the Borough received a Charter, Newson Garrett became the first Mayor.

Garrett was a vigorous thrusting man and proceeded to develop the Snape Maltings on the monumental scale which may still be seen, albeit the greater part is given over to its latter-day function as the home of the Aldeburgh Festival of Music and Drama. He also took an active part in the development of the town and in spite of his somewhat arrogant personality the epitaph on his monument in the Parish Church, "God gave him largeness of Heart", may not be undeserved. His daughter, Elizabeth Garrett Anderson, who made history by battling her way into the medical profession, hitherto a preserve of the opposite sex, also achieved the distinction of being the first woman to serve as Mayor of a Borough.

A son of Newson married a daughter of Peter Schuyler Bruff, who as we have seen brought prosperity to East Anglia through his outstanding work as a Civil Engineer. Bruff acquired land in

Aldeburgh and might have brought enhanced prosperity to the town had a scheme to make a harbour directly open to the sea at Slaughden been allowed to proceed to fulfilment. Unfortunately opposition was whipped up in Parliament by a caucus of objectors to whom, whether through stupidity or conflicting interests, the plan was obnoxious.

The matter of flotsam and jetsam which occurs often as a manorial incident in early times has always been of material interest to those who dwell by the seashore. The right to take up what the sea cast with such prodigality on our beaches could be of considerable consequence before the days of insurance and salvage and we find along the coast that the 'beachmen', who in fair weather are fishermen, turn the foul weather to good account by salvaging the results of other men's misfortune. Unkind chroniclers have been prone to blur the distinction between the act of salvaging from a wreck and encouraging a wreck and there certainly have been times in history when the matter of least importance in times of tempest was the saving of human life.

Before the days of life-boats specially designed and provided for the purpose of saving life that function, when it did not interfere overmuch with the recovery of the spoils of the wreck, was usually carried out by the beachmen who in their specially built gigs would brave most seas and, to be fair to them were as forthcoming in the saving of life as any could wish. A further interest for these beachmen was pilotage and although this was generally an exclusive right of pilots licensed by Trinity House there were certain local exceptions where the local pilots reserved their own rights. In any case the pilot had to get out to the ship in need of his services and here the beachmen were in fierce rivalry with each other to get their respective pilot on board first. Meantime the race was watched eagerly by the longshoremen and the wives; for much depended on the outcome. The pilot's fee was fixed by Trinity House; but a poundage was paid to the crew for getting him aboard. Not much at two shillings a time; but in those hard times it was a worthwhile supplement to what they earned by fishing. Each Beach Company had its own look-out and the two towers, from each of which many a bet must have been wagered on the result, still stand sentinel today. In some cases a beachman was also a Trinity House pilot himself. The beachmen at Aldeborough were organised in two Beach Companies, the Up-Towners and the Down-Towners, each with its own look-out.

It was natural that at Aldeburgh as elsewhere on this coast the beachmen were the hardcore of the first lifeboat service. The beachboat built for Joshua Chard in 1870 was only a 28-footer, but she was designed to serve equally well as a fishing boat for life-saving operations. By then, however, the Suffolk Association for saving the lives of shipwrecked seamen had had a purpose-built lifeboat stationed at Sizewell, and when the National Life-boat Institution came on the scene, this was moved to Aldeburgh. To enumerate all the families who, generation by generation, have had men in the Aldeburgh boats, for until from 1905 until a few years ago there were two, would be invidious; but no story of Aldeburgh can be told without the names of James Cable and William Mann who as coxswains have become legendary. Over the years nearly six hundred lives have been saved and not without price. In 1859 the lifeboat —a self-righter— capsized and drowned three of the crew and forty years later the worst lifeboat disaster on this stretch of coast occurred when the *Aldeburgh* so soon as she was launched broached to and was cast back, bottom-up, on the beach. Seven men died and up in the churchyard they lie looking out to the cruel sea whence they had snatched so many back to life with incomparable heroism. On the great marble block displaying the emblems of their calling are the words:

> "On December 7th, 1899, in response to the signals of distress, a crew of 18 brave men manned the lifeboat, *Aldeburgh*, which was speedily launched in the teeth of an easterly gale and a heavy rolling sea. At duty's call to rescue others, with their own lives in their hands, these brave men went afloat, when alas, the boat capsizing, seven of them met their end and lie buried here."

There is also a copper plaque inside the church where most of them probably were sealed with the Sign in token that they should continue Christ's soldiers and servants unto their life's end.

So Aldeburgh stands today, a quiet tolerant, well-mannered town, gracious with the courtesies of yesteryear, yet vitally interested in the world of the present. At Festival time when visitors throng the town and nearby Snape, the musical idioms of old and new meet, yet do not clash. It is at times like these that Aldeburgh likes to glance over her shoulder, remembering her past, rich in historical memories. Is it perhaps for this, and no more esoteric reason that when the Sergeant-at-Mace appears in full fig he wears his tricorne hat back to front? Or so it seems to simple souls!

A SHORT two miles along the coast from Thorpe brings us to what is still known as Sizewell Gap, although the Gap is not so prominent as formerly. This is partly due to the landscaping around the power station which stands up like a huge fortress almost on the very foreshore itself. The levelling-off process had been going on for a considerable time before the station was built and it would seem to have been caused chiefly by the action of wind and tide on the 'pentlands' which stretch along the coastline. The word is probably a corruption of bent lands or bent hills so called from the bent grass with which they are clad.

Sizewell — Sisa's well — is traditionally wrapped in an aura of the smuggling which was formerly prevalent here. A hundred and fifty years ago this was a deserted stretch of beach and inland there lay an area of wild heath and lonely marsh land, ideal for running cargoes. At Leiston and Knodishall and Theberton there were ideal points of distribution. The story of the *White Horse Inn* at Leiston which was a 'command post' of the 'free trade' under the master-mind of the formidable Mrs Gildersleeves, has often been told. Even the Society of Friends was involved, possibly without their cognisance; on at least one occasion a store of smuggled spirits were hidden beneath the clerk's table in the Meeting House.

At Theberton, "Old Shuck" the phantom black dog, was known to roam. This fearsome creature was reputed to have but one fiery eye, in the centre of his forehead, and it has been remarked by the sceptical that even where he appeared headless, as in some versions, the eye still blazed with undiminished vigour. He is usually identified by the folklorists with the hound of Odin and it is certainly true that the legend is prevalent principally in those parts of the country where the Danes or Norsemen settled.*

---

*Scandinavian mythology is a tangled skein and its ramifications are complex and various, Odin is often represented with two creatures at his feet described alternatively as wolves or hunting-dogs. It may not be irrevelant to recall the demon wolf Fenris, offspring of Loki, the god of mischief. This unlovely quadruped was of uncivil demeanour, as when he bit off the hand of Tyr, the god of war. Shuck's monocular handicap may have been a reflection of Odin himself, who had only one eye; perhaps it was "like master like dog".

What is even more certain is that where the terrifying creature haunted the lanes and heathlands at night the smugglers moved with impunity. Who would want to meet "Old Shuck", the sight of whom presaged the death of the beholder? This was a fairly safe prophecy, for anyone who saw what he was not intended to see had the best possible chance of having his throat cut — or worse!

Opinions vary as to the importance of Sizewell in mediaeval times. Its Anglo-Saxon origin is self-evident from its name, although no one knows who Sisa was or exactly where he dug his well. The place is mentioned occasionally in post-Conquest times and always in a maritime connection. The fact that Sizewell is recorded as finding a ship or ships for the King's service is often assumed to be evidence that there was a port of consequence here; but it seems doubtful if it was more than a settlement of fishermen who would have built their ships on the beach. It must be remembered that such a mention in contemporary records is merely evidence that the King's officers who were charged with the task of assembling a fleet whenever one was required had found one here or there on the coast which served their purpose. Many of these ships thus impressed were used to carry men or horses or victuals or simply to serve as tenders for larger craft. For example, when one ship from Sizewell was taken for the Earl of Surrey's invasion of Scotland in 1497 it was probably in such a capacity. Another factor which must not be overlooked is that when vessels were smaller, of forty or fifty tons burthen, it was practicable to breach a ship at any convenient point on the coast where there was a safe shelving beach with no more ceremony or circumspection than would attend the beaching of a large smack. Most ships were built very solidly with massive planking and doubled wales and would take no harm from such a manoeuvre.

In 1528 there were Sizewell ships in the Iceland fishery; but that was fishing on a large scale and there were a hundred and forty-nine vessels that year, which may have included escorting ships. Although it was necessary for this escort to accompany a fishing fleet it is an interesting and sobering thought that there was often greater danger from piracy in home waters than on the high seas — and that not always from foreign marauders!

A further argument against any exaggerated estimate of Sizewell's size and importance is its nearness to Thorpe. While this was still Aldeburgh's chief haven there would be little hope of gain for another port less than two miles away.

Until the turn of this century Sizewell was still a mere handful of cottages inhabited by fishermen and coastguards and over the past fifty years these have been joined by some villas. The name of this ancient hamlet is perpetuated in the name of the Urban District of Leiston-cum-Sizewell; but for the last few years it has become world-famous by reason of the huge nuclear-powered generating station erected on the very dunes themselves. Despite the fears of those who value this incomparable stretch of coastline, this great cubical mass of concrete has blended quite happily with the landscape. It cannot be ignored and whether in sunlight or against a cloudy sky it is a stark uncompromising fact; but its clean functional lines are probably no more unsightly than those of the castles when they were built for less peaceful purposes eight centuries ago. The element of this vast plan which disfigures the countryside far more and over a much larger radius is the web of power lines with their supporting pylons which stride contemptuously across some of the fairest land in England.

Two miles north of the Gap through a sad and strictly regulated sluice flows that River Minsmere or Mismer which once offered both a haven and an entry to seagoing ships. A modest concourse of small streams in the countryside between Badingham and Ubbeston gives birth to the Mismer just above Sibton whence it flows through Yoxford where for some reason, not very apparent, it is known for the next mile or so as the Yox. This has set some enthusiasts off on fruitless etymological meanderings as various as those of the river itself and to less purpose until it reaches Middleton where it seems finally to have decided where it wants to go. Formerly it was a really determined stream; but its valley is now so wide and poorly drained that for some centuries it wandered delta-like through a marshy area which was constantly subject to flooding. For this reason and in an endeavour to reclaim some of this marshland for more profitable agricultural use it was decided about 1810 to canalise it and it is as the 'New Cut' that it finally joins the grey waters of the German Ocean.

> "Even the weariest river
> Winds somewhere safe to sea" —

but it was not always so. The haven to which the river gives its name and which is still marked on the map was once a safe anchorage for ships and there is no doubt that vessels of moderate draught could work up at least as far as Yoxford and possibly even to Sibton. There is no very clear evidence on this point; but it does not seem improbable that before the strict operation of the Staple a certain amount of wool found its way out to the weavers of the Low Countries by way of this unobtrusive stream. Sibton was an Abbey of the Cistercians and at Leiston were the Praemonstatensian White Canons and these two Orders were pioneers in developing that high quality wool which only England could produce. It is true that the great abbeys of Yorkshire were able to farm on a larger scale; but it seems inconceivable that the White Monks of Sibton and the White Canons of Leiston were not a material factor in the early development of sheep-farming in Suffolk. In those days the sheep was esteemed for the wool which it yielded in its life and the skin at its death. Moreover its dung manured the fallow land which was further enriched by the 'golden hoof'. The mutton which we esteem so highly today was then considered a very trivial end-product and of little interest as food.

Even when the Staple was fully established to confirm and control the dealing in wool it is probable that the river and sea provided a quick, cheap and safe means of transport from farm to market.

At Eastbridge, which is still a small hamlet, there surely could never have been a man-made bridge spanning the river so long as ships were passing and one may hazard a guess that this may have been a gravel ridge like the others we have met. Today the local hostelry, *The Eel's Foot* is frequented by locals and visitors who explore this wholly delightful stretch of country between Theberton and the sea; but in the bad old smuggling days it was the scene of a surprise encounter between a party of troops and a gang of smugglers in which shots were exchanged and at least one of the smugglers was killed.

Theberton has another unusual link with the past, more recent than "Old Shuck". During the Great War of 1914-18 a German Zeppelin was brought down in flames and for some years the airmen who died lay buried in Theberton churchyard with the moving inscription over their grave:

"Who are thou that judgest another man's servant?
to his own master he standeth or falleth". Romans 14.4.

Whatever may be the calamitous causes of a bloody war between nations, this is the spirit which should govern the peace. The bodies of the Germans were taken back to their Fatherland after the war; but the inscription remains and there are times when St Paul's words could be noted with profit today.

On a knoll overlooking the sluice outfall there is a ruined chapel. Known locally as the 'Hermit's Chapel' this constitutes the only remains of the first Abbey of White Canons founded in 1182 by Sir Ranulf de Glanvill, Justiciar to Henry II and author of that first exposition of the Laws of England which every law-student is expected to pretend to know to this day. It was this same Ranulf who, as we have seen, also founded Butley Priory. In 1365 the Canons petitioned the Pope to permit them to remove farther inland to avoid the damp and inhospitable site and a large part of the building materials were conveyed to the present site near Leiston where the Abbey was refounded by Robert de Ufford, Earl of Suffolk. The circumstances of this removal are some evidence against the assumption that there was ever a port at the mouth of the Mismer River.

For two centuries the Abbey kept this last relic of their first house as a hermitage and hither came the last abbot but one, who was permitted to resign his abbacy to finish his days in the peace and austerity of this retreat, exchanging the chanting of the Canons for the cries of the gulls.

After the Dissolution the chapel remained and gradually decayed from lack of use. It was still however fully recognisable for what it had been until the Second World War upon which this country embarked to defend the freedom of Europe and the preservation of our English tradition. In pursuance of this eminently desirable aim some unknown heroes in uniform, who had probably never heard a shot fired in anger, used this ancient monument as a target for their mortars. It is easy to condemn such clownishness; but it is probably no more reprehensible than the behaviour of many municipal gauleiters who dig up an ancient earthwork to lay a sewer, notwithstanding its 'protected' status, and get away with it because no one protests!

From the Minsmere we move on beyond the incomparable bird sanctuary and nature reserve of that name, so admirably administered by the Royal Society for the Protection of Birds, and upon which we resist the temptation to expatiate, to what is the most fascinating, yet over-written part of the East Anglian coast, Dunwich.

Before we set foot on the site of this much debated, decayed port it is above all things necessary that we take a firm hold of ourselves. Between the highly coloured chronicles of the far past and the equally highly imaginative speculations of more recent times, Dunwich has been bathed in a kind of magic afterglow. It has all the aura of Lyonesse and Atlantis rolled into one. Writers have wandered over the area and claimed to be aware of an "atmosphere". They have been aware of the men who built this town and lived here and worked here. They have heard the ringing of the bells of the churches engulfed by the all-devouring sea; they have heard the chanting of the Grey Friars whose boundary wall and gateway is the only monastic relic of an Order which spent less time in liturgical observance than any other! Dunwich was most certainly a port of importance, in its day possibly the greatest in this part of England; but it is essential to keep our feet on the ground and the wilder and more rosy-coloured the claims, the more important that we should rely on what is known rather than on what has been day-dreamed by the romantically-minded writers of the past century. It is a little odd that so many should have been carried away; for the Revd. Alfred Suckling, writing in 1847, himself utters this *caveat*:

> "Dunwich is so enveloped in the halo of traditionary splendour that he who ventures to elucidate its history by pursuing the path of topographical inquiry must exercise unusual caution, lest he be misled by imaginary light. The steady ray which truth might have shed over its earliest origin is almost wholly extinguished by the violent assaults of the ocean, for, unlike those ruined cities whose fragments attest their former grandeur, Dunwich is wasted, desolate and void. Its palaces and temples are no more, and its very environs present an aspect lonely, stern and wild — assimilating well with the wreck of its former prosperity".

Suckling must have been convinced of the need for caution on this score; for he had to rely a great deal on the history of Dunwich written by Thomas Gardner, a century earlier. Gardner was Salt Officer at Southwold and was so intrigued by the romantic tales of Dunwich which were current gossip that he decided to cross over one day to see what he could. This was only some fifteen years after the last storm so that a great deal of the remains left by that ultimate catastrophe were still to be seen and these so stirred the imagination of a middle-aged man that he determined to write the history of the town. It is obvious that he consulted every earlier chronicle he could lay hands on; but it is equally obvious that the story lost nothing in the telling.

In spite of the apparent Anglo-Saxon origin of the name
Dunanwic — Duna's village, it is possible that the claim for the
Celtic origin *Domnoc* (which Bede calls it) may be justifiable
Dumnoc is said to suggest the meaning of 'deep' and this is assumed
to refer to the deep water of the ancient port; but it could just as
well signify a place in a deep hollow, — *dom* in Gaelic means
'hollow' as well as 'deep'— in bosky shades embowered. This is a
common and acceptable Celtic application of the word and is borne
out by the belief that there was once a forest of Eastwood between
the ancient Dunwich and the sea on the south-east of the town, while
the forest of Westwood lay towards the west. Eastwood is now
completely swallowed by the sea and Gardner recounts that in
1740 the storm left tree roots exposed; Westwood is perpetuated
today in the marshes which lie to the north of the last remains of
this once prosperous city.

That there was once a considerable settlement here in Roman
times is without question, although the belief that it was the
original site of *Sitomagus* is more than doubtful. It is also highly
likely that the town had a strong and well-nigh impregnable stone
wall or *murus,* but the romantic picture of the 'brazen gates' is
strongly reminiscent of the mediaeval trappings with which the
dim memory of King Arthur was endowed by the troubadours
In the same category must be placed the story of how the Earl of
Leicester with his Flemish mercenaries after landing near Walton
planned to attack Dunwich; but when he saw the strength of the
place, "it was terror and feare unto him to behold it". This seems
a slight overstatement, for all he had to do to rid himself of this
phobia was to go away — which he did! It was perhaps as well
because Jordan de Fantosme, the Monk who seems to have got
about a lot in the reign of Henry II and has left a long chronicle
in verse of the rising, describes how, besides the fighting men of
Dunwich,

> "There was within the town neither maid or woman
> Who did not carry a stone to the palisade to cast".

Perhaps it was the prospect of facing this monstrous regiment of
women which changed the noble Earl's plan of campaign!

What sort of place was Dunwich in terms of sober reality — or
at least so far as we can gather from such records as have survived?
It is certain that there was a Roman settlement here and probably
the galleys found their way to the town with supplies by way of

what was the Blyth estuary. With the coming of the Angles and the Dark Age which intervened the early stages of its revival are hidden in the mists of time. It seems to have become a place of importance in the days of the Wuffingas, the first royal house of the East Angles and we learn that Sigebert who acceded about 629 had his capital here. He it was who induced Felix of Burgundy to bring a Christian mission here and for this reason Felix is usually referred to, somewhat uncertainly, as the first Bishop of Dunwich. In fact, he should be more properly styled as of the East Angles, there being no bishop of Dunwich until the senior See had been established at Elmham in 673. Sigebert did not occupy his throne for long; for in 634 he abdicated to enter a monastery, whence he was induced to emerge when the kingdom was attacked by the heathen Mercians under Penda. This proved to be a gesture of spiritual fervour rather than military effectiveness; for having gone into battle armed with nothing but a white staff, he was slain together with the King, Ecgric, whom he had been called to assist. Most of this we know from Bede, but a great part of the history of this part of East Anglia is very obscure for another century and a half, indeed right up to the death of Edmund, King and Martyr, at the hands of the Danes. Thereafter it fell first into the Kingdom of Guthrum the Dane, christianised as Athelstan, and later into the Danelaw. During all this time the town of Dunwich seems to have continued to grow and the advent of the more practical sea-going Danes must have contributed materially to its activity as a seaport on a modest scale.

After the Conquest there is abundant evidence of the growth and importance of this town which speedily became the largest Suffolk port. The continual outbreaks of war with France, even before the commencement of the Hundred Years War, called constantly for ships and the references to Dunwich confirm her importance. At about the middle of the thirteenth century she is credited with having as many as eighty ships. Here again it must be remembered that these figures would almost certainly have included ships of every conceivable type and size; but the overall fact remains that the port was regarded as highly important. The mere fact that in 1295 it was subject to attacks by pirates which justified special provisions for the defence of the coast is evidence that there must have been ships and merchandise worth plundering.

In 1294 when a galley was built at Dunwich for Edward I there was a very precise account not only of her equipment, her one hundred and twenty oars, her sails and banners, but also of the provision of one hundred plates and dishes for the crew. One wonders whether twenty oars were carried as spares or whether twenty hungry mariners had to wait their turn before satisfying their hunger.

In 1341 we have a list of the Dunwich ships which were assembled at Plymouth for war service. This gives the names of the ships, their owners and captains and the number of mariners from which it would seem that the total complement consisted of eleven ships and about six hundred men. It does not follow that the whole of each ship's company came from Dunwich; but it is probable that the majority did and from this and other evidence it is clear that the town also enjoyed a high reputation for the shipbuilders who were active at that time. It is interesting to observe that in 1497 one William Pette, a shipbuilder, died and it is tempting to see in this master craftsman the beginning of that great dynasty of ship-builders at Harwich, Chatham and Woolwich, of whom sprang the Phineas and Sir Peter Pett whom we have met at Woodbridge.

Dunwich, in common with other Suffolk ports, frequently had to find craftsmen of skill without whom the greatest shipbuilders could never have attained their success. Whether they wished to go or not was of little consequence in the days of the Tudors and if Dunwich carpenters and caulkers were needed at Woolwich to build the *Henry Grace à Dieu,* then to Woolwich they had to go.

Another family of Dunwich shipbuilders was that of Jentleman or Gentleman, a name which is still not unknown in East Anglia and representatives were found also at both Southwold and Yarmouth.

In the early days of the development of the Iceland trade there were always Dunwich ships. Much profit resulted from sending these considerable fleets; but the profit was not always derived from fishing. As we have seen elsewhere, the English seamen were not above a fair share in the skullduggery which was rife in those days; for there was no law on the High Seas but that of the strong right arm. It is no wonder that from time to time the King of Denmark remonstrated with his cousin of England in no uncertain terms over the behaviour of Englishmen in his waters. The Orkneys and Shetlands knew of their depredations as well and there is more than one case of a captain sailing for home with some of his sick men left behind in Iceland to fend for themselves at the tender mercies of the Icelanders who can scarcely have cared much how they fared.

We have seen how Dunwich had grown in size and importance. Some of the earlier writers have given us highly coloured accounts of the great size of the town which can often be guessed at by the number of churches. When however we are told that at the height of her power Dunwich had fifty churches we must take this with a large pinch of salt, even if the total included monastic establishments. The actual number of parish churches was probably eight or nine, to which must be added three chapels, and the houses of the Dominicans and the Franciscans, as well as two Hospitals and a preceptory of Knights Templars taken over after the fall of that Order by the Knights of St John. From this it is evident that the town was sufficiently large and there is no doubt of its prosperity for churches of any kind and especially the two orders of mendicant friars argue a flow of alms to supply their needs.

With prosperity came temptation to do business whenever and however opportunity offered and so we find Richard I imposing a fine of 1,000 marks on the burgesses for selling corn to the King's enemies. Some have taken this as evidence of the importance of the town; but as Suckling has pointed out, the size of the fine may have been commensurate with the enormity of the offence. Nevertheless it does not seem that the town had much difficulty in paying and Orford, Ipswich and Yarmouth seem to have been engaged in similar activities; they were, however, mulcted of lesser sums, Orford 15 marks, and Ipswich and Yarmouth 200 marks each. Pelf and patriotism are an ill-matched pair.

But even by the time of Edward I the sands were running out — or perhaps it would be truer to say, notwithstanding the metaphor, that other sands were coming in. The continual inroads of the sea which eventually was to swallow the whole town alternatively washed away large parts of the town while silting up the approaches to the harbour. As far back as the Conquest there is a record of one holding of two carrucates having been halved by the sea having carried one away. A carrucate was, of course, the amount of land which could be ploughed by one team of oxen in a farming year, say 120 acres by modern admeasurement. This encroachment went on from time to time and the men of Dunwich seemed unable to do much about it. Periodically at times of exceptional tempest larger areas of the town were swallowed up. One of the earliest of these catastrophes was on 1st January, 1286, which is recorded as having destroyed several churches. A lamentable result of this storm was that the harbour was so blocked by mud and shingle that a new one had to be opened up farther up the Blyth estuary and near enough to Blythburgh to detract considerably from the importance of Dunwich. All through history the fortunes of the four Blyth ports, Dunwich, Walberswick or Walderswick, Blythburgh and Southwold have been inextricably interwoven; for however the channel changed they were all dependent on this great estuary for their access to the sea, the shelter of their ships and the traffic in merchandise upon which they all to a greater or a lesser degree depended. One can hardly describe this relationship as founded on any complex pattern of love-hate; for there was little love between them. As at Orford and Yarmouth, and to some extent at Orwell Haven, the town which sat on the river mouth exploited its opportunities to obstruct the traffic to the ports higher up. In this case Dunwich being the first to develop dominated the affairs of its neighbours so long as it could and when they sought to protect their own interests by cutting fresh outlets to counter the forces of Nature Dunwich was deeply aggrieved. In 1351 came another great storm which engulfed four hundred houses and many shops and windmills, the latter always an essential part of a trading port shipping or receiving grain.

Over and above the ravages of the sea at about this time the whole country was visited by the Black Death, that appalling plague which carried off between a third and a half of the population of England and Scotland, and its results had a profound effect upon the social, economic and religious structure of this country. It has been compared, not without reason, to the probable death-dealing effects of a major attack with nuclear weapons under modern conditions.

Hardly had the town recovered from this disaster when, in 1385, a fresh attack by the sea destroyed three more churches and that must have involved most of the houses in their parishes. Meanwhile the status of Blythburgh increased, which is not a little ironic seeing that the practice of 'inning' much of the foreshore at the head of the estuary undoubtedly contributed in no small measure to the slowing down of the natural tidal flow and the increasing tendency for the outlet to silt-up. It was when the clouds began to gather over Dunwich that Blythburgh pressed its claims for tolls on goods brought into Dunwich on the grounds of somewhat shadowy rights over the foreshore. Eventually some kind of compromise was reached between the two towns; but now a fresh element entered on the scene resulting from Dunwich's political affinity during the Wars of the Roses when the town gave its support to the House of York. Why this came about is not very clear unless it was a gesture of defiance to Southwold which supported the Lancastrian faction. All seemed to be going well after the ascendancy of the Sun of York; but alas! it was soon to be in eclipse and with it fell the hopes of Dunwich. After Bosworth Field Henry Tudor looked with a somewhat jaundiced eye on this pocket of legitimist zeal; he granted a charter of incorporation to Southwold and with it went a remission of harbour dues, thus depriving Dunwich of a source of her income. She had lost her harbour, more than half her town had been swallowed by the sea and now she found part of her dues given away to her rival. The following reign brought the dissolution of the religious houses which were an important factor in the economic balance of the town and if the burgesses regarded a further succession of storms as a judgment of Heaven, who can blame them?

In the first year of Elizabeth, Dunwich received a Charter and so honours were even. She had been sending two members to Parliament since the reign of Edward I so that the Queen could give nothing more on this score. However, she ensured a further claim upon the loyalty of this hard-luck borough by making them a loan, from the proceeds of bells, lead and so forth from churches at Beccles, and Kessingland, which had, most opportunely, come into "her Majesty's dysposycion". Most writers refer to this typical example of Tudor munificence without precise details of its value, which could not have been of much consequence; it has even been suggested that the Queen had aspirations to being regarded as a humorist!

Nevertheless the sea still continued to attack the town. In 1608 the road to the beach was destroyed and shortly afterwards the foundations of the former house of the Knights of St John disappeared. In 1677 the sea had reached the market-place and within forty years the church of St Peter was so damaged that it had to be pulled down together with the town gaol. When Defoe visited the town in 1722, he wrote that there was but one church left and that not half-full of people. That in an age when church-going was a normal feature of life is an eloquent testimony to the decay of the town. After some moralising comparison between the ruined cities of antiquity and this wasted town in an age of comparative civilisation and affluence, the loquacious Daniel goes on to say —

"Yet Dunwich however ruined, retains some share of trade as particularly for the shipping of butter, cheese and corn which is so great business in this county that it employs a great many people and ships also, and this port lies right against the particular part of the county for butter as Framlingham, Halstead, etc., also a very great quantity of corn is brought up hereabout for the London market; for I shall still touch that point how all the counties in England contribute something, towards the subsistence of the great City of London, of which the butter here is a very consider- able article; as also coarse cheese, which I mentioned before, used chiefly for the King's ships.

Hereabouts they begin to talk of herrings and the fishery, and we find in the ancient records that this town, which was then equal to a large city, paid among other tribute to the Government, 50,000 of herrings; here also and at Swole, or Southole, the next sea-port, they cure sprats in the same manner as they do herrings at Yarmouth, that is to say, speaking in their own language, they make red sprats, or to speak good English, they make sprats red.

It is remarkable that this town is now so much washed away by the sea that what trade they have is carried on by Walderswick, a little town near Swole, the vessels coming in there because the ruins of Dunwich make the shore there unsafe and uneasy to the boats; from whence the northern coasting seamen to a rude verse of their own using and I suppose of their own making, as follows:

Swoul and Dunwich and Walderswick
All go in at one lousy creek.

This lousy* creek, in short is a little river at Swoul, which our late famous atlas-maker calls a good harbour for ships and rendezvous of the Royal Navy, but that by the bye; the author it seems knew no better."

---

*It has been suggested that this rhyme is less uncomplimentary than it seems, since the 'lice' are crabs; I bow to higher authority, although this seems to my untutored mind to be reading etymology backwards. Moreover it is the habit of the northerners to disparage those who live in the effete south!

"Peter Pett with the *Sovereign of the Seas*". This picture, in the National Maritime Museum, cognised as an imaginative composition by two artists and was formerly believed to have been ted, the ship by Willem Van de Velde the Elder and the portrait by Willem Van de Velde the nger. More recent opinion leans to Sir Peter Lely as the painter of the portrait of Peter Pett.

National Maritime Museum, Greenwich

(xiii) "The Battle of Solebay". From the painting by Willem Van de Velde the Younger who was present at the Battle.

National Maritime Museum, Greenwich

) Woodbridge viewed across the Deben from the Sutton shore and showing the Tide Mill.

Seckford Library

) The Port of Felixstowe. The *Europic Ferry* lying moored by the Quay at night.

David Kindred, East Anglian Daily Times

(xvi) Walberswick showing the 'Anchor Boat' moored in the Blyth estuary.

Signed N. R. Gowers. Great Yarmouth Libr

(xvii) *The Parrot and Punchbowl Inn*, Aldringham. Renowned as a 'Clearing-House' for smugg
cargoes from Thorpeness and Sizewell.

iii) Martello Tower, Slaughden. Note the unusual quatrefoil plan of this, the largest of the
wers. The erection on the top of the Tower is a relic of the Second World War when it was
d as an observation-post.

) Cottages, Southwold Beach.   *Signed N. R. Gowers. Great Yarmouth Library*

(xx) East Indiaman *Orwell*, launched August, 1817, on the stocks at Jabez Bayley's, Halifax Y
Ipswich.
Ipswich Dock Commi

(xxi) Ships locking through at Ipswich Wet Dock at about the end of the nineteenth cent
Ipswich Dock Comm

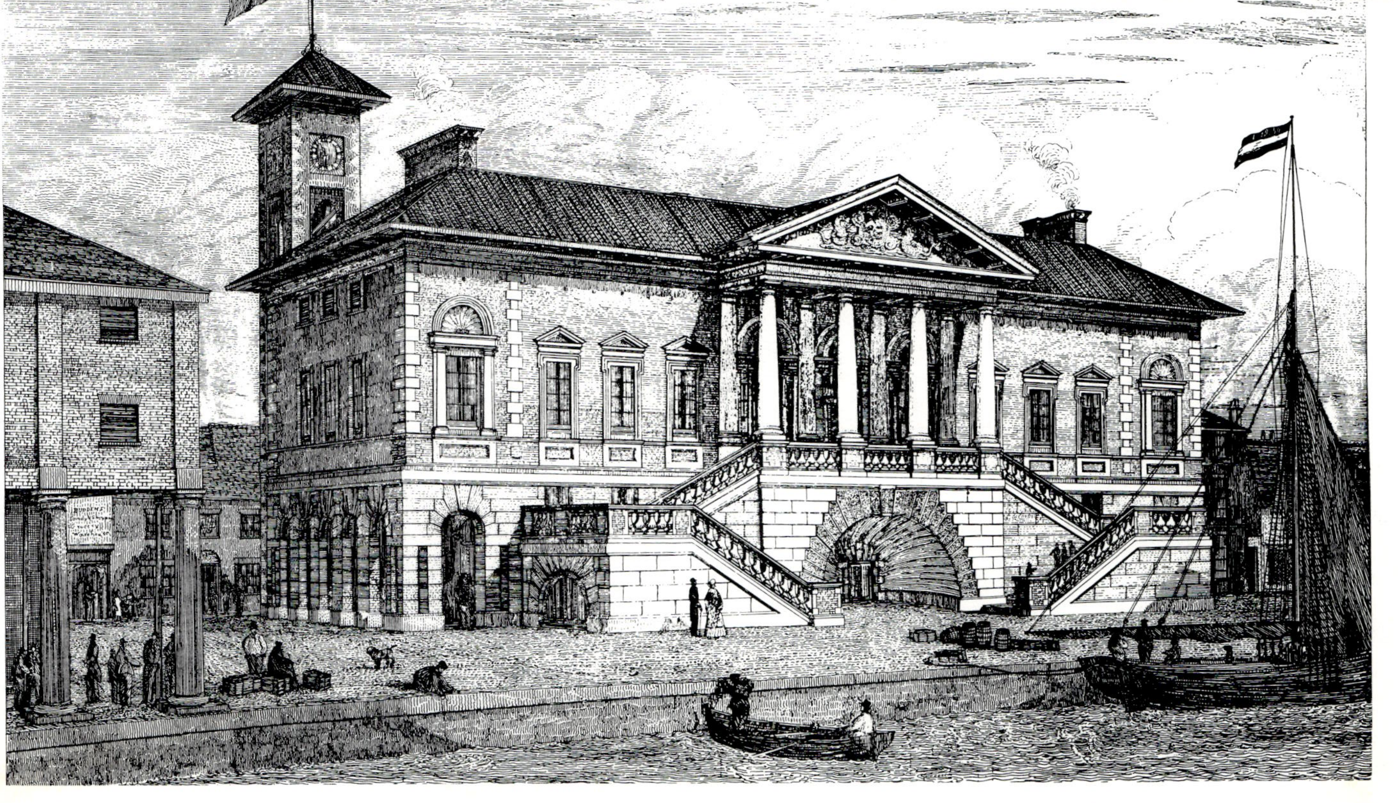

(xxii) The old Custom House, Ipswich, erected in 1845 as a 'Hall of Commerce' to replace the former Custom House, part of the colonnade of which can be seen on the left. This building also houses the Office of the Ipswich Dock Commission.

Ipswich Dock Commission

(xxiii) Old Stoke Bridge, Ipswich. Date unknown, but probably latter half of the eightee
century.   *Ipswich Dock Commis*

(xxiv) The latter days of sail. Ships unloading at Ipswich Docks, 1923.   *Ipswich Dock Commis*

Defoe is as patronising in his view of the 'little river' as he is of the 'late atlas-maker' whoever he may have been. The fact remains that there are few rivers on this side of England which have provided the natural factors for the growth of four ports in such close proximity to each other. It is true that through the combination of a continuous process of silting up, shingle drift and coast erosion the opening of the river has shifted from its original position which gave Dunwich such a magnificent sheltered anchorage to a position some two miles farther north favouring Walberswick. Nevertheless, the fortunes of these four Blyth towns have been so bound up one with the other that it is impossible to consider their maritime rise and fall apart. Today only one survives and that a mere shadow of her former self; but more of that in due course. Let us return to Dunwich as Defoe saw it in his day. It is clear that, decayed though she was, the town still battled gallantly on with her roads and houses and churches constantly under attack by the ravenous waves, her only outlet to the sea parlously involved with her near neighbour sitting athwart it. Still some farm produce was shipped to London, including that Suffolk cheese which was so maligned by those who found it hard going, and we may be sure that the comments of the lower deck must have been explosive enough for it to have served as a blistering broadside.

However, the sea had still not done its worst to Dunwich. In December, 1740, one of the worst storms in the town's history took place. Further portions of cliff were washed away, yet another church was finally destroyed, shingle and sand were spread across arable land and two hills, the Cock and Hen hills between forty and fifty feet high, were levelled to the ground. This was really the end of the town as a live community and thenceforward it became a fishing village living with the memories of the past. It still remained as a corporate borough in name with the symbols of municipal state and its two members of Parliament; these went with the Reform Act of 1832 and in 1883 the Corporation was dissolved. The property and regalia of the town were handed over to a Dunwich Town Trust as happened in Orford.

Today the site of the last remnants of the town are visited by many visitors, most of whom are lured by the sentimental hope that they will be impressed in some mystic manner by the spirit of this city beneath the waves; but surely the true magic of the place is to be found in the wild beauty of shore and marsh, the view across the bay to where Southwold lighthouse gleams in

the sunshine like an up-pointing finger of warning and of hope —
and over all the cries of the seabirds.

Walberswick, Walbert's settlement, was always a small fishing
village and probably regarded as of small consequence by her rich
and powerful neighbour when the Blyth ran out by the King's
River, which was the Dunwich estuary and haven. As this outlet
became blocked and the main river turned farther north to meet
the sea the men of Walberswick found a new sense of importance
and began to take part in the continual squabbles with Southwold
on the other bank which also benefited by this new state of affairs.
Between them they thought to hold proud Dunwich to ransom.
As between Dunwich and Blythburgh Walberswick seems to
have played the part of the trimmer, backing one or the other
according as opportunity suggested. Partly due to these circumstances and partly from the very considerable fishing trade
Walberswick prospered and built a fine church in the last quarter
of the fifteenth century. However in spite of the attempts to keep
the fishermen in business by enforcing such rules of abstinence as
survived the Reformation, Walberswick found that prosperity was
a fickle jade and in 1633 suffered a further set-back through a
disastrous fire. So impoverished were the townsfolk that they
could not restore their church and part of it was demolished to
avoid further expense. Today it is a popular and picturesque
village much frequented by artists and visitors, especially by those
who enjoy messing about in boats. Between Walberswick and
Southwold there is easy communication by ferry. There was
formerly a steam ferry plying across the river; but this fell into disuse some years ago.

At the head of the estuary stands Blythburgh, now a mere
shadow of her former self but once a town which bid fair to rival
Dunwich, with a weekly market and three annual fairs and with
sundry manorial rights which extended down the estuary through
Walberswick and sharing dues by covenant with Dunwich. In the
reign of Henry II it might be said that the whole mercantile and
maritime life of the Blyth estuary was completely controlled by
these two towns. Today Blythburgh is a tiny village lying
astraddle the main road between Saxmundham and Lowestoft,
very charming but best known for an inn of deservedly high
reputation and a church which is one of the finest in the county,
both for its architecture and its commanding position on a knoll
above the main road and looking across to an incomparable

vista of the upper tidal waters of the Blyth. Formerly there was also a priory of Austin Canons, a daughter house of the Abbey of St Osyth, Essex. Without going into ecclesiastical technicalities, it should be made clear that when the Priory is referred to as a 'cell' of St Osyth this is also true. It was an example of those few monastic houses which had a double status being independent in some things but subject to the mother-house in others. It most certainly was not a house of Black Friars, as some writers have stated, the confusion having probably arisen because at one time the Dominicans of Dunwich contemplated moving to Blythburgh after their house had suffered from the ravages of the sea.

What concerns us much more than the Priory, of which only a few scanty fragments of masonry remain, is the Church which is exceptionally large and because of this it has been assumed that the town was formerly of considerable extent. This may well have been true; but it would be rash to base this assumption on mere congregational space. For a town of wealth and consequence the size and magnificence of the church was frequently a status symbol and it is on this basis that we are justified in assessing the importance of the town. There is no historical evidence of more than one church, although there was a chapel of the Holy Rood on the main street near the bridge, and there was of course the priory chapel which would not be used by townsfolk generally. The town had a gaol and at one time miscreants from Dunwich were sent there to receive their just deserts. Over the administration of justice there were occasions when the two towns were far from being in accord, as for example when the Dunwich serjeant having been sent to arrest certain transgressors was denied the right so to do on the grounds that the north side of the river was part of the manor of Blythburgh. Moreover —horribile dictu!— they took away his serjeant's mace by force and kept it for a whole day. It conjures up a delicious picture of a battle of the Bumbles. According to one version of this story the Dunwich serjeant had been sent to arrest the Blythburgh freebooters who had forced a ship bound for Dunwich to put into Walberswick where she was relieved of her cargo. Dunwich regarded this as piracy, Blythburgh as free enterprise.

It has been stated that after the decay of Dunwich shipments of wool took place at Blythburgh; if so it must have been after the strict enforcement of the Staple ordinances. This also supposes the ability of sea-going ships to get up so far; for the general silting up of the river was by then affecting Blythburgh too. This drying out of the navigation was not the sole cause for Blythburgh's decline, for as at Walberswick two fires devastated the town, the latter in 1676, and it was for this reason besides that of general decay that there are no very ancient houses there today.

After the failure of trade and commerce, the church, magnificent though it was, became very dilapidated and Suckling reports it as being in a state of desolation and neglect. Since then it has been the subject of extensive and careful restoration and as it stands today it is a magnificent monument not only of its former splendour as a place of worship but also a reminder in heraldic and monumental pomp of the great families, the members of which once worshipped here.

As one stands by the church on a summer day and gazes across the spacious waters of the estuary it comes as a shock to discover that Blythburgh has had its share of the eerie and macabre. According to a contemporary account:

> "On Sunday, 4 August, 1577, between the hours of nine and ten of the clock in the forenoon, whilst the minister was reading the second lesson in the parish church of Blithburgh, a town in Suffolk, a strange and terrible tempest of Lightening and Thunder strucke through the wall of the same church into the grownde, almost a yarde deep; drove down all the people on that side, above twenty persons, then renting the wall up to the Revestry, cleft the door and returned to the steeple, rent the timber brake the chains of the bells and then fled towards Bungay. The people that were stricken down were found grovelling more than half an hour after, whereof a man and a boy were found dead, the others scorched."

This might seem sufficiently alarming, although lightning can play strange tricks as we know well. But the writer adds that the people of Blythburgh were firmly of opinion that this was a diabolical visitation and that when the Lord of Evil departed through the north door of the church he left his red-hot claw-print on the woodwork. This was probably to express his annoyance that the north door — the 'Devil's Door' — had not been left open for him, as it always was at the consecration of a church. If any there be who are sceptical of this circumstantial story, let them visit the church today and inspect the north door!

But hear what happened when the Evil One got to Bungay which was his next port of call. After the manifestations of storm as at Blythburgh —

> "Immediately hereupon there appeared in the most horrible similitude and likeness to the congregation then and there assembled a dog as they might discerne it, of a black colour, as the sight thereof with fearful flashes of fire then were seen, moved such in the minds of the assemblie that they thought Doom's Day was already come upon them.
>
> This Black Dog or the Devil in such likeness (God he knoweth all who worketh all) running along down the body of the church with great swiftness and incredible haste, among the people in visible shape and forme, passed between two persons kneeling upon their knees, occupied in prayer as it seemed, wronge the necks of each clene backwards at one instant insomuch in a moment where they kneeled they strangely dyed. The same Black Dog still continuing and resembling one and the self same shape, passing another man of the congregation of the church, gave him such a gripe i' the back, that therwith all he was presently drawen together and shrunk up as if he were a piece of leather scorched in a hot fire, or lik unto the mouth of a purss or bag drawne togither with string. This mischief thus wrought he flew with wonderful force, to no little fear of the congregation out of the church in a hideous and hellish darkness. Leving the church dore marvelously rented and torne, bearing ye marks as it werr of his claws or talans."

This is all very reminiscent of our friend "Shuck" but this time in broad daylight. Certainly neither town intended to be outdone by the other in the telling of the tale; and as to the physical evidence of this supernatural visitation, let the reader be the best judge of the validity of this.

There is another happening in the neighbourhood of Blythburgh which has caused cold shivers down many local spines — Black Toby.

In June, 1750, Ann Blakemore of Walberswick was found dead and suspicion fell upon Tobias Gill, one of the negro drummers of Rich's Dragoons. He protested his innocence but was duly convicted at Bury and brought back to Blythburgh to be hanged. Right up to the last he pleaded vehemently and seemed to be searching for someone whose evidence could save his life. When he was finally and irrevocably despatched someone remembered that the victim's body had shown no sign of violence and gradually the whisper spread that the girl may have come upon this black-faced figure in the gloaming and have been just "frit to death".

Thereafter the uneasy spirit of the Black Drummer was said to haunt the lonely heath as he galloped along and if this kept the country folk indoors when the 'gentry' were abroad, then poor Toby may not have died in vain.

In due course Rich's Dragoons became the 4th Light Dragoons and thence by a succession of those deathless feats of 're-organisation' so beloved of the chair-borne generals they eventually became the 4th Queen's Own Hussars. This gallant regiment distinguished alike in war and peace nurtured that Man of Destiny, Sir Winston Churchill, who steered his country to eventual victory in the Second World War.

It is an irony of history that of our Blithe Company the only one to survive with any semblance of its former status was the last to achieve the dignity of a borough. The charter incorporating Southwold dates only from 1485 and as late as the thirteenth century the place was only a hamlet of Reydon, although the manor was held by the Abbot of Bury. The changes and chances which had come upon its neighbour had brought some advantage to Southwold and although it had suffered damage from a fire which destroyed its church in 1430 the magnificent building which arose upon its site and stands today testifies to the prosperity of this flourishing town.

Through the century or so before the first Tudor sat on the throne of England, Southwold had been content to profit as opportunity offered; but during the Wars of the Roses, having given her allegiance to the Lancastrians, she did not take easily to the House of York, the less so since Dunwich for some reason decided to back that side. As it fell out, Southwold found her policy paid off; for after Bosworth Henry VII gave her a charter of incorporation and other privileges, which did Dunwich no manner of good at all. No doubt the men of Southwold lifted their heads the higher for the recital of the said charter that "the navigation of the inhabitants of that Town by their industry exceeded and excelled above that of the ancient privileged Towns of these parts". The effectiveness of Southwold's harbour was in the earlier days a factor of uncertain value, because the shifting of the Blyth estuary which had ruined Dunwich did not cease and Southwold was always in a state of some uncertainty which was not alleviated by a severe fire in 1596. What they did have was the haven provided by the inshore curve of Sole Bay from Easton Ness to Thorpe Ness. Neither ness is there today, having been swept away by centuries of gnawing and worrying by the devouring sea. The town stands on what is nearly an island site; for besides the river Blyth on the south there is on the north a fleet or creek known as Buss Creek from the fishing 'busses' which used to lie here joining the Blyth about a mile above its mouth. Looking at the map today it is not easy to see Sole Bay as other than a name on paper, but remembering the former Easton Ness which jutted out perhaps a further two miles to the east, it is manifest that this must once have offered a sheltered anchorage for many ships.

We have already referred to the magnificence of Southwold church as an indication of the wealth and importance of the town and this is not the place to elaborate on its ecclesiastical importance and architectural magnificence; but it cannot be ignored as a landmark as well as being one of the finest parish churches in the whole of Suffolk, comparable only to Blythburgh, Long Melford and Lavenham. Apart from the disastrous destruction wrought by the unspeakable Will Dowsing in the Commonwealth period it stands very much as it did when the rich merchants of the town built it in the mid-fifteenth century. Defoe who came here in 1722 remarked on its size and quality, adding:—

> "there is no occasion for its being so large, for staying there one Sabbath Day I was surprised to see an extraordinary large church, capable of receiving five or six thousand people and but twenty seven in it besides the parson and the clerk, but at the same time the meeting house of the dissenters was full to the very doors having, as I guessed, from six to 800 people in it".

He also recalled that on a previous visit he had noticed many thousands of swallows gathering for their winter exodus to warmer lands and that the wind changing overnight they were all gone in the morning.

On 25th April, 1659, the town was again devastated by fire when three quarters of the town was destroyed and three hundred families left destitute. The result here as at Blythburgh is that the town, pleasant and gracious though it appears today, lacks any really ancient buildings.

Piratic attacks by the 'Dunkirkers' were always a pest and there were times when peaceful shipping from East coast ports was brought virtually to a halt, especially during those periods when our naval strength was not always up to proper convoying. On one occasion the marauders took a 100-ton ship out of Southwold Road and did not scruple to bombard the town to prevent a rescue.

The one outstanding historical event which has been associated with Southwold did not happen here at all but at sea just offshore and if no one had ever looked at a chart, the story of the Battle of Sole Bay would ensure that this part of the East Anglian coast could never be forgotten.

As we have seen there had from time to time been a state of war between England and Holland, each outbreak being based nominally on one ground of difference or another. There had been a sea-engagement off Lowestoft in April, 1665, when the Dutch were sent packing back to their own waters in great haste. In 1667, largely due to the instigation of English refugees in Holland the Netherlanders took advantage of the unpreparedness of the English fleet to raid the Medway and the Thames with humiliating results as we have seen in connection with the persecution of Peter Pett.

In March, 1672 an attempt was made to seize the Dutch Smyrna fleet, an attempt which failed but in its inception reflected little credit on us. To what extent this provoked an expedition against our eastern coast is a little obscure; but it was obviously not entirely unexpected. A fleet of English and French ships amounting to 101 sail was anchored in Sole Bay in three divisions reaching from Easton Ness to Mismer Haven. Lord Sandwich commanded the northern division, the Duke of York the centre and the French made up the Southern division. That they were expecting something to happen is very obvious from the fact that they were getting into position on 20th and 21st May and the time seems to have passed in a certain amount of junketing interspersed with somewhat acrimonious Councils of War at which Lord Sandwich and the Duke did not see eye to eye.

During the night of the 27th the wind changed and left us on a lee shore with the Dutch suddenly appearing in the early hours of the morning running before the wind. There was little time to weigh anchor and many ships had to cut their cables and get under way as best they could, leaving some of their crews ashore. The French found an urgent reason to stand off on the port tack and so headed south, their interest in further operations seeming to have waned. This left 65 English ships to take on the considerable Dutch fleet of 91 ships of war, 54 fire ships and 23 yachts in one of which was Van de Velde the Elder, the sea painter and to his sketches which he developed when he got back to Holland we owe some of our colourful records of the battle.

Lord Sandwich engaged the enemy first in his flagship *Royal James*. The Duke of York, whose courage has never been in doubt, whatever blunders of statecraft he may have made as James II, was hotly involved and twice had to shift his flag from *Prince* to *St Michael* and finally to *London*.

It was a tough fight and the coast was crowded with spectators who ran no little risk from stray cannon balls fired by some of the more inshore ships. There seems to have been none of the panic shown by the Londoners five years earlier when the Dutch ships were having a party of their own some miles down the Thames, although the fact that clouds of smoke mingled with sea-mist hid a great deal of what was going on and may have masked the danger from the onlookers.

Eventually the *Royal James* while grappling with the Dutch *Great Holland*, was locked on to by a fire ship and drifted on to Easton Ness where she* blew up with the loss of her whole gallant crew, including Lord Sandwich. A fortnight later his body was found floating near the Sunk sand and could be recognised chiefly by his Garter ribbon and star. It was taken to Landguard Fort and thence to London for a state funeral in Westminster Abbey. A local historian of recent years has written that this gallant gentleman was buried at St Paul's, but alas! there was no

---

*There is some doubt as to whether the dramatic picture of the *Royal James* vanishing in one great roseate burst of flame is founded on fact. Some authorities claim that she was burnt to the water's edge by fire. It was believed that Sandwich, though singed, actually died from the shock of jumping into the sea from the quarter-deck.

St Paul's in 1672! The old Cathedral was destroyed in the Great Fire of 1666 and they did not even begin to clear the site until 1674.

Although the Dutch fleet were not chased home as in 1665 there can be no doubt that the result of the action was to our credit, having in mind the discrepancy in the numbers of the opposing fleets. It is surely not too much to claim that it was the greatest naval action fought in home waters. Even the Armada affair, important though it was, owed a large part of its outcome to other ancillary factors to back up the valour of the Elizabethan seamen. *Afflavit Deus et dissipantur;* it says so on the Armada medal!

There is a rumbustious story in verse written by an anonymous bard, who whether he saw the action or not, would have us think he did. It has been quoted so often that its authenticity as a contemporary composition might well be questioned; but the sentiments expressed in the last two verses suggest that it was written before Jacobitism became a dirty word.

> "One day as I was sitting still
> Upon the side of Dunwich hill,
> And looking on the ocean,
> By chance I saw De Ruyter's fleet
> With royal James's squadron meet;
> In sooth, it was a noble treat
> To see that brave commotion.
>
> I cannot stay to name the names
> Of all the ships that fought with James,
> Their number or their tonnage;
> But this I say, the noble host
> Right gallantly did take its post,
> And covered all the hollow coast
> From Walberswyck to Dunwich.
>
> The French, who should have joined the Duke,
> Full far astern did lag and look,
> Although their hulls were lighter;
> But nobly faced the Duke of York,
> (Though some may wink and some may talk)
> Right stoutly did his vessel stalk
> To buffet with De Ruyter.

Well might you hear their guns, I guess
From Sizewell Gap to Easton Ness,
The show was rare and sightly;
They battled without let or stay
Until the evening of that day,
'Twas then the Dutchmen ran away,
The Duke had beat them tightly.

Of all the battles gained at sea
This was the rarest victory
Since Philip's grand armada;
I will not name the rebel Blake,
He fought for Whoreson Cromwell's sake;
And yet was forced three days to take
To quell the Dutch bravado.

So now we've seen them take to flight,
This way and that, where'er they might,
To windward or to Lew'ard;
Here's to King Charles and here's to James,
And here's to all the captains' names,
And here's to all the Suffolk dames;
And here's the house of Stuart."

When all the loud bangs were over the French ships slipped primly back to proffer their felicitations to the victors; for however the historians view the strategical outcome of the battle, when 65 ships can give 91 such a bloody nose that they decide that their best course is to head for home it can hardly be regarded as a drawn game. The comments of the English captains on the behaviour of their 'allies' have not come down for the edification of posterity.

It is worthy of record that at the battle of Sole Bay there were scattered through the English fleet a number of soldiers and among these a detachment of the 'Admiral's Regiment' which had been raised eight years previously for service in the King's ships. They are said to have been raised from Thames Watermen and their first uniform was yellow with scarlet facings. Today the uniform of their successors is less flamboyant, but their name is written in letters of gold – the Royal Marines. Besides the Thames Watermen who may have formed the hard-core of this hardy band there were others who from the discomforts of debtors' prisons besought the privilege of saving His Majesty in His Majesty's ships. That they did so with credit is attested by one of their officers who wrote: "Those marines of whom I soe oft have write to you behaved themselves stoutly".

One of the ensigns who escaped from the *Royal James* was little the worse for his scorching and immersion in the water. Another was one John Churchill, destined to go down to posterity as the most brilliant strategical general in British military history.

A feature of the Southwold scene today is the nine open spaces or 'greens' which are dotted about the town, some of which are believed to mark the sites of buildings destroyed by the fire of 1659 and not re-built. A notable one is Gun Hill on the cliff top with its six old guns pointing out to sea and keeping watch and ward over the waters beneath which sleep the fine ships and their gallant crews who fought so valiantly on that May day three three centuries ago.

Historians have wrangled loud and long over the true origin of those guns. Some have believed them to be of Elizabethan vintage on the strength of the Tudor Rose and Crown cast on their breeches, others cling to the romantic story that they were taken from the Jacobites at Culloden and given to the town by an appreciative Duke of Cumberland. The late Major General P. J. Mackesy went very carefully into the Privy Council records so far as they were available to throw light upon the problem and it is very evident that they were never used by Prince Charles Edward. They are not field pieces at all and that is all the Young Pretender ever had, besides two 18 pounders of French origin which he abandoned after the siege of Stirling. It is pretty certain on all the evidence that these were the guns which had been asked for in the latter part of 1745 for the town's defence. They were old pieces and all that Cumberland may have had to do in the matter is that when he called at Southwold the Borough Fathers may have asked him to put in a good word for their petition when he went to London.* The local historians, Wake and Gardner, did the rest and after a deal of gossip it is very easy for a somewhat vague and fanciful story to take hold of people's memories until they come to believe in the utter veracity of what old men will mutter over a pint-pot. Nay! the time was to come when loose and foolish talk was so nearly to be the undoing of these old veterans.

---

*If Cumberland ever came to Southwold at all (which is not certain) it would have been on his return from the Low Countries in October 1745; Culloden was fought on 16th April, 1746.

During the Second World War an hysterical demand for scrap metal demanded the surrender of anything which might catch the eye of some chairbound patriot. The fact that cast-iron is rarely of convertible value, and most certainly of no value at all if its metallurgical content is uncertain, did not prevent many priceless and irreplaceable examples of art or craftsmanship being carried off to rust into oblivion in a war being fought to preserve the Heritage of the Nation. The guns were doomed to go; whither and why and to what end mattered not. Fortunately there were a few educated Englishmen who protested vigorously; officialdom was persuaded to hold its hand and the guns were saved. After the War they were brought from their hiding place and restored to their former position. The old wooden carriages had disappeared and probably ended their days supporting pot-plants in someone's greenhouse, unless indeed they were hewn asunder to keep the home fires burning! However, in 1956 new carriages were made for them and today they are back where they belong, to remind us of the days when Englishmen were ready and willing to deny their land to the enemy, come what may.

The history of the harbour itself is one of alternate endeavour and failure; endeavour to overcome the ancient enemies of sea and storm, of sand and silt and failure to press the fight to a successful outcome. It is believed that the tempest which carried the hapless Spanish ships to death and destruction in the northern seas was the same fury which dealt the final blow to Dunwich by destroying the last remains of her independent outlet to the sea. This was the opportunity for her rivals to profit by her disaster and Walberswick and Southwold brought themselves to combine sufficiently to dig a new channel for the Blyth which should provide both a haven and a harbour for the ships of greater burthen than they had been able to take of yore. This was completed in the spring of 1590 but it did not prosper. The supersitious may have thought that the ghost of Dunwich brooded over this dastardly attempt by her neighbours to deal a death blow in her last struggles to survive. A more practical cause was probably the failure to provide proper piering and for over a hundred years the actual harbour mouth was always shifting, by as much as four hundred yards back and forth, it was said. Indeed it was not until 1749 and 1752 that the first piers, north and south, were built. It seems incredible that anyone should think of making an artificial entry on this type of coast without piering, but this hazy habit of entering upon a warfare without counting the cost or even making a proper plan of campaign seems to have been endemic in the maritime history of the eastern counties.

In 1750 the Society of the Free British Fishery was formed and incorporated by an Act of Parliament with the laudable intention of combining to compete with the highly successful Dutch trade in both deep-sea fishery and also curing techniques. With headquarters at Southwold great hopes were entertained of a fishing boom and for a time the future seemed to be hopeful. The piers were improved and extended; but by the time the harbour had taken on a new lease of life the fishing boom had exhausted itself and the only ship traffic consisted of a moderate flow of small coasters. The harbour had to be dug out not less than thirteen times in as many years and no port can prosper on that basis; in fact by 1888 the situation had become completely hopeless. Further capital expenditure of a large order was incurred in the present century but without any very tangible results.

With the decay of the other Blyth ports and given the will to tackle and overcome the natural hazards of tide and silt there should have been nothing to stop Southwold stepping into a position of unchallenged supremacy in the estuary. There were however other factors involved which were not wholly of a natural order. To understand these we must take another look at the river where it enters the salt flats at the head of the estuary. The water which flooded these saltings at high tide had provided on the ebb the necessary outflow to scour the channel at the river mouth.

Five miles above Blythburgh there lies Halesworth, which in the middle of the eighteenth century was a flourishing market town, and it stood to gain from a direct waterway to the estuary whereby the principal of its commodities consisting of malt, grain and iron products could reach Southwold for shipment and in return could receive the coal and timber from the ships unloading there. Accordingly Parliamentary powers were obtained for the construction of a navigation channel which was completed and in use by the middle of 1761. At first keels were used for this shuttle traffic but later wherries were found to be a better proposition because they could more easily negotiate the narrow and twisting course of the river.

Things went very well for a few years but there was constant trouble owing to the harbour mouth being blocked with silt and it sometimes happened that ships were trapped in the harbour while others were lying outside unable to get in. On at least one occasion a ship was lost completely in bad weather while milling around in the roads.

Reference has already been made to the pernicious land-grabbing which had been going on at the head of the estuary by 'inning' large parts of the saltings below Blythburgh and this had reached the stage when it was preventing the outflow necessary to keep the channel open at the harbour mouth. Even Southwold Corporation whose interests would have seemed to demand that the acceptability of the harbour should come first was as guilty as the private landowners in this respect and between 1770 and 1845 no less than 4¼ square miles were 'reclaimed' to the profit of the land-grabbers and the ruin of the harbour. Some mathematically minded people have calculated that if the saltings had been covered by only one foot of water at high tide, this embanking must have robbed the outflow of 800 million gallons of water twice a day.

The whole situation was thoroughly disreputable and the chicanery which was practised between the landowners and the Harbour Commissioners — often the same individuals — seems almost unbelievable. Nor could any one plead ignorance of the facts: a galaxy of competent engineers, including such famous men as John Rennie, William Cubitt and James Walker, reported on the matter, pointed out the cause of the trouble and its obvious remedies, were thanked for their services and politely bowed out!

Eventually a courageous Scotsman, Patrick Stead, who owned a maltings in Halesworth and was one of the chief users of the navigation, went into battle and fought this conspiracy of corruption with such consistency and vigour that a public inquiry was held at Southwold in 1839 to the disgust and near-panic of many highly placed local magnates. The evidence given at the Inquiry brought out exact figures testifying to the falling off of traffic and the financial losses occasioned thereby, moreover ample and convincing evidence was given of the causes of such deterioration of the channel as had occurred. By the time the Inquiry was concluded there were some red — and white — faces on the other side of the table as the whole story thus brought to light constituted a damning indictment of the roguery which had been going on. It was a complete vindication of Stead's case; but time was against him and the users of the river. The General Enclosure Act of 1845, the purpose of which was to prevent this wholesale filching of land without so much as a by-your-leave, confirmed the owners of such land as had already been enclosed in their unsavoury titles. This was the death-knell of the Halesworth Navigation, which in a short time was not to be needed when the railway offered alternative facilities; but by the same token it prevented Southwold ever becoming the port she might have been. Today the River Blyth flows serenely under Blythburgh Bridge, a haunt of wildfowl and a paradise for canoeists and dinghy-sailors; but it carries no serious traffic and if it did, that traffic could never reach Southwold and the sea.

A distinctive feature of the Southwold scene is the lighthouse which, as we have already noticed, is prominent in the distant vista along the coast. It is not, however, an old one and dates only from 1890 when it replaced two temporary ones, themselves built only a few years earlier.

Here, as we have seen elsewhere on the coast, the beach yawls, or yolls, were manned by the Beachmen who were combined in close-knit corporations, or Beach Companies, ever watchful for a chance to profit from salvage or to take out a pilot. Probably the most famous yawl on this stretch of coast was the Southwold *Bittern* built by Beechings of Yarmouth. After a long and honourable life as a working boat and a brilliant performer at the Southwold Regattas for many years she ended her days in decay on the beach, surely worthy of a more glorious end; a model of her is still to be seen in the Sailors' Reading Room.

From the tradition of the beach yawls and the men who manned them sprang the early lifeboat service. Although the Suffolk Humane Society was formed in 1806, as is told elsewhere, Southwold determined to have their own society with its own boat and so in 1840 the Southwold Lifeboat Society was formed; but it did not last for many years. Looking forward, perhaps ahead of its time, the Society had a new boat built in 1853 which incorporated all the latest improvements of self-righting design. But alas! local prejudice which has so often bedevilled the lifeboat service prevailed; the local crew would not sail in a self-righter. The Society gave up the unequal struggle and asked the National Institution to take over; and from that time many lives were saved by the same brave men sailing the boats they understood.

Southwold might once have been great. In Anglian times it paid 20,000 herrings to its manorial lord, the Abbot of Bury, a levy to which William the Norman added a further 5,000 for himself; and still the town survived. She still has a quay and one sometimes sees an odd ship moored here; but as a port she is no more. The town is a serene smiling place with neat, brightly painted houses, a genial home for retired people and a sunny, welcoming holiday place for visitors of the more discerning sort.

Two miles north of Southwold, beyond Easton Cliffs where formerly was that Easton Ness, once the easternmost point of England and cited, albeit poetically, in the poem we have quoted, there lies the little lagoon-like Easton Broad. Now barely separated from the sea by a shingle bank it may well have been once the estuary of a river; for the little stream which wanders shyly down from Frostenden bottom, like the Hundred River at Thorpeness, was probably wide enough to take a galley. There is a good evidence of Roman occupation hereabouts and there are remains of Roman masonry in at least one house near Frostenden Rectory. It is also known that the Romans rated it a *portus maris* and with a *salina* or salt-pan to boot. As Froxedena the place figures in Domesday when one Ran held two church glebes here; it is well that this individual has been recorded in an ecclesiastical role or we might be tempted to think that this was the Scandinavian sea-goddess who was reputed to tangle drowning men in her net.

As a sea-port the place does not seem to have any established history beyond these stray mentions; although one East Anglian writer of high repute, the late Major Ernest Cooper, speculated on the possibility that just such a place as this could have provided the terrain for the Beowulf legend. This is not the place to discourse on the mixed provenance of that story with its Anglo-Danish implications; the plain fact remains that once this was a sea-port and now it is not. A beautiful and nostalgic corner of East Anglia remains also where in our rough island story so many great deeds were done and where we rightly honour the memory of the men who did them.

FOR centuries the most easterly point of England was recognised to be Easton Ness; but the sea has eroded it to an extent where it can be said to have ceased to be. Whether it was still a recognisable promontory when the *Battle of Solebay* was written —

> "Well might you hear their guns I guess
> From Sizewell Gap to Easton Ness".

or whether it was already a folk memory may be open to conjecture. What is certain is that 600 feet had been lost between 1836 and 1907; no longer was it the first point of England to be kissed by the first rays of the rising sun and even Lowestoft Ness is not much more than a name. Nevertheless the town was fully justified in claiming as its motto "Pointe du Jour" when the Corporation received its Grant of Arms in 1915.

The origin of the place-name Lowestoft has long been a matter of conjecture and not a little dispute among the learned. It has taken many forms, including *Lothuwistoffe, Laistoft* and *Lestoff,* and some have suggested that it may originally have been Hludwig's or Ludwig's toft or homestead. A side issue might be made of the name of Lake Lothing which has by a curious chain of circumstance, become the harbour of Lowestoft. For long regarded as a near-island, the Hundred of Lothingland, enclosed by the Lake, the Waveney and the Yare, is now completely so, although in a merely technical sense. The wise men have sought to derive this name from a people called the Luthings, whoever they may have been — if indeed they ever were! An entertaining feature of the town's name is that it has become sort of shibboleth. The true East Anglian usually pronounces it as a dissyllable, Lowstoft, or better still, Lowstoff, while the incomer or the holiday visitor tends to make a real meal of it as Lowiestoft. Thanks to the pernicious effect of broadcasting and other mass media there seems a kind of Gresham's Law in operation whereby the speech of our fathers is driven out by the brash jargon of the metropolis.

Lowestoft, by one name or another, is mentioned in Domesday Book only as part of the manor of Gorleston and within the Hundred of Lothingland; but it was early recognised as of some maritime importance. In 1250 it was included among a number of places where ships temporarily released after impressed by the King were to remain in his service until Michaelmas Day. This was probably in connection with John's proposed descent upon Normandy; for each of these towns was to find seamen and masters to navigate the ships to London when required.

Although Lowestoft is mentioned from time to time as involved in one warlike preparation or another, it would seem from an early date that most of its triumphs and tribulations were tied up with fishing or trading in fish. The comings and goings of the humble but succulent and essential herring have been the chief concern, not only of Lowestoft but also of many other places and peoples in these parts. It has been a staple diet ever since men first took fish from the sea and its periodic disappearance or scarcity has probably had a direct influence on the movements of whole communities. It has been suggested that a shortage of this fish in Scandinavian waters may have brought the Danes and Norsemen to come foraging in our waters. This is by no means the only cause of their voyaging; but it may have had some slight contributory significance. It has moreover been surmised that the exodus of the herring from Baltic waters is a result of the migration of the whales which formerly preyed upon them.

Lowestoft was not granted a market until 1442: but the fishermen were bringing fish ashore and selling it much earlier than that. There used to be a belief that the market was originally held on the beach; but this may be because of a mistranslation of the Latin *infra villam* as 'below the town' instead of 'within the town'. The exact whereabouts of the earlier market-place can be debated *ad nauseam;* all that matters is that Lowestoft soon became a thriving and important place. In fact it throve too well; for it never ceased by its self-sufficiency to annoy its more assertive neighbour, Great Yarmouth. This powerful town from its early beginnings perched precariously on a cluster of sandbanks had secured a dominating position at the mouth of the Gar, or Yare, and the men of Yarmouth brooked no rivals. By the Statute of Herrings of Edward III, 1357, it was decreed that no herring should be bought within the compass of fourteen 'lukes' about the town of Yarmouth but only at the town and haven of the same. A great deal of wrangling went on for a great many years as to the right interpretation of the statute and not least as to what constituted a luke. Like the mile it has been divers things to divers men at divers times and in divers places and one gets the impression that, like Humpty-Dumpty, Yarmouth made the word mean just what it chose it to mean. However the statute might be read, the stretch of coastline over which Yarmouth claimed jurisdiction extended from Winterton Ness in Norfolk to Easton Ness in Suffolk — and that is a mort of miles. Moreover, lest any trading should take place out at sea between ship and ship, the restriction was claimed to apply up to seven miles from the shore.

For centuries the battle went on and the men of Yarmouth were prepared to enforce their rights by every physical means in their power. Lowestoft pointed out in many a legal argument that this clog on free trade was to the hurt not only of themselves but of any of the King's subjects; but to no purpose. Ships were taken, cargoes pillaged and men of Lowestoft or other ports were haled before the Yarmouth bailiffs and fined and their boats as well as catches confiscated. Nor was this all; for Yarmouth exploited to the full their position to hold up or penalise traffic to or from Norwich, itself a port — and a staple town to boot. There seemed no limit to which Yarmouth would not go. In 1344 a hundred and twenty nine men boarded ships belonging to Robert de Morley, admiral of the Northern Fleet, then lying off Lowestoft and plundered them of cargo to the value of five thousand pounds. This raiding party was led by four of the bailiffs of Yarmouth and although this could have been a fishing dispute, the value of the cargo suggests a graver motive.

To some extent the rival ports had to come to terms from time to time and in 1400 by an 'accord of compromise' agreed that the Lowestoft men could buy fish from all ships not 'hosted' to Yarmouth or from ships whose catches were not required by the host town for itself. However the Lowestoft ships had to pay half a mark per last to the hosts in addition to the normal market value of the fish.

In spite of this campaign of repression by their acquisitive neighbours, Lowestoft was not prepared to take it all lying down. In 1359 it was enacted that the merchants of Lowestoft should be able to buy herrings of the "fishers as free of the London pykers, to serve their carts and horses that come thither from other countries, and to hang them". The hanging would relate to the fish for smoking, not the men! A pyker was an itinerant salesman, one who travelled on the pike or road; it is still used in some parts of the country for a tramp; a peddar or pedlar was so named because he carried his goods in a ped, or basket, not because he necessarily travelled on foot. It seems fairly obvious that the Lowestoft men reserved the right to buy their fish from any fishing vessels, whencesoever they came and to dispose of them as they willed.

In this way, Lowestoft flourished in its quiet way. In 1428 large consignments of herring were taken coastwise to Southampton and all the ports in this part of Suffolk took their share of this traffic. Covehithe, Dunwich, Southwold, Lowestoft, Walberswick sent their ships with their holds full to the coamings. Whether the main proportion was salted or smoked is not very certain, but at that time the full refinements of smoking may well have been better known to the Scandinavians and the Dutch. Nevertheless, the time was to come when the Scotsmen were going to be eager to learn from the Eastcoasters.

It is not very certain when the practice of deep-sea fishing, usually referred to in contemporary accounts as the 'Iceland' trade, commenced. In 1415 there was a proclamation made at Ipswich and other maritime towns that for a year there was to be no fishing in Danish or Iceland waters, "other than has been customary as of old"; this would make it seem that ships had been going there from England for some time. In 1379 one notices a difference in the amount of the convoy levy as between herring boats and "other fishers". There appears to have been quite a degree of competition for the task of convoying the fishing boats both in home waters and farther afield, and this gives a very fair idea of the volume of traffic in the trade. It is true that there were times when things were not so well, as for example when, under a statute of 1430, Englishmen were forbidden to go to Iceland or Denmark for the fishing, but only to North Bergen. This was, because, of "the riotous and piratical behaviour" of English fishermen and traders. Henry V who was anxious to avoid friction with the King of Denmark had taken similar action; but apparently the Danish king did not want to lost the trade indefinitely, because in 1523 he wrote to Henry VIII, who in 1509 had repealed the earlier statute, asking that more English ships should come to Iceland. Of all the deep-sea boats in those days, the majority came usually from Dunwich, but although Lowestoft seems to have concentrated more on the herring fisheries, there were always some of their ships in the Icelandic fleets.

Both from the herring fishers and those in the Icelandic trade, the parsons of the maritime towns expected and received the tithe of fish called Christ's half-dole. This depended in theory on the catch, the other half-dole of equal value being paid to the town for the repair of the pier and havens; in practice it usually amounted to £1 per boat to each recipient of the half-dole. This went on for centuries and when in 1845 a fisherman of Lowestoft demurred, he received no support from his fellows who all bore witness that it was a perfectly legal demand which had never been disputed. It is interesting that in these spiritual — or semi-spiritual— issues fishermen are, by and large, on the Lord's side. Some might attribute this to superstition; or could it be that the stark realities of a sailorman's life make it more natural to observe the ethical decencies?

In those days shipbuilding was on the basis of local self-sufficiency; ships were of course smaller and they were usually built on the strand like our smacks of today. They would be launched on rollers or more often floated off on a high spring tide. This practice went on for quite a while and in fact as late as 1599 there is a record of the *Susan* of 160 tons being built on the beach at Lowestoft by Edward Stephens. Certainly Suffolk craftsmen were in demand and in 1513 shipwrights and caulkers were pressed in Ipswich, Dunwich, Southwold and Lowestoft to help build the *Henri Grace à Dieu* at the new dockyard at Woolwich.

At the same time as ships were being built considerable attention was paid to land defences and while the south coast received its full measure on this score the Eastern seaboard was recognised as a vulnerable area. Commissioners were appointed to report on the construction of 'bulwarks' and batteries; but the armaments allocated to these strong points were frequently ludicrous as were the numbers of men competent to handle them. In 1522 the bulwark which had been made at Lowestoft some time previously was furnished with one gun. It seems that this formidable weapon cannot have been in danger of being worn out; for not until 1542 was a gunner appointed to serve it! On a contemporary map there appears a three gun battery commanding the Stanford channel and another serving a like function for St Nicholas Gat. It may be that this map was produced by the planners of those days and the scheme never got beyond the drawing board. Alternatively one can only conclude that the gunner must have been a very busy man! When the threat of a Spanish invasion loomed in 1587 things began to move; but the batteries were planned to occupy the same relative position as those of Henry VIII. Apparently Lowestoft still had only two guns, although a grand scheme was mooted to construct a parapet along the cliff-top between Lowestoft and Gorleston with a 'sconce' or redoubt at Gorleston. The following year Lowestoft built a bulwark at a cost of £80; but this was presumably only a part of the whole expense of fortifications, guns and ammunition for which the town had to raise £200. The Queen sent six guns which remained there until in 1643 Oliver Cromwell took them away in circumstances to be recounted in due course.

The vexed problem of providing ships for the country's defence was paramount. For centuries it had been customary for the King to impress ships or to make a levy in aid of their provision. In the following century this question of 'Ship Money' was to be blown up to a size which helped materially to rend the whole realm in a bloody and disastrous Civil War. At no time were people happy to pay, whether they lived within range of maritime attack or not; but one did not push argument too far with the Tudors. When Lowestoft protested that it was too poor to contribute to any ships the Council ordered the bailiffs to send to London any townsmen who would not pay! After the threat of the Armada had passed, the wrangle still went on and when there was peace between England and Spain the men of Lowestoft had other troubles. As invariably happened, the threat of war was succeeded by the reality of piracy and then the coastal towns protested to the Crown that they needed protection — to be found, of course, by the King! For reasons which we have no room to discuss here, the royal money-bags were empty; but the unhappy sovereign was still expected to make bricks without straw and if he could not, so much the worse for him. Off with his head!

During the conflict between King and Parliament, although in the earlier stages there were a few 'pockets' of Royalist supporters in Norfolk and Suffolk, the general trend in East Anglia was for the Parliamentary cause. Whether it was for some deep-seated reason of loyalty or merely because Yarmouth stood for the Parliament is difficult to be certain; but Lowestoft supported the King, and that openly. From this proceeded the inevitable result that so far as these two towns were concerned the war was a private affair to be pursued on every possible occasion and with unabated fury. On the whole, Yarmouth got the worst of these encounters largely due to the warlike enterprise of one Captain Allin who carried out a successful raid upon the Yarmouth Icelandic fleet, destroying twenty of their ships.

As the Royalist cause waned the tide turned against Lowestoft and after an abortive attempt in 1643 to hold the town for the King the more cautious townsmen decided that discretion was the better part of valour and offered no opposition when Cromwell entered. He made prisoners of about a dozen of the most prominent townsmen and carried them off to Cambridge as well as taking possession of the six guns which the town had had since Queen Elizabeth's time. The soldiery having stripped the tradesmen of every part of their stock-in-trade which could be of use, and probably much more beside, the Parliamentary forces withdrew, leaving Lowestoft licking its wounds while Yarmouth preened itself with virtuous glee.

With the Restoration of the Monarchy in 1660, the Royalists plucked up heart again and Lowestoft was soon in the news for a different reason. One of the things which Charles II inherited from the Commonwealth government besides a depleted purse, was a navy consisting of incomparable seamen, but an indifferent collection of ships and an uneasy confrontation with the Netherlands. Fortunately his brother, James Duke of York, although not always the best judge of a political situation was a courageous soldier and a dedicated naval commander. The peace made with Holland in 1654 had never been more than an armed truce and in 1665 war was declared again. The English fleet was commanded by the Duke of York, assisted by Prince Rupert and the Earl of Sandwich, and putting to sea in April blockaded the Dutch in their own ports. Bad weather forced the English to stand off and gave the Dutch the opportunity to break out; but they were engaged off Lowestoft on 3rd June, defeated and chased home to Holland with a loss of nearly forty ships and 6,000 men. Among the Lowestoft men who distinguished themselves was the Thomas Allin who had fought with such vigour against Yarmouth and the Parliament over twenty years before. Rear-Admiral Riches Utber and his son Captain John Utber, each prominent among Lowestoft sea captains, also added to their reputations. The fleet returned to the Kent coast with their prizes and prisoners but arrived at a bad time, the plague having just reached England, and many of the former foes must have been united in death.

In 1609 an event had occurred at Lowestoft which has secured for this small Suffolk town a place in history. Not since the days of the Roman occupation had there been any proper form of lighting the coast. The pharos at Dover is well known and was one of two which lit the entrance to the Roman *Portus Dubrae;* the other one on the opposite side of the harbour has disappeared. There were probably lights on certain headlands at various times during the eleven and a half centuries following the departure of the Eagles; but it was not until 1609 that a lighthouse was built in Britain, and this was at Lowestoft. Indeed this was only second in the world, the earliest being the Skaw on the northernmost point of Denmark which was built in 1564. Others followed and those which concern us are mentioned in their proper places. Why the East Coast should have received priority in this lighting of the coast is difficult to understand unless it is because of the continuous traffic in colliers which passed between Newcastle and the capital city and which tended to sail closer inshore than foreign going craft. The first lighthouse was much lower down than the present High Light and was opposite the Stanport or Stanford Channel; but as this tended to shift its position it was soon thought necessary to have another light and in 1627 a second was fixed higher up the cliff. This was in a fixed position and was lighted by an open coal brazier like the early Roman pharos, while the lower light on a timber structure could be moved from time to time so that the alignment of the two lights corresponded with the position and direction of the channel. In 1676 the 'High Light' was rebuilt in approximately the same position as it occupies today. Although the tower was again rebuilt in 1873 it still bears the plaque fixed to its predecessor which records the fact that it was "Erected by the Brotherhood of the Trinity House of Deptford Strond in the Mastership of Samuel Pepys Esq., Secretary of the Admiralty of England Anno Dom. 1676". This plaque bears the arms of Trinity House and also those of Samuel Pepys. Seeing that Pepys seemed to take his duties as Master of Trinity House very seriously — he certainly enjoyed their hospitality — his remark to the Duke of York on one occasion that he thought all lighthouses useless and a burden on trade, has always seemed a little odd. For all his selfishness and pettiness in his personal prejudices, Pepys was a brilliant and competent administrator, but great men often say some silly things in their less guarded moments. As we have seen for many years the majority of lighthouses were privately built and proved a fruitful source of income to the speculators who owned them.

The Low Light was eventually abandoned and replaced by a second light lower down the tower of the High Light. When the second High Light was built in 1676, the base of its predecessor was left for some time and there was a story of an old crone who sat on this base and practised witchcraft for conjuring up storms. Could this have been a garbled memory of a woman employed to tend the light who had failed to do her job? Up and down the coast one constantly comes upon cases where the lights have been ill-tended by old or drunken women and certainly in 1663 the official lightkeeper was alleged to have been negligent in his duties.

A few months after the rebuilding in 1676, the open coal fire was enclosed, owing to the risk of fire. The tower stood within eighty yards of the nearest houses and the risk would seem to be a real one which had been anticipated by the original design. In 1778 oil lighting was installed after experimental observations from the Trinity House yacht lying twenty miles out to sea. The design of the mirror containing four thousand one-inch facets gave it the name of the spangle light and this was then shipped to the Scilly Isles to be replaced at Lowestoft by another light of the same design.

Not the least of the hazards of the fisherman's calling can be the added risks in time of war. During the American War of Independence when we found ourselves once again at war with France, Louis XVI ordered that fishermen should not be molested; but the revolutionary government had no such scruples and the risk of being robbed, captured or sent to the bottom resulted in a considerable reduction in the number of fishing boats. Nevertheless it took a deal of intimidation to keep the fisherman ashore as is evidenced by the notice which appeared in the Ipswich Journal of 5th June, 1744:

> "Whereas it has been represented and repeated by some ill-designing People, that the Boats do not go to sea from Lowestoft to catch Mackarels as usual, on account with the war with France; This is to give notice to all Buyers and others, that we have now at sea thirteen Boats, employed in catching mackarels, and that, during the season, all Pedlars and others may be duly supplied with the said Fish at Lowestoft as in former years."

In 1776 Lowestoft decided to look farther afield for the fresh fish for curing and for this reason sent some of its boats into Manx and Scottish waters to secure the larger herrings which were abundant there. Unfortunately the home curing industry was nearly wrecked because the curers in Scotland and the Isle of Man began to realise that the Lowestoft process was far better than their own and began to offer tempting premiums to the Suffolk men to migrate north to teach the secrets of their trade. A 'tower' or head man could earn a fee of twenty guineas which in those days would be a substantial inducement, even after he had paid his assistant 'roarers' who rored, or stirred, the fish about during the smoking process. Liverpool followed suit and this unexpected competition created alarm and despondency in the home town, especially as the French wars limited the considerable export of smoked fish to the Mediterranean. This serious setback brought a compensatory advantage; for the town occupied the time in strengthening its sea-defences which in the years to come was to help materially in rebuilding the fishing trade.

It may be no more than a coincidence that here, as at Aldeburgh, the name of Johnson is remembered in connection with ship-building. In 1785 Thomas Johnson of Yarmouth, having served his apprenticeship in that town, was in due course admitted a freeman of the Borough and soon after obtained permission of the Lord of the Manor of Lowestoft to build a shed on part of the beach. This seems to have been on a copyhold plot measuring no more than forty feet by twenty; but here he laid down his first Lowestoft ship, the brigantine *London* (140 tons) which was completed in 1787 and registered at London.

From this beginning a succession of fine ships came off the stocks over the next thirty years and it seems obvious that more working space must have been acquired as time went on. It is not certain how many vessels were actually built by Johnson because there are gaps in the Custom House Register; but there is evidence of over thirty and it may be that the total was over twice that number and ranged from small luggers and schooners to a full-rigged ship, the *Young Henry* (260 tons) built in 1801 to a London order.

In 1817 Thomas Johnson was joined by his son, also named Thomas; but the partnership did not last long as for some reason or another they ran into financial trouble and in 1820 went bank-rupt. Nevertheless while they were in business they established a reputation which extended far beyond Lowestoft and besides their

London orders their commission came from as far afield as Sunderland and Glasgow. An interesting feature is that whereas the other Lowestoft builders kept to clinker construction the Johnsons always turned out carvel hulls. This may have been a point of difference between them and their more traditionally minded neighbours who were perhaps not above regarding the downfall of these Yarmouth incomers with a certain prim malice in their hearts.

With the failure of the Johnsons the building of trading vessels at Lowestoft seems to have ceased until after the construction of the harbour when John Korff built two schooners in Lake Lothing, but he too failed and it was not until the harbour had outgrown its own initial difficulties that shipbuilding gradually revived.

On 14th January, 1747, King George II landed on the North Beach on his return from Hanover and was brought ashore sitting spectacularly in his ship's boat, which was lifted bodily from the surf by a band of Lowestoft stalwarts dressed up for the occasion as seamen. It must have been a solemn and awe-inspiring affair and it is a matter for regret that there is no record of its effect upon the spectators! It would not be fair to say that the second George was entirely devoid of any sense of humour, although such examples as have come down to us are mostly on the heavy side. He seems to have taken this as a matter of course consistent with his royal dignity and climbing into his coach was driven up Rant's Score and so away.

The Scores are a distinctive feature of Lowestoft, although today most of them, partly through neglect, partly through haphazard development have lost any claim to be even picturesque. The origin of the word 'score' has been variously explained. The obvious suggestion that they are the deep channels made in the cliff by the 'scouring' action of floodwater has been challenged by an alternative derivation from the Anglo-Saxon verb *scearan*, to cut as with a plough-share. It all sounds very learned; but is it not a verbal journey 'all round Will's mothers'? After all, there is another Anglo-Saxon word, *score* which just means the shore! We are back again in the etymological jungle. The trouble with all these speculations is that we are apt to forget that Anglo-Saxon was already a fully developed and expressive language when its speakers first reached these shores and that was five hundred years before the Norman Conquest. If today we look back five hundred years, we are back in the days of Edward IV before the much-maligned Richard III had came to the throne. Discounting the synthetic jargon of the past hundred years, five-eighths of the words which we use today are Anglo-Saxon in origin. One is tempted to sympathise with Humpty Dumpty!

The continual erosion of the coast line has been referred to before and nowhere has this problem been more acute than at Lowestoft. After the disappearance of Easton Ness, the distinction of being the most easterly point of Great Britain fell to Lowestoft Ness which formerly jutted out opposite the High Light; but within the last hundred years this too has gone and the Ness Point is its only memorial. Much attention and capital has been given to the never-ending battle of coast defence; but here as elsewhere it has often happened that the strengthening at one point has resulted in increased erosion at another.

Apart from the continual damage by scour and shingle drift there have from time to time been grim reminders of the hazards to which this part of the coast is exposed at times when the sea, so peaceful at times of fair weather, can be a ravening monster in seasons of storm and tempest; and there have been times when disaster has struck at those in peril on the deep, especially in days when there was far more traffic than we see today. As we look at contemporary 'prospects' of the coast hereabouts, it is easy to assume that the artist has given full rein to his imagination in showing such an enormous concourse of shipping. Some of the vessels were undoubtedly at anchor or hove to in the roads; but there were still many under way. There are however many of us who can remember the days when there were still ships a-plenty whenever one looked out to sea. One of the most dramatic and tragic occasions when calamity came to this part of the coast was on the 19th December, 1770. Let the account speak for itself as it appeared in the *Ipswich Journal* ten days later:—

"The dreadful storm of Wednesday the 19th inst. began about 1 o'c in the morning and continued with increasing violence till five when the wind suddenly changed from the north-east to the south-west and for two hours raged with a fury that was hardly ever equalled. Anchors and cables proved too feeble a security for the ships, which instantly parting from them, and running on board each other, produced a confusion neither to be described nor conceived; not a few immediately foundered, others were dismasted, and none escaped unhurt. At daylight a scene of the most tragic distress was exhibited;

those who first beheld it assert that no less than 18 ships were on the sand at one and the same time, and many others were seen to sink; of those on the sand, one half were entirely demolished with their crews before 9 o'clock; the rest were preserved a few hours longer; but this dreadful pause served only to aggravate the destruction of the unhappy men who belonged to them, who betook themselves to the masts and rigging; these continually breaking 8 or 10 men were not unfrequently seen to perish at a time without the possibility of being assisted. Fifteen only, about 2 in the afternoon, were taken off one of the wrecks, and about as many more were saved by taking to their boats or by getting on board other ships when they boarded each other. It is impossible to collect with certainty how many lives or how many ships were lost in this terrible hurricane, 25 at least, perhaps 30 ships and 200 men do not seem to be an exaggerated account. This indeed is too small a calculation if credit is to be given to one of the seamen who declares he saw 6 vessels sink not far without the Stanford among which was a large ship bound for Lisbon with 60 or 70 passengers on board. The concern this destructive scene occasioned to the spectators of it was increased by the following circumstances: when the masts of one of the ships on which were 8 or 9 men fell, 2 of them were sometime afterwards seen struggling among the wreck, and at length, after unremitted efforts, got upon the hull. In the afternoon a pilot boat ventured from the shore, but it was found impracticable to administer any relief to the unfortunate sufferers whom they were compelled to leave in their forlorn state. An approaching dark stormy night heightened the horrors of their situation. The next day, to the astonishment of everybody, one of the men was observed to be alive, and about noon the boat again attempted to save him and approached so near as to ask the poor fellow several questions; but the hull on which he was, being surrounded with wreck, and the sea running high, it was impossible to rescue him from the impending danger. He was to the stern of the ship, towards her head the sailors con-sidered it barely possible to board her with safety; this they told the unhappy man they would attempt and bid him walk to the place, but he replied that he was too weak to change his situation and they were again obliged to leave him. The ensuing night put a period to his misfortune and his life."

In the eighteenth and nineteenth centuries, the traditional practice of salvaging from wrecks resulted in the formation of Beach Companies at towns with sizeable populations of fishermen and longshoremen. They were especially well-organised at Yarmouth with seven companies and Lowestoft with three. They were not content merely to salvage what the sea had cast up, and in that case there was much competition to be on the spot first and also to put out to endeavour to salvage what had not yet become a total wreck. They were rough days and the standards applied to decide whether a wreck really was a wreck, that is that no man escaped alive, were not above suspicion.

Nevertheless, the record of the Beachmen is not all wholly a black one and many a mariner owed his life to the toughness and, yes! bravery of these men. The yawls, or yolls, which they used were almost legendary in their ability to stand up to the worse seas. Before some purist points out that by pedantic standards some of these boats would seem to be lug-rigged or ketch-rigged, let it be emphasised that yawls they were called, so yawls they were! In any case the classification of many vessels in those days was not so precisely governed by sail-plan and the word is derived from the Dutch *jol,* so that the local pronunciation is very right. In fact the yawls were usually lug-rigged and until the middle of the nineteenth century were often three-masters.

The unity of each Beach Company was promoted by its having its own hut or 'shod' where the Beachmen kept their gear and settled their own affairs, which no doubt included dividing the spoils of a salvage!

The tragedies of the 1770 storm were to be repeated from time to time for many years until the public conscience was sufficiently roused to evoke some active action. According to one account by a local historian a Lifeboat Society was formed in 1800 but this does not seem to have come to anything very effective until in 1807 the Suffolk Humane Society took the matter seriously into its hands and the *Frances Ann* was built at Lowestoft by a local boat builder, Bareham, at a cost of £200. She remained in service until 1850 and alone was credited with the saving of three hundred lives. It is from the *Frances Ann* that the famous Norfolk and Suffolk type of boat was evolved.

The coming of the lifeboats was greeted with deep suspicion by the Beach Companies who saw in jeopardy their own profits from salvage. There was great competition between the various 'rescue' crews as to who would get out to a wreck first and we must piously hope that the cause of saving human lives was treated as the most urgent. A third element entered into the race when in addition to the voluntary 'Society' boats there were also boats provided by the National Life-boat Institution founded in London in 1824, as well as the Suffolk Association for Saving the Lives of Ship-wrecked Seamen. It would be wearisome to describe in detail how the two societies between them established boats up and down the coast at Landguard, Bawdsey, Sizewell, Aldeburgh, Thorpeness and Southwold; but Lowestoft must still take pride of place and time. Various designs were produced, the Greathead, the Norfolk and Suffolk, the Watson, but it was the same then as it still is today; wherever you find a boat the question of whether it is self-righting or not, of this standard of buoyancy or another, the local men have their own prejudices and nothing that architects or designers may say will reconcile them to any model but their own traditional favourite. How many gallant lives have been sacrificed to this local bias? And yet may it not be on balance that the local men handle best their local boat?

In 1805 the victory of Trafalgar eased the tension of France's threat to these islands by sea, although the North Sea remained a place of uncertainty for those who sought to pursue their lawful occupations. There was still the odd privateer — or worse — on the prowl and in this atmosphere an amusing episode occurred in 1807 when the skippers of two Lowestoft yawls spotted a brig which they took to be a prize in enemy hands making for French waters. Filled with patriotic zeal —and maybe the incentive of prize-money— they gave chase and like a pair of well-trained terriers they came up with her simultaneously, one on each quarter. She, taking the yawls for privateers, was about to defend herself with what guns she had; but hesitation could have proved her undoing had that been the case. When the Lowestoft men came alongside they found that she was a British ship bound on lawful business for the West Indies. Fortunately, no harm was done, 'refreshments' — to borrow the newspaper term — were offered and gracefully received, and in general it would seem that a good time was had by all before the 'valiant sons of Neptune' returned with a good story to tell in their local hostelry.

Eight years later came Waterloo and peace for good, or so it seemed until the statesmen of Europe sat down around the conference table and wrangled themselves into the next international crisis.

But in 1814, a year before Wellington's "damn close run thing", an idea was born in the mind of one Alderman Crisp Brown which was to change the pattern of Lowestoft and lay the foundation for much prosperity in the years to be.

For long it had been thought that the River Waveney originally found its way to the sea through Lake Lothing as well as if not instead of, the estuary of the Yare, and that the narrow isthmus between Lowestoft and Kirkley was merely a silting-up of the original river mouth. Although there was a corduroy road whereby traffic of a sort could pass on this which was the most direct route along the coast and ultimately to London, yet the sea broke through this from time to time and it frequently happened that on occasions when there was special need for people to pass on foot such as for Pakefield Fair or the like there would be an opportunist ready with a boat to ferry people across or maybe to carry children over dry-foot. Subsequent research has given strong support to the belief that Lake Lothing never was estuarine — at least in historical times; but that is not greatly relevant to our story.

Alderman Crisp Brown conceived the idea of linking up Lake Lothing, Oulton Broad and the Waveney, with certain ancillary 'cuts' to provide a way through to Norwich which would free that town from the onerous harbour dues exacted by Great Yarmouth as well as the other restrictions which had caused continual friction between the two towns for centuries. A Private Bill was promoted to further this scheme which was vigorously opposed at great cost by Great Yarmouth; but with the support of their Lordships of the Admiralty who saw the advantage of making Lowestoft a Harbour of Refuge, the Bill received the Royal Assent on 28th May, 1827, as "An Act for making and maintaining a navigable communication for ships and other vessels between the City of Norwich and the Sea, at or near Lowestoft in the County of Suffolk".

The first meeting of the proprietors of the Norwich and Lowestoft Navigation Company was held at Norwich in the following July and work was started at the sea end almost immediately under the distinguished engineer, William Cubitt. On the 3rd September, 1827 the proceedings opened ceremonially with the cutting of the first sod, as is reported in the *Norwich Mercury* five days later:

"On Monday (3rd September, 1827) the Directors proceeded to St Olaves in a steam boat, then changed into the yacht Rob Roy which was towed by three 6-oared gigs manned by Pilots and Beachmen who towed the yacht up reaches of the river where the wind was adverse and arrived at Lowestoft about 3 p.m.

On Tuesday (4th) morning the Directors walked from the Crown Inn to the edge of Lake Lothing in the following order:—

Preventive Men with their colours.
Crews of several boats with various colours.
Band.
Master Disney carrying the Act of Parliament.
Mr Disney carrying the flag of Norwich, a Port.
Mr Cubitt, the Engineer.
Mr Green, the contractor with the Spade.
Aldermen, Sheriffs and Others."

Presumably, the Aldermen and Sheriffs were from Norwich, because at that time Lowestoft was not a Borough; the Sheriffs of Norwich were reduced from two to one by the Municipal Corporations Act 1835.

The entry from the sea was originally by means of a sea-lock; but the lock gates having deteriorated after some years use they were not used and dredging was relied upon to keep the channel clear. The cost of the whole undertaking in the first place was of the order of £150,000, of which £54,000 was advanced by the Exchequer; but as the scheme was slow to achieve success after seven years the Government foreclosed, closed down the undertaking and put in an engineer who was in fact nothing less than a caretaker-bailiff. But Lowestoft was not to be beaten. Six local business men acquired the dock and when the situation got beyond them Sir Morton Peto, a building contractor on a large scale, bought the whole concern and from that stage the Dock never looked back. Peto it was who linked the town and its dock to Reedham by a railway line, thus enabling merchandise to be rapidly transported to London, Norwich and the rest of England.

For various reasons which do not concern us here the original scheme to link up Norwich with the sea was not proceeded with;

but Lowestoft was now a real port and the merchandise flowed through; with the additional advantage that the town now had an adequate harbour of refuge, the only effective one between Yarmouth and the Orwell ports of Harwich and Ipswich. No longer did fishing boats have to discharge their cargoes laboriously on the beach and as the harbour was extended throughout the years more and more ships could be docked and the subsidiary but no less essential processes of salting and smoking the fish could be carried out expeditiously and effectively.

The original piers 500 feet long were found to hold up the north-south shingle drift and there was reason to fear that a substantial harbour bar might be formed. Two outer piers were therefore built to north and south of the existing piers to act as breakwaters, and these are still incorporated with modifications into the very considerable harbour complex with its two inner basins to which were added still later the Waveney Dock and the Hamilton Dock. Meantime the Inner Harbour in Lake Lothing itself as it developed provided berthage for large cargo vessels, and shipbuilding was encouraged to revive and flourish and keep pace with current changes of hull construction and the coming of steam.

The opening up of the sea entrance had necessitated a bridge which, while maintaining the main roadway to the south would permit the passage of ships. This was a double-leaf swing bridge, but in 1897 the year of Queen Victoria's Diamond Jubilee, it was replaced by a single-leaf swing bridge which served until recently when it was decided to provide a more modern bridge to accommodate the road traffic of today.

Lowestoft would be a strange town if it had not drawn to itself some odd characters such as George Borrow, that eccentric and turbulent genius of language and Edward Fitzgerald, whom we have met also at Woodbridge and Aldeburgh. Finally, out of a great galaxy of men of note, we must not forget Joseph Conrad who arrived in Lowestoft from his native Poland not speaking a word of English but who grew to love his 'Lowestoft chaps' and who gave to us such a brilliant succession of masterpieces of English literature.

While it has had no significant impact upon the development of the town as a fishing town and a port, mention in passing must be made of the famous Lowestoft China, the production of which flourished from 1757 to 1802; but by reason of that short period of output, pieces are eagerly sought by discerning collectors of ceramics. Its scarcity no less than its quality ensures a high price in the sale-rooms.

In 1885 Lowestoft at last received its charter of incorporation; this may seem somewhat overdue for a town which has played such a prominent part in the history of our land. It took a further thirty years for the Corporation to get round to securing a Grant of Arms and when this was eventually done there must have been some surprise that the Heralds in their design had commemorated the china industry which had lasted a bare half-century as well as the fact that Lowestoft receives the first light of the rising sun; but of the herring, the king of fish, which for centuries had made the town rich and famous and over which so many valiant battles had been fought with other town, no mention whatever was made!

This omission which at the time may have been due to mere snobbery has in the result proved sadly prophetic. Today the port flourishes and many thousands of holiday visitors flock to Lowestoft every summer; but the fishing industry languishes for lack of herring. It may be that the North Sea grounds have been overfished and that the herring is going the way of so many other creatures who have succumbed to man's stupidity and greed; it may be that the scarcity is merely seasonal. It is certainly a matter for concern and although the deep-sea ships still go out and brave the hardships and perils of the sea to fill our larders, who knows how long they will survive?

FROM Great Yarmouth to King's Lynn is ninety miles of what can sometimes be a very dodgy sea and today the greater part of this coast-line —the rump of the pig— makes a massive curve breasting the grey relentless German Ocean. True, the curve is broken between Blakeney Point and Brancaster Bay where the sea has eaten deep and left vast areas of sand and saltings; for here there is no land mass between England and the Arctic. Yarmouth itself sits between the line of the pleasure beaches, which every year draw thousands of holiday-makers from all parts of England, and the estuary of the Yare which gives the town an unrivalled water-front for a port of this size. This channel takes the united waters of the Gar or Yare, the Bure and the Waveney in a southward direction, thus providing the chief outlet from the large and complicated system of the Broads to the open sea.

It was not always thus. Once the whole confluence of these rivers swept out to sea in a great estuary which stretched from Caister to Corton. Up to the end of the Roman occupation this must still have been the pattern of the land and from Garionnonum, Burgh Castle, the Commander of the Stablesian Horse would have had something like six miles of water between him and the little walled town at Caister.

Across the mouth of this estuary there lay a long sandbank which was originally surrounded by water but was later added to at its northern end so as to link up with the main coast line at Caister. On the westward side of this bank there arose a little settlement of fishermen's huts. This was the infant which grew into the formidable walled town destined to play such a prominent and dominant part in the history of this part of England. But all this was well away in the future and when Swein of Denmark took his longships up the estuary in 1004 to burn Norwich they do not seem to have taken much count of the handful of Angles who must have trembled to see this host sail past. Today Breydon Water is all that is left of the estuary; but it would seem possible that the small settlement on the sandbank was able to catch herrings in sufficient numbers to make it worth taking them to Norwich. Some writers suggest that herrings were actually caught at Norwich; but this hardly accords with the migrating habits of the fish. There are records in later years of sturgeon being taken from the river; but this is another matter.

It took some centuries for the coastline to take shape and one of Yarmouth's chief problems was to secure a haven which would not be choked by the ever-shifting sand. It is believed that when the sandbank was still an island the channel at its northern end was used as an entry and a shelter for ships and that this was the mysterious 'Grubbs Haven' which was regarded as the northern town boundary. When this was choked the townsmen had to look towards the southern end which was their only, though less desirable, outlet. The position of Grubbs Haven is thought to be marked by the 'Cross in the Midsands', a cairn of stone regarded as Yarmouth's most Ancient Monument.

Between 1346 and 1560 six attempts were made to establish a permanent haven and each eventually failed. The sixth, begun in 1549, seemed doomed to disaster from the start. In spite of a special service in the parish church to invoke a blessing on the enterprise there may have been some pious souls who doubted the efficacy of this operation, seeing that plate and vestments from the church had been sold to raise funds for the harbour works. In the same year the Kett Rebellion brought Robert Kett to Yarmouth and although his forces were repelled some of the insurgents returned after cover of darkness and so handled the works that they were never completed.

Finally the assistance of a Dutchman, Joost Jansen, was enlisted and under his direction and by a mighty effort to utilise the services of every available man, woman and child the seventh attempt was made. Revetments were made from masonry salvaged from church buildings and one cannot but admire the touching picture of the magistrates 'encouraging' their toiling townsfolk, who laboured in water up to their waists with shovel and bucket to give Yarmouth a harbour mouth. The task had been accomplished by colossal effort, not only of human sweat and endurance, but also at enormous cost. Six years after the work had begun and even before it was completed the sea broke through. The financial cost of the work and of the subsequent maintenance of the port could only be recovered in tolls on shipping and even so there was never enough. In 1650 the desperate town asked Parliament for the lead from the roof of the 'useless cathedral at Norwich'. Fortunately, although surprisingly coming from a puritan Parliament, the application was refused. One wonders how far the suggestion was prompted by desperation, vandalism or a desire to humble Norwich with which Yarmouth had been at loggerheads for centuries!

But let us return to the story of Yarmouth itself. It is probable that when Swein's dragon-ships had passed the fishing village on the sandbank the Danes did not think it worth landing to sack the place, for it cannot have been of any size by appearance or repute. Eighty years later the Domesday survey recorded that Yarmouth had only 70 burgesses compared with 665 at Norwich, 110 at Ipswich and 720 at Thetford; and be it remembered that those other three towns had suffered heavily when Swein was on the rampage which eventually brought his son Cnut to the throne of England.

Whether because of the relative insignificance of this small maritime town, or as seems more likely, on account of its strategic significance, the King reserved the town as a royal demesne and all dues were paid to the sheriff instead of to a feudal mesne lord. In due course as the town grew and prospered the sheriff was assisted by a port-reeve, but Yarmouth longed to be a chartered town in its own right with the right to form its own trade guilds.

Eventually by the good will of King John, and a certain financial consideration, the town received a charter in 1209 and Yarmouth became a free borough ruled over by four bailiffs, who were each responsible for his own ward. In 1272 Henry III granted Letters Patent under which the town was authorised to appoint twenty-four jurats to assist the bailiffs. Later a council of twenty-four councillors afterwards increased to forty-eight, was appointed and this in addition to the jurats, came in the fifteenth century to take on the form of one of the greater boroughs. The jurats in due course became aldermen and there was a time when this office became in fact if not in theory hereditary in some of the more prominent families. Many great cities like London had already acquired this hereditary element in their government. It was one which could easily lend itself to abuse; but like many institutions against which the charge of nepotism is often levelled, there was another side to the picture. It may not seem to us today that it could ever be a good thing for overmuch power to reside in the hands of a few wealthy citizens; but in those days it was more important for a town to be subject to stable government by a responsible minority than for the body politic to be at the mercy of an irresponsible multitude which could easily be swayed.

From this time Yarmouth is known as Great Yarmouth to distinguish it from Southtown which was for long known as Little Yarmouth. In 1426 the number of bailiffs was reduced to two and this figure remained constant until the first mayor was appointed in 1684.

It is evident that from very early times the aspirations of Yarmouth were maritime. From the first we see the town beginning in a very small way as a fishing village; but as it began to prosper in trade it was inevitable that it would not be content to carry out its operations with other men's ships, and where trading ships went they would need a modicum of protection. When therefore we find that in 1205 Yarmouth had three galleys of its own it is reasonable to assume that these were ships of war. It is also very evident that Yarmouth was a town with whom it was unwise to be on bad terms. The circumstances in which all vessels carrying Scottish merchandise and lying in Yarmouth Roads were arrested in 1216 are obscure; but it must be remembered that at that time England was in turmoil. King John was seeking to repudiate the terms of Magna Carta which he claimed to have entered into the previous year under duress — and with good reason. The Barons who do not seem to have been over-sure of themselves had come to terms with King Alexander of Scotland and done homage to him. Yarmouth could not but feel itself bound to the King who had so recently enfranchised the town. Moreover together with Ipswich, Colchester and other towns it had been subject to a heavy ransom, those towns which did not pay having been plundered. Hence Yarmouth was very much involved in the King's war.

It is evident that Yarmouth was already recognised as a place of reputation for the building of ships; in 1290 a ship was commissioned for Edward I to be sent to Norway to fetch Margaret 'the Maid of Norway', grand-daughter of Alexander III of Scotland and heiress to the Scottish throne. It was intended that she should marry the young Edward, first Prince of Wales. Alas! on the voyage home the ship only got so far as Orkney, then part of the Kingdom of Norway, where the Maid died at the tender age of seven years. How different might have been the life of the ill-starred Edward II, to say nothing of the histories of England and Scotland, had this child of destiny lived to unite the two thrones by marriage.

Instead, that Union was to come three centuries later when the throne of England, left vacant by the failure of a tainted line, passed to the 'wisest fool in Christendom'.*

In 1294 Yarmouth was summoned to send four burgesses to Parliament, so it is apparent that the town was recognised as a port and borough of substance. In 1260 Henry III had given authority by letters patent for the construction of a wall and moat; but it was nearly a quarter of a century before the town got round to making a start upon this essential job. Essential because the existence of an important sea-port on the coast so nearly exposed to our neighbours on the European mainland was a constant reminder of how easily England could be wounded in a vulnerable part of her commercial wellbeing.

While Yarmouth men were possessed of an effective naval force to deny to an enemy the approach by sea, it was none the less essential to guard their back and this was accomplished by building a substantial wall twenty-three feet high and a mile and a quarter long. It was a major operation, for even in those days material and labour was costly and it was over a hundred years before the work was complete. The total area thus enclosed by the wall on the south, east and north, and the river on the west amounted to less than 150 acres and it may well be that from this sense of being a compact well-knit community proceeds not only the distinctive lay-out of the town but also its tight cohesion and determination which made Great Yarmouth a force to be reckoned with in war or in peace. To this day, in spite of neglect and planning improvements, in spite of the effects of time and weather and the devastation wrought by the King's enemies in the last destructive war, Great Yarmouth has a large part of this wall intact and in this respect is probably nearly equal to Chester and York. Here and there the wall or some of its original eight gates and eighteen towers have succumbed to time or the hand of the destroyer; but there is sufficient left to show why the Tudor monarchs regarded Yarmouth as a key-point in the defence of the realm. Thomas Nashe, the dramatist wrote in 1558:

> "Do but convert the slenderest twinkling reflex of your eyesight to this flinty ring that engirds it, these towered walls, portculised gates, look wistly upon the walls, which, if you mark, make a stretched-out quadrangle with the

---

*James I of England and VI of Scotland.

haven. They have sixteen towers, mounts underponging and inflasking them, which have their thundering tools to compel Diego Spaniard to duck, and strike the wind cholic into his paunch, if he prance too near them and will not vail to the Queen of England. Gates to let in her friends, and shut out her enemies, Yarmouth hath ten, lanes, seven score: as for her streets they are as long as three score streets in London, and yet they divide them into but three".

And all this panegyric from a native of Lowestoft!

Within the limited perimeter of the wall the town had to be contained and with the least possible expenditure of ground. One result of this need for economy of space is the distinctive feature known for centuries as the Rows. Learned opinion has exercised itself to find a satisfactory reason for this 'grid-iron' layout without coming to any very definitive conclusion. One theory is that by having these narrow 'flues' between houses the sea wind could blow through and so purify the air; another is that they helped to drain the town of surface water; yet another is that if an enemy gained a hold in the town he could be more easily impeded; perhaps the true reason is the most obvious — economy of space. Today, alas, the bombs of the Lüftwaffe have wrought nearly as much havoc as the planners—and neglect has done the rest. Few of the original 145 are left today and of these fewer still have kept their characteristic atmosphere. Even the famous 'troll carts' which were built especially narrow so as to pass through the Rows — are no more; their demise is due as much to the passing of the horse as to any other cause — *tempora mutantur*, etc.

Another tragic casualty of the Second World War was the parish church of St Nicholas, which was completely gutted. Despite some caustic criticism of the nondescript collection of irrelevant articles which had found their way into this ancient House of God, St Nicholas was the very embodiment of Yarmouth's whole colourful history. It was for long a moot point as to whether Yarmouth or Hull had the largest parish church in England and now that St Nicholas has been completely re-constructed it presumably still remains a good ground for argument.

Over the centuries the church has not been without its despoilers and these have not always been the agents of an alien power. At the Reformation the reredos and rood-loft were destroyed and in 1551 the monumental brasses were ripped out to be turned into standard weights; ten years later a number of grave-stones were sent to Newcastle to be cut into millstones and, as we have seen, the vestments and plate were sold to pay for harbour works.

The defences were overhauled during the Armada scare; but as so often happens in this country, once the scare had passed they were allowed to lapse into decay so that further works of reparation were called for at the time of the Civil War. This time however, unlike King's Lynn, Yarmouth sided with the Parliamentary cause from the beginning, which spared the town a somewhat undignified capitulation like that of Lynn.

While Yarmouth prospered it would not be in the nature of things for good fortune to smile without sometimes averting her gaze with something suspiciously like a smirk. Even in the days before the town was born the denizens of the sandbank were not allowed to carry on their fishing undisturbed. Away down in the south were those Kentish towns destined to come down through history as the Cinque Ports. Five there were in the beginning:— Sandwich, Romney, Hastings, Hythe and Dover, to which were later added Winchelsea and Rye. How long the original Confederation goes back in history is disputed; some say as far as Edward the Confessor or earlier, some say the latter days of the Conqueror. Be this as it may, they had long claimed the right to take herring wheresoever they pleased and this went for the island in the estuary of the Gar. Consequently there was ever a state of strife between Yarmouth and the Ports and most especially with the more assertive ports such as Sandwich and Winchelsea. The Ports were always very much a law unto themselves, they had their own Court of Shepway and they claimed a kind of suzerainty over certain other ports and even inland towns. Yarmouth they treated as if it were a 'limb' of the Ports, which it never was, and the Bailiffs of each party to this uneasy and reluctant partnership were for ever coming to blows — and worse.

In return for the privileges which the Cinque Ports had wheedled out of the King, he looked to them to provide him with a fleet whenever he needed one. He also looked to them to rid the Narrow Seas of pirates, which meant in practice that they were free to attack any ship on any pretence and for centuries the Ports were pre-eminent in piracy themselves. How they fared with their south coast neighbours is not the concern of this story; but between

Great Yarmouth and the Portsmen the fur was always liable to fly on any pretext, or none, and neither side was particularly concerned to confine themselves to the mere shedding of fur! While the Ports contented themselves with waging unofficial and murderous war on the French — even in French waters — that was their own affair and a continual embarrassment to the King, who had little control over them; but when they insisted on visiting Great Yarmouth to oversee their 'limb' there was always trouble.

This state of affairs went on for centuries, and on two occasions the men of Yarmouth and the Portsmen confronted each other even in the middle of a campaign as happened twice near Sluys. In 1297 they were supposed to be escorting Edward I to Flanders when the two factions turned aside to fight each other in the most bloody manner. Edward I shrugged it off as being a case of "boys will be boys". When at the outset of the Hundred Years War Edward III set sail from Orwell Haven on the voyage which resulted in the successful sea battle at Sluys there does not seem to have been any open hostility; but this may have been because the ships found by Great Yarmouth were more numerous than the whole of the Cinque Ports fleet. Moreover the 'Admiral', a word which had only recently found its way into our language, was a Yarmouth man, one John Perebrowne who brought much honour to himself and to his home-town of which he was a bailiff many times, as was his predecessor, Thomas de Drayton.

At about this time, Great Yarmouth began to use the arms which the town has borne ever since. Originally the device was of three herrings* and the 'dimidiation' of this with the leopards of England is claimed to be a mark of royal favour. This may be true and the dating is probably accurate; for it was in the latter half of the fourteenth century that this heraldic method of 'marshalling' fell into disuse. It may not be without a certain significance that most of the Cinque Ports used arms which were similar except that 'demi-hulks of ships' took the place of the demi-herrings. One heraldic writer of the present century has hazarded a tentative guess that the conjunction of lions and ships might have been a naval ensign of Edward III himself.

Be all this as it may, the friction between the portsmen and the men of Yarmouth continued for another three centuries both at

---

*It is interesting and significant that the House of the Herring Fishers in Lübeck also bore three herrings, the herring fishery being a basic source of the fortunes of the Hanseatic League.

sea and whenever the barons of the Cinque Ports asserted their claims to be present at the annual Herring Fair. This lasted from Michaelmas to Martinmas, thus giving six good weeks of riotous bad manners on each side. The sight of the Cinque Ports banner and the sound of the 'brazen horn of saylence', which the portsmen persisted in tootling in the streets of Yarmouth, was sufficient to infuriate the East Anglians who were quite as proud as, and far more wealthy than, the Men of Kent. Eventually this unprofitable war, against which Kings and Archbishops had protested in vain for centuries, was ended by the diplomatic offices of Charles II in 1662. Nine years later the King visited the town in company with the Duke of York and the Duke of Monmouth and the Corporation entertained them right royally, at a cost of £1,000. The King was presented with four golden herrings which shewed that the town was justifiably proud of the source of so much wealth and influence. From Yarmouth Charles II proceeded to Norwich where he was joined by Queen Catherine and no doubt the City Fathers strove to outdo in their hospitality that profferred by their rivals down river.

The herring was indeed an outstanding factor not only in the wealth of Yarmouth but also in its relations with others besides the Cinque Ports. We have already seen how Lowestoft had been at loggerheads with its assertive neighbour as the result of the enforcement of the Statute of Herrings of 1357. The Dutch were also deadly rivals in this field and that rivalry was based not so much on where the fish were taken — for the Hollanders had fishing rights in Yarmouth waters under a treaty of 1494 — but because they had perfected methods of curing which enabled them to command a wider market. They continued to come to the Michaelmas Fair, which had now widened in scope to include all sorts of merchandise and was held on the South Denes amid a certain amount of junketing; this went on well into the nineteenth century.

In 1427 the first bridge was built to replace the ferry but it seems to have been a fixed bridge which would have obstructed the passage of most ships and it was replaced in 1553 by the first of a succession of opening bridges. The earlier ones appear to have been based on the lever principle, rather on the lines of what is known in the eastern counties as a 'cock-up-bridge', the last of which was replaced by pulley-operated bascules about 1836. The present Haven Bridge is still a twin bascule bridge.

All this time there is abundant evidence that while the town increased in importance the harbour was a constant cause for concern. Yarmouth was no more exempt from the constant attacks of the sea than any other East Coast port and while trade flourished in fish and other commodities the maintenance of the quays and jetties was an ever-recurring source of expense. Moreover, Yarmouth was not without troubles on the landward side. From very early times there had been bad feeling between the town at the Yare's mouth and the proud city of Norwich whose only access to the sea was by that same Yare, or Wensum — call the river what you will. The men of Yarmouth were in a strong position and they knew it, although in later days there are signs that the tension had eased somewhat, as for example when in 1636 there was an outbreak of plague which was believed to be conveyed by incoming travellers by sea. Norwich wrote to Yarmouth asking them to exercise strict control of such travellers and particularly where they embarked for their journey up to Norwich by wherry. Immediately, a reply came from Yarmouth promising their entire co-operation. The letter from Norwich was dated 1st September; the reply from Yarmouth was dated 3rd September. Public Servants of today, please note!

But earlier in history things had not been always so easy. One thing which must have niggled Yarmouth was the knowledge that Norwich was a Staple town in the days when the trade in wool was rigidly controlled by that great two-way monopoly. As a result Yarmouth proceeded to hold up all vessels passing through on their way to or from Norwich; but they soon found that they were up against the determined will of Edward III to whom the strengthening of the Staple was essential for fiscal reasons. Yarmouth saw the red light and desisted; but it did not improve relations with Norwich. Later in the reign of Henry IV the town was granted certain limited control over the passage of wool, which was good policy on Henry's part. As a usurper he could do with all the friends he could make and the stricter control of the passage of wool became less needful when England was turning so much of her wool into cloth on her own looms.

Yarmouth was very prone to stand on its dignity both in the exploitation of its geographical location and also in the display of its own wealth and magnificence. There seemed to be a great tendency to 'keep up with the Joneses' and while its leading citizens could not always compete with the more exalted social life of

Norwich, yet many a wealthy merchant of Yarmouth could dip his hand just as deep into his well-lined pocket as the more cultivated men of the capital city on the Wensum.

The truth is of course that the relation between the two towns, however it may seem to have been a compound of love and hate, must necessarily have been close. When Norwich was at its richest most of its imports and exports passed through Yarmouth and being transhipped there from ship to wherry or vice-versa, brought great wealth to Yarmouth merchants and ship-owners. There have been times when Norwich has yearned to be a port in her own right; today small coasters from European ports find their way to Norwich without difficulty; but before the days of power it was usually more practicable to send goods from Yarmouth by wherry or keel. In the survival of these famous craft there was not only an interesting link with the ships of our Scandinavian forebears but a vigorous and efficient means of traffic in goods and passengers for centuries.

The keel — Anglo Saxon *ceol,* a ship — was a direct descendant of the flat-bottomed oared boats which had brought the first Anglians to this country except that it had acquired the square sail of the Viking longship. This served for both men and goods until in the later sixteenth century the single fore-and-aft sail found its way here from the Low Countries and married to a more manageable hull, gave us the wherry. The exact derivation of this word is a matter upon which even the wise men are hesitant; but it seems likely that it is connected with an Icelandic word *hverfa* — to turn — and the wherry certainly was faster and handier than the keel, not only because of her fore-and-aft rig but also by reason of her hull design.

It is commonly said that in clinging to the huge square sail of the keel England was lagging behind the rest of western Europe and that the loose-footed gaff-sail was in general use not only in the Netherlands but also farther north by the middle of the sixteenth century. This is not entirely true. In 1770 Bernard Belotto, nephew of Canaletto and as meticulous in detail as his uncle, painted a view of Warsaw from the opposite side of the Vistula in which are river ships very like our wherries in hull-shape, but each with a huge single square-sail like a keel — with also a bonnet. The main differences are that they appear to have both fore-stays and back-stays but no braces and are steered with a sweep. So perhaps East Anglia was not very far out of step. It is unlikely that the ships on the Vistula would be very different from those of the other Baltic nations.

The traffic between Yarmouth and Norwich by keel or wherry was brisk and fast. The wherry had the advantage in adverse winds; but either craft could always fall back on quants if the wind failed altogether. And how many modern East Anglian argonauts know that the Greeks had a word for that too, *kontos,* which meant — a quant!

The hull form of the wherry which needed no lee-boards made it a very manageable craft in spite of its one huge gaff-sail hoisted on a mast stepped well forw'd and there were occasions when some adventurous Norfolk skippers ventured down the coast not merely as far as Southwold or Ipswich but beyond the Nore, through the Straits and into Portsmouth Harbour.

Daniel Defoe visited Yarmouth in the course of his *Tour through the Eastern Counties* and was very impressed. He commences by saying, "Yarmouth is an ancient town, much older than Norwich. And at present, though not standing on so much ground, yet better built, much more complete; for number of inhabitants, not much inferior and for wealth, trade and advantage of its situation, infinitely superior to Norwich." This encomium is a little strange; for he has just described Norwich itself an ancient, large, rich and populous city" in the most euphuistic terms. Nor is it very likely that Yarmouth is older than Norwich seeing that when Swein sailed past to sack Norwich, as we have noticed, Yarmouth was still not much more than a group of fishermen's huts on an island sandbank.

Nevertheless while Defoe cannot be relied upon for data of strict historical accuracy he paints for us a fascinating and generally reliable word-picture of the Yarmouth of his day. Having described the position of the town situate on its 'peninsula' he goes on to eulogise the "finest quay in England, if not in Europe, not inferior to that of Marseilles itself". He continues:

> "The ships ride here so close and as it were keeping up one another, with their head-fasts on shore, that for a half a mile together they go cross the stream with their bowsprits over the land, their bows or heads, touching the very wharf, so that one may walk from ship to ship as on a floating bridge, all along by the shore side, the quay reaching from the draw-bridge almost to the South-gate is so spacious and wide that in some places it is near one hundred yards from the houses

to the wharf. In this pleasant and agreeable range of houses
are some very magnificent buildings, and among the rest, the
Custom house and Town Hall, and some merchants houses
which look like little palaces, rather than the dwelling houses
of private men.

The quay and the harbour of this town during the fishing
fair, as they call it, which is every Michaelmas, one sees the
land covered with people and the river with barques and
boats, busy day and night landing and carrying off the
herrings which they catch here in such prodigious quantities
that it is incredible. I happened to be there during their
fishing-fair, when I told in one tide, one hundred and ten
barques and fishing vessels coming up the river all laden with
herrings and all taken the night before; and this was besides
what was brought on shore on the Dean (that is the sea-side
of the town) by open boats which they call cobles* and
which often bring in two or three last of fish at a time. The
barques often bring in ten last a piece."

Defoe then mentions the considerable trade in other commodities, besides the export of smoked herring to the Mediterranean
ports, as we have seen at Lowestoft, there were the worsteds,
camblets** and silk manufactured at Norwich and thereabouts
which went both to the Mediterranean and to Holland. From the
Baltic and Norway came timber, pitch tar and hemp. He suggests
that a deal of the Newcastle coal trade had passed from Ipswich to
Yarmouth, although of course Ipswich had a considerable trade in
coal for another hundred and fifty years.

In describing the town Defoe mentions with commendation the
'Rows' which formed the street plan of Yarmouth, as we have
already seen. Some writers have commented on Defoe's knowledge
of the town and of this part of the coast which is thought to have
supplied him with the local atmosphere for his dramatic description
of the storm in Yarmouth Roads in the opening part of *Robinson
Crusoe*. It may well be that for this he drew on his imagination as
freely as for the details of the *Desert Island* or the *Travels in
Tartary*. If however he had any personal knowledge of Yarmouth
before writing, it must have been acquired on a previous

---

*The cobles of course came down from Whitby and Scarborough and the barques from the
Kentish and Sussex coast on seasonal charter.

**Camblet, or chamblet was a mixture of wool, silk and hair, or any two of these.

occasion; for *Robinson Crusoe* was published three years before he visited the town in the course of the Tour. His topography is by no means faultless; for he describes Winterton Ness as the most northerly point of Norfolk.

Defoe mentioned an example of the Borough's self-sufficiency in administering justice, when the captain of a King's ship was tried and executed for committing a murder in the street. This was Captain Booth who by stabbing a seaman in 1677 drew down upon himself the righteous wrath of the law in this town which prized its Admiralty jurisdiction over all comers. The silver oar which still forms part of the Borough insignia is one of the largest and most magnificent in the country.

Although it may not seem pertinent to the story of Great Yarmouth as a port, some mention may be made of the Borough Sword of State, or as it is usually called, the 'Sword of Justice'*.

When Charles II granted the town a fresh charter in 1684 by which the two bailiffs were superseded by a Mayor he also granted the privilege of having a Sword borne before his Worship. In 1688 the charter was abrogated by James II and the sword was put away into cold storage in the Town 'Hutch'; apparently the Borough Fathers were not prepared to accept this set-back as more than temporary. In the reign of Anne the office of Mayor was restored and out of hiding came the Sword which is carried to this day. An unusual and interesting custom at Yarmouth is that on ceremonial occasions in time of war the Sword is carried naked.

In this same year of Queen Anne's accession was founded the Fishermen's Hospital, a gracious and genial home for twenty fishermen and their wives who had fallen on hard times. Formerly occupants who were widowed could not —save by special consent of the Trustees— marry again except to persons already residing in the Hospital: which seems to demand a certain modicum of planning between couples before a partner shuffled off this mortal coil!

In 1681 the Duke of York was again in Yarmouth where after being entertained to a 'sumptuous' dinner he embarked in the *Gloucester* frigate. It is not recorded that the Master and crew

---

*In early times justice in Yarmouth was sometimes draconian, as in 1368 when John Lawyers was hanged for not paying Customs dues!

had also been the recipients of mayoral hospitality and it would therefore be charitable to regard it as a pure Act of God that the ship struck the Leman and Ower bank and sank. The Duke escaped in a shallop together with Colonel Churchill, the Earl of Aberdeen, the Duke of Montrose, and a few other persons. The fate of the remainder of the ship's company is apparently not deemed worthy of record!

In spite of the constant attention that the harbour was now receiving, nothing could control the unruly sea and in 1694 further work was called for to clear the bar which had built up across the harbour mouth. As the years went by and ships got larger and larger this problem of silting up became more and more urgent.

Yarmouth was still known as a town where fine ships were built and the freemen's roll included names which were to become historic, such as Drury and Crabtree and that famous apprentice of theirs, Thomas Johnson, who moved to Lowestoft to set up business on his own account.

In 1784 Yarmouth began to take a serious interest in the Greenland whaling trade and two vessels were fitted out for this purpose. King's Lynn and Hull had been prominent in this field for years and although, as we have seen, Ipswich did not derive much profit in this way, ships from Yarmouth continued to fish with success for quite a time. Of course the odd whale stranded or killed off shore turns up from time in history; in 1475 a whale was stranded at Grubbs Haven where it was cut up and the blubber carried in carts to the town, although whether there were any permanent blubberhouses at this time is not certain. There is a record of a 'bloberhouse' at Cromer in 1483 and at Wells in 1309 the Earl of Surrey complained that certain persons had cut up and carried a whale cast ashore at Burnham which he claimed to be his. There was one occasion in recent years when in 1891 an unfortunate rorqual whale found its way into the harbour and after an exciting and somewhat revolting struggle by fishermen who attacked it with boathooks, it died of its injuries. A local taxidermist having preserved and mounted the carcass, it was taken on tour for the edification of those who were prepared to pay for the experience. One is tempted to wonder if the slaughter of this harmless cetacean would not have been better justified if it had been turned into useful trane oil!

The French war with Napoleon found Yarmouth still an important naval station. Ships were putting in and refitting, important personages were coming and going and the estuary, narrow though it was, could not be overlooked in the scheme of national defence. In 1782 a fort armed with six 24-pounders and nine 18-pounders was erected on the Gorleston Heights to cover St Nicholas Gat.

On 6th November, 1800, Nelson landed after the Battle of the Nile. He was carried off by a wildly huzzaing crowd to the *Wrestlers Inn,* which seems an odd place at which to present him with the Freedom of the Borough. Perhaps it was the strangeness of the venue which caused the Town Clerk to commit the gaffe which has written this occasion on the page of history. Observing that the hero had laid his left hand on the Bible preparatory to taking the oath, the Town Clerk interposed: "Your right hand, my Lord." The terse reply: "I left it at Teneriffe," was received with rapturous cheers, which we hope gave the embarrassed dignitary an opportunity to dissemble his confusion.

Whether this story is authentic or not is uncertain; Robert Southey in his *Life of Nelson* does not recount it, although he records that Nelson was granted the Freedom of the Borough on this occasion after which the whole assembly went in procession to church.

The next time Nelson landed at Yarmouth was after the battle of Copenhagen and on this occasion he pushed through the crowd and went straight to the hospital where the sailors wounded in the engagement were lying. It was then that he said to a sailor who had lost his right arm: "Well, Jack, what's the matter?"; "Lost my right arm, your honour." "Well, Jack, then you and I are spoilt for fishermen. Cheer up my brave fellow."

It was not long after Nelson's death at Trafalgar that one Captain G. W. Manby, barrack master at Yarmouth, a Norfolk man from Denver, was a witness in 1807 of the wreck of the gun brig, *Snipe* with the loss of all hands within sight of the shore. This spurred him on to perfect the Rocket Apparatus (actually the first form of this was a projectile fired from a mortar) which during the inventor's life resulted in the saving of over a thousand lives. It is satisfactory to record that contrary to the experience of most inventors who have conferred benefits on their fellowmen, Manby's enterprise was recognised by Parliament and he received grants totalling £6,700 before he died at Yarmouth at the age of ninety. Even today, in spite of such modern devices as the helicopter, the rocket apparatus is still a standard and efficient part of coastguard equipment.

It was centuries since the northern limit of the estuary had been by Caister; but no reference of life-saving can omit the Caister life-boat which after a magnificent record of service suffered in November 1901 a disaster surpassing even that at Aldeburgh two years previously; No. 2 boat capsized and nine of the crew of twelve were drowned. Their memorial, not unlike the Aldeburgh one, stands in the churchyard and it was at the inquest that the ex-Coxswain, James Haylett —who, at the age of 78 had rescued two men from the surf— made the memorable statement: "Caister men never turn back".

It was also during the 'Napoleonic' period that a visual signalling apparatus of the system commonly used at that time consisting of a frame of pivoted shutters — and commonly mis-named a semaphore — was mounted on the South Gate. This linked up with a chain of such signal stations covering the whole country between London and the coast, the signal being relayed from station to station. It is on record that a message could be passed in this way from London to Yarmouth in seventeen minutes! It might improve our modern Post Office communications if the system could be revived.*

Although the growth of Yarmouth outside the walls at the end of the eighteenth century was still limited, the population, according to a census taken in 1801, was 14,854 for Great Yarmouth which, together with Gorleston and Southtown, totalled 16,573. The population of Yarmouth and its constituent parts today is estimated in the neighbourhood of 52,000, but of course this will not include casual visitors except such as might technically qualify on the basis of a National Census.

At Yarmouth, as elsewhere on the East coast, the Beachmen were ever alert to profit by salvage and there were seven Beach Companies in intense rivalry with each other. Gradually they were weaned from that primitive doctrine that salvage could be

---

*This type of telegraph was invented in 1796 by Lord George Murray, Archdeacon of Man. As a result he was appointed the first Director of Telegraphs in the Admiralty. After five years of this unusual manifestation of the Church Militant the Venerable gentleman was made Bishop of St. David's!

claimed only if nothing living, not even a dog, survived, to the more civilised view that the saving of life was of paramount importance and it was from this change of heart that the early lifeboat services were born.

After the Napoleonic crisis had passed most the Volunteer units which had sprung up to reinforce the regular forces in the event of invasion were disbanded and it was not until 1860 that the idea was revived. By that time Yarmouth was no longer a port which lent itself to any considerable naval concentration; but the town was not lacking in patriotic enthusiasm. When the various volunteer units in Norfolk paraded on Mousehold Heath at Norwich in 1863 out of a total of 1,800 volunteers Yarmouth provided 415, nearly a quarter of the whole county strength.

This part of our story began with herring and no history of Yarmouth as a port or as a town can get very far from the silver harvest of the sea. Without the skill in seamanship and the prosperity which came from that skill Yarmouth would never have attained the importance she enjoyed. Yarmouth ships and Yarmouth men were the backbone of English naval supremacy from those three galleys which the town owned in 1205 to the fleet which fought for Edward III at Sluys in 1340. If they claimed to the full their rights of fishing to the exclusion of their coastal neighbours, they were always a match for the Men of Kent. In 1597 there were 700 vessels in the haven at one time and there was no class of merchandise that came amiss to these hardy voyagers. Whether on the Icelandic fishery or living it hard at Spitzbergen after whale, Yarmouth men were there. Even the Baltic in the days of the Hanseatic League and the bloodthirsty Victual Brothers saw ships from Yarmouth venturing into those perilous waters. In 1394 Thomas Adams and John Walters, merchants of Yarmouth, and Robert Caumbrigge (Cambridge) and Reginald Leman, merchants of Norwich, were captured by 'malefactors' who relieved them of woollen cloth to the value of one thousand marks and then held them to ransom.

Like most East Coast ports Yarmouth had her ups and downs. In her struggle with Norwich for absolute control of the trade going through to that great city, she always seemed to come out of the tussle better than she went in. Even the attempt by Lowestoft and Norwich to by-pass her in 1830 came to naught, although this was due chiefly to the promoters' failure to pursue their plans to fruition, and the eventual result was to the great profit of Lowestoft.

Still the drifters went in and out and in 1913 well over a thousand boats were fishing from the port. Two world wars severely curtailed their activities and many fishing boats were diverted to defence duties. Now they could recover if the fish were there to catch; but as with Lowestoft and other fishing ports there has been a great falling off in catches. Some of this has been due to over-fishing and the activities of ruthless foreign competitors; some has been due to natural fluctuations in the fish population. Even now at this eleventh hour there are signs of an improvement, if all the parties concerned can be sensible enough to let the fisheries recover. But if this slight improvement continues, shall we have sufficient ships to cope with better catches? And if we had the ships should we have the men to man them, and to follow the hard life of the sea? Time alone can show.

There is still activity in timber and general merchandise and to wander down the quays is a fascinating experience. Still the little ships from our European neighbours creep through the quiet waterway up to Norwich; but now the port tends to be a place for holidaymakers to gaze and it is their money which pours into Yarmouth pockets.

IN ALL the maritime history of Norfolk Great Yarmouth and King's Lynn are outstanding in age, in wealth and in prestige. In age King's Lynn may have the advantage of Yarmouth by a few centuries for it was already a sea-port of repute when the first huddle of huts was still sitting uneasily on its native sandbank. As in any human family, they had much in common and yet each fulfilled its destiny in its own way. Each had to fight a persistent battle with the forces of nature to secure an outlet to the sea, and although Lynn was securely shore-based, the ever shifting sandbanks of the Wash made the approaches to the town hazardous and erratic.

In the stormy history of sea-warfare Yarmouth was ever more active than Lynn, it seeming to be the nature of the Yarmouth men to be for ever scrapping with their neighbours, whether it were over herring or the profits of piracy. It must be remembered that in those days Yarmouth was not much better than its old enemy the Cinque Ports in this respect; the suppression of piracy and a little quiet enterprise 'on the side' in that sphere were often indistinguishable. Moreover the warlike qualities of the Yarmouth men were of great value to the King. As we have seen, the port was often called upon to find ships for the royal service and at times these and their commanders formed the backbone of the English naval forces.

Lynn was never laggard in its response to the King's needs; but it was easier and more profitable for the Plantagenet monarchs to be assisted with the financial sinews of war by this opulent town, although when Edward III invaded Normandy in 1346 Lynn sent 19 ships which compares favourably with London's 24. It is, of course, dangerous to assess the importance of towns on the strength of a 'league table' of ship impressment. It may be that London had fewer ships suitable—or perhaps the East Coast men were the better sailors. It is certain that at this time and for long after Lynn ranked as the third port of England for trade and importance and in King John's reign the port dues collected were two-thirds those of London.

At that time Lynn and Yarmouth were equally prominent in Norfolk and each secured charters from that troubled sovereign which were to confer the privileges so esteemed by any self-respecting borough in those early days. While John always needed money, he was also in urgent need of friends and supporters and who would back the king more wholeheartedly against the feudal lords than the towns who stood to be at their mercy? But more of this hereafter, let us keep our minds coast-wise.

In all the ninety miles, or thereabouts, between Yarmouth and Lynn, there are few places on that great coastal curve where a storm-beset vessel can take shelter. There have always been fishermen plying their trade along the coast; but for the most part they have laid their boats on the beach. Hence the provision of coastal lights as at Winterton, nearly co-eval with Lowestoft and later together with that at Orfordness to be owned by those hardy speculators Sir John Meldrum and Gerald Gore. There was some slight haven just south of Winterton Ness but nothing which would give any real shelter.

At Sea Palling where the first lifeboats were manned by the old Beach Companies before the National Institution took over, there were constant calls upon their services. In 1842 within a month both the Beach boats were lost, with the deaths of twelve brave men. The service was taken over in 1852 by the Norfolk Shipwreck Association and in 1858 the National Institution assumed responsibility for the lifeboat. The *British Workman,* which from 1870 to 1893 was Sea Palling's No. 2 boat, established a classic reputation with a total of 321 lives saved.

In any weather the off-shore sandbanks were a constant hazard to shipping and in times of storm this inevitably resulted in total loss with a tragic toll of human lives. Of all these banks one of the worst was the 'Hasebro', and it was here that many of the gallant exploits of the Sea Palling and Cromer boats took place. At Happisburgh itself there is a lighthouse as well as the Halisbro' lightship moored with a whole family of warning buoys out at the sands.

Cromer, where there is also a lighthouse, has figured largely in the history of life-saving and in more modern times the name of its famous lifeboat coxswain, Henry Blogg, has achieved world-wide fame, with a score of 873 lives saved by him and his gallant crews. The lighthouse on the cliff replaces an earlier one which 'went down cliff' in 1867 and although of no great height itself, is 274 ft. above sea-level with a range of well over 20 miles. The first light to be established here was in 1674 and like most early lighthouses employed an open coal fire until 1792. For a great part of its life it was maintained by the coalmasters of Newcastle and Ipswich, whose brigs represented the most numerous of any class of coastal traffic hereabouts; no doubt they found it easy to find the wherewithal of their own protection.

As a town Cromer has quite a respectable antiquity, although Defoe could only say that he knew nothing it was famous for except good lobsters which were taken in such quantities as to warrant their being sent to Norwich and even to London. Surely such a reputation should merit some measure of fame both then and thereafter! He also tells us that Cromer Bay had a reputation of a very different sort among seamen who called it 'the Devil's Throat'.

As in other places this is an example of a hamlet owing its rise in the world to the caprice of Nature. Cromer originally was a mere 'place' on the outskirts of the town and port of Shipden or Chipden which is believed to have extended for at least a quarter of a mile to the east of the present coastline and perhaps even farther. In the fourteenth century it probably included a mere similar to that at Thorpe and at a guess we may think of the town as being comparable to Aldeburgh before the sea swallowed it up. Two hundred years later we find Cromer rated as a port of sorts; for the town sought help in maintaining its piers. It is true that in Henry VIII's reign the statement was made that Haven Courts had been held "Tyme oute of Mynde", but this may have been based on the sense of continuity with Shipden. Certainly at about the same time Cromer was sending out ships on the Iceland fishery, and as we have seen, there was a 'blobberhouse' there in 1483. It does not seem to have maintained its prestige as a port and the sea continued to encroach until the town was confined to that area which the older part of Cromer occupies today.

Beyond Cromer and Sheringham lies Weybourne, or 'Webb'n', which was once regarded as our Achilles Heel.

> "He who would old England win
> Must at Weybourne Hope begin" —

So runs the old jingle and in the days when any serious attempt at invasion involved the landing of horses and guns, the deep water close inshore would seem to invite a presumptuous foe to establish a beachhead here. William Le Queux in his novel *The Invasion*, written nearly seventy years ago, described the landing of a German force as seen by a Sheringham fisherman. The Elizabethans regarded this as a vulnerable point and in 1588 a bulwark was thrown up and a 'Home Guard' mustered under the local gentry for "the deforcing of the Spannyeardes". The significance of the 'Hope' or 'Hoop' is disputed. There is an Anglo-Saxon word, *haga*, which means a gap between hills and this lends itself to the alternative name 'Weybourne Gap'. 'Hope' in the sense of a valley surrounded by hills is a common inland place-name in the North Country. There is also the meaning of a rounded inlet or haven; but if this be so it seems to have vanished. Both meanings seem to be compatible with the place so it may well be left to the learned to wrangle over the matter and perhaps one day they will enlighten us lesser mortals. Another four or five miles and the coast breaks back, leaving a vast area of saltings. Here are Cley-next-the-Sea and Blakeney on each side of the Glaven. Once they were quite busy little ports; but the approaches had so silted up that they 'decayed'. As at Blythburgh the blame has been laid on enclosures which have prevented the full force of the ebb from keeping the river channels flushed; but unlike the Blyth the Glaven may never have made the same head against the sea. Be all that as it may, there are few places on the East Coast where the sea has deserted the ports of yesteryear as here at Cley, Blakeney and Stiffkey. The modern love of sailing has brought some slight revival and behind the strange promontory of Blakeney Point there is still scope for those little ships to find their way to the old staithes.

Once the saltings provided sport for the wild-fowler and indeed there are still plenty of birds for the shooting of the right type and at the right time; but the stupid slaughter of such birds as the avocet and indeed any species formerly at the mercy of any lout with a gun is a thing of the past: at least we like to think so.

Once Blakeney was called upon to send two ships to Calais in the service of Edward III and a quiet but busy trade to the German ports brought prosperity; today that is a nostalgic memory.

In 1406 the young Prince James of Scotland, while on his way to seek refuge in France, was captured by an English 'merchant' ship off Flamborough Head. There is reason to believe that this was a Cley ship 'and that the royal captive was brought ashore here before being handed over to King Henry IV. Henry made sure of his safety by incarcerating him in the Tower for eighteen years, during which time the luckless youth was used as a pawn in the intrigues of Anglo-Scottish affairs. For this it might have been thought that the King would have been grateful to the men of Cley; but here, as in many other matters, the Lancastrian usurper had a sadly elusive memory.

Wells is the only one of these north Norfolk ports which has kept even a semblance of its former state. It has always been at war with the ever-present menace of the sea and sand. It has also suffered at the hands of the 'reclaimers' of the saltings and the Tidal Harbours Commission in 1846, in spite of its pious lamentations over these enclosures, did little to remedy things. This is not surprising seeing that the harbour was put under the jurisdiction of one Commissioner who not only controlled the harbour dues but also owned the one single tug!

In its day Wells was a port of some consequence. In 1297 the King demanded that all Wells ships after due and expeditious discharge of their cargoes should proceed to Winchelsea to set out again "on the King's service" and in 1324 the masters of ships were enjoined to "proceed cautiously. . . . . . so that they do not fall into the hands of their adversaries, pirates and others". In 1528 Wells was sending six ships on the 'Iceland trade', presumably the fishery. In 1580 a certificate of ships of sixteen tons and upwards showed Wells as having nineteen ranging in size from 20 to 160 tons.

In the following century it is evident from the Port Books that there was a considerable volume of trade with the Continent and other parts of England or Scotland. Much of the Icelandic cod was shipped to London and it is apparent from a comparison of the export and import commodities that there was a great deal of exchange trade, the same goods both coming in and going out. Before the Reformation there must have been a certain amount of passenger trade; for by reason of its proximity to Walsingham a number of pilgrims landed at Wells, though probably nothing like the number who passed through Lynn.

Although the Wells lifeboat is a comparative newcomer to these veterans of the East Coast, (the station was established in 1869), it has done good service. In 1946 it figured in an attempt by seven German prisoners of war to use her to make their journey back to the Fatherland. They probably felt that now the fighting was over they wanted to be back home — and who could blame them? However, their technical skill fell short of their enterprise and they failed to get the engine to start!

Scolt Head Island is best known today as an interesting factor in the involved study of the salt marshes and shingle spits of this part of the Norfolk Coast and perhaps even better as a nature reserve under the guardianship of the National Trust. Behind its odd outline there lies the channel still known as Burnham Harbour leading to what was the port of the Burnhams, Overy Staithe; apart from an involvement in the mussel and cockle fishery — if that is the right word — its maritime days are past. The same might be said of Brancaster Staithe, three or four miles to the west and also sheltering in the lee of Scolt Head. A lovely country and a paradise for the small yachtsman and naturalist.

At Brancaster village we are back in history over fifteen centuries ago; for here stood Branodunum, the northernmost of the strong forts of the Saxon Shore. It was doubly important, for it was the headquarters of the Count of the Saxon Shore himself. Like Gariannonum, it was garrisoned by cavalry, the Dalmatian Horse, and it is probable that some part of the *Classis Britannica* may have harboured in Brancaster Bay or what is now Brancaster Harbour. It is unlikely that there would have been any large concentration of galleys here because after the goings-on of Carausius towards the end of the third century it was considered safer to keep the fleet dispersed in smaller units. In this way there was less likelihood of another naval-minded opportunist making a bid for power. Branodunum has left little for us to see today and there is nothing comparable with the massive remains at Burgh Castle. It seems, however, to have been built on a similar scale, rather more square in plan and slightly larger in superficial measurements than the fort on the Waveney. What the passage of time had left was plundered in 1797 to provide material for the 'Great Malt House' which was intended to be the largest malthouse in England. Like all grandiose things of this nature it shared the usual fate, being pulled down eighty years later.

Whilst it may not be immediately relevant to our search for ports, there is a subject for speculation connected with this monument of the Pax Romana. Four and a half miles to the west is Holme-next-the-Sea, which is at the northern end of the Peddars Way. This ancient trackway was almost certainly there before the Romans came; but it is equally certain that they used it, as was often their wont, where an existing line of road fitted in with their plans. There has always been a mystery about this termination at Holme, although it has been conjectured that from here there was a ferry link with the other side of the Wash. This may be so; but if this ferry existed before Roman times it would seem to argue a higher standard of seafaring than we are accustomed to credit to the Britons or their predecessors. Failing this explanation, why should the road stop at Holme or indeed why should it ever go to Holme at all?

If it was used by the Romans, why should it not run straight to Branodunum or was there some reason of a strategic or tactical nature which demanded that it should end where it does. A glance at the map shows that the Peddars Way lies as a chord across the arc of the coast-line here which suggests that the fastest way to deploy reinforcements to any part of the coast would be from such a road. Once again it must be remembered that the presence of cavalry at these forts implies the importance of reinforcements, since at this time Roman cavalry was an exploratory and not a striking arm. By the same token the forts were of exceptionally massive construction and capable of repelling attacks until such time as they could be relieved.

On the coast near Holme there is Gore Point, a small spear-shaped promontory, the name of which recalls the origin of Landguard Point at Felixstowe; so we head south past Hunstanton into the Wash.

To consider the origin of this huge inlet of the North Sea 220 square miles in extent is no part of our plan, nor have we time to assess the various proposals which have been made from time to time to reclaim all this land for agriculture. Once it was thought that this was impracticable because of the salinity of the soil which would be yielded in this way; but the opinion nowadays is that this is not an insuperable objection. The advocates of a Wash Barrage which is supposed to be the panacea for all our problems of shifting sand, angry tides, and the full development of the Fens point to the success which Holland has achieved with the Zuider Zee. The two cases are not entirely alike and there may be some failure fully to recognise and evaluate the points of difference; but this is no place to enter upon this highly contentious subject. We are concerned with the coastline as it has been in the past and as it is today and in doing so we are now at a point where we come to the most traditional and romantic sea-port in all Anglia and indeed on this side of England.

The approach to King's Lynn from the sea in fair weather can be at first a very straightforward affair until one is past the Roaring Middle and Lynn Well and then without local knowledge a pilot is essential. To look at the names of the sands in the southern end of the Wash can conjure up a slightly sinister picture unless you are a real sailorman — and if you are not, you have no business to be afloat without a pilot! The 'Blackguard,' the 'Thief,' the 'Bulldog' — even the 'Pandora' may be a giver of the wrong kind of gifts — and we all remember that it is when they bring gifts that the Greeks are most to be feared! And the channel is never so constant that even the pilots can afford to take it for granted.

Once perchance when vessels were smaller the hazards of the banks were less significant; but today the buoyage is essential if you want to make the Lynn Channel and the Ouse without complications. But let us assume we have made the entrance to Lynn Docks safely and take a look at this ancient town in retrospect and in comfort.

If Yarmouth is an ancient town — and Defoe told us so — Lynn is more ancient. Some have satisfied themselves that the name of the town is of Celtic, that is, Brythonic, origin and is derived from *llyn*, a lake. An alternative *lin*, a waterfall, is unthinkable for a place which at the earliest stage of its existence can have been no more hilly than it is today. Whatever may have been the true origin of the name of the town — and in etymology one is tempted, with jesting Pilate, to ask, *"Quid est veritas?"* — it is certain that before the Conquest it was already a very busy place and it is equally certain that most of this business was with ships. Yet Lynn might never have attained this eminence without the change of circumstances which changed the course of the Ouse so that instead of entering the Wash at Wisbech it came out by Lynn. Whether this change was entirely natural or whether the hand of man brought it about is still somewhat obscure. Once it was thought to be a result of the sea wall which meandered between Wisbech and Lynn and which has for long been called the Roman Bank, although Belloc could not believe that the Roman engineers could have contrived anything so irregular and thought that it could be of earlier date. Certainly the Romans were responsible for other works of embankment and canalisation in the Fens; but whoever or whatever was the cause — and be it remembered that throughout the centuries there have been recurring alternations in the balance of land and water in this area — the fact remains that the Ouse had changed its course considerably even within the last thousand years. At the time of the Conquest both Lynn and Wisbech were coastal towns in the sense that each was situate on an inlet of the Wash itself. The streams which we now know as the Ouse, the Wissey, the Little Ouse and the Lark all combined to flow in one conjoined river to enter the Wash at Wisbech. The Nene in those days formed its estuary approximately where the Welland flows today. The Nar which now joins the Ouse Estuary at Lynn then flowed into the Wash at the head of the inlet on which lay Lynn, already a town of some consequence.

Gradually and for reasons which, as we have admitted, are not entirely clear the Ouse changed course and flowed towards Lynn while at the same time the natural coastline between Lynn and Wisbech built up at its south-western end so that the latter town was eventually separated from the Wash by a long channel, as it is today. Lynn, now on the Ouse, was connected by a navigable inland waterway with the area lying between Cambridge, Thetford and Bedford, while Wisbech was on a direct channel linking it with Northampton and Stamford.

Incoming ships could thus pass into the heart of England by either Wisbech or Lynn; but the supremacy in this regard fell inevitably to the latter town which had such unrivalled land links with East Anglia in addition to its facilities for maritime and river-borne traffic. Ships could discharge at Lynn and then their cargoes could be transhipped by barge to Bedford to Cambridge to Peterborough to Stamford to Northampton. In some cases the sea-going vessels could themselves go far up the rivers without transhipment of cargo; but of this more later.

After the Conquest Lynn grew apace in importance and that same Herbert, first Norman bishop of Norwich, who had founded St Nicholas at Yarmouth, built the great church of St Margaret which still stands, although much altered and added to, and may be said to embody much of the tradition of Lynn both as a town and as a port. From this ecclesiastical patronage the town was known for the next four-and-a-half centuries as Lynn Episcopi, Bishops Lynn.

xv) 'The extreme Eastern point of England'. The Low Light at Lowestoft, 1867.

Lowestoft Borough Library

(xxvi) Lowestoft High Light. Drawn and engraved by W. Daniell in 1822. The Low Light, as
appeared at that date, is seen in the middle distance.   *Lowestoft Borough Libr*

(xxvii) Lowestoft Harbour Mouth showing drifters working out to their fishing grounds.

xviii) A sailing ship being towed by steam tug through the swing-bridge into the inner harbour ..sin at Lowestoft.   *Lowestoft Borough Library*

xxix) ''Conversation Piece, The Fisherman's Hospital'', Great Yarmouth.

Yarmouth Borough Library

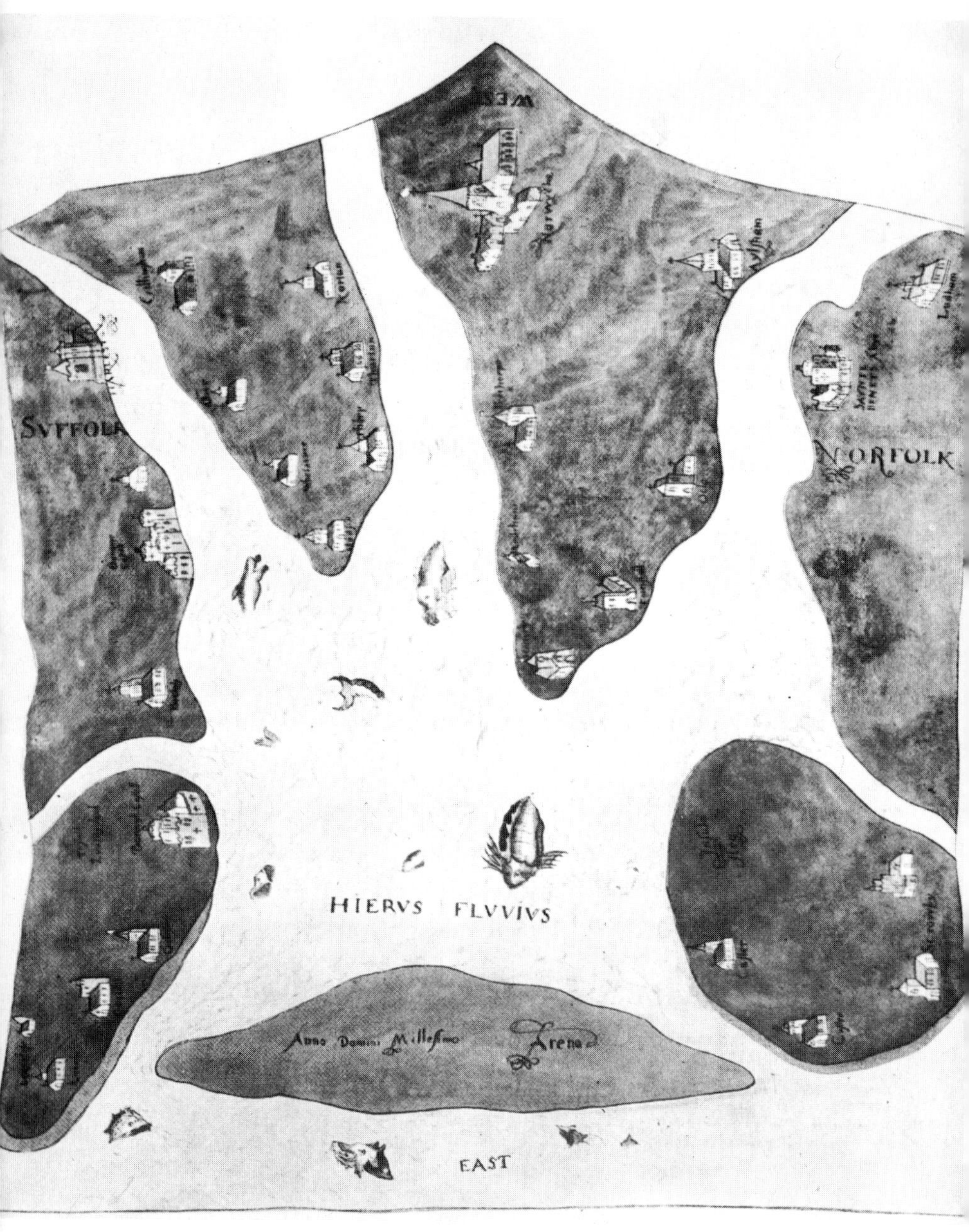

(xxx) The 'Hutch Map' Great Yarmouth. This old map, so named because it was found in the Tow[n]
Hutch, or Chest, shows an early attempt to depict the formation of the sandbanks in the Yar[e]
estuary from which Great Yarmouth arose. The relative position of other towns, such as Harwich[,]
discounts its value as geographical evidence to any further extent. *Yarmouth Borough Librar[y]*

(xxxi) Ships moored near Great Yarmouth. This is of especial interest as illustrating, from left to right, a spritsail barge, a Norfolk wherry and a Norwich keel.

Engraved by W. Lloyd after an original drawing by T. S. Cotman

(xxxii) The North Gate, Great Yarmouth, showing the distinctive 'Troll-Carts' which were built to pass through the 'Rows'.

Yarmouth Borough Library

(xxxiii) The South Gate, Great Yarmouth, showing the telegraph—often miscalled Semaphore—by which a message could be passed from London to Yarmouth in seventeen minutes!

Yarmouth Borough Library

xxxiv) The Haven, Great Yarmouth, showing the dignified Palladian front of the old Town Hall built in 1713 and sacrificed in 1882 to be succeeded by the architectural monstrosity in Aberdeen granite from which the County Borough is governed today.   *Yarmouth Borough Library*

xxxv) The exterior of the Chapel of St Mary of the Red Mount, King's Lynn.   *Revd. L. Hammond*

(xxxvi) The Custom House, King's Lynn. Built in 1683 by the local architect, Henry Bell, as a Merchants' Exchange and still used by H.M. Customs and Excise.

King John, who tried so hard to win support from the richer and more powerful towns by granting charters wherever he went, did not omit to call at Lynn. Of course every schoolboy knows, or used to know, that this much maligned monarch lost his treasure crossing the Wash, although whether this really happened is now very much an unsolved mystery. Arising from his visit to the town in 1204 Lynn has equipped itself with its two most celebrated myths. Among the civic insignia is a singularly beautiful covered cup of silver-gilt and enamel which for centuries has been known as King John's Cup, the tradition being that he gave it to the town on his visit. Alas! it has been authentically ascribed to the middle of the following century and now it is known more cautiously as the 'King John Cup' — without the apostrophe. He was also alleged to have taken the sword from his side and bestowed it on the town to be borne before the Mayor; but the iconoclasts have dated this as of about the time of Henry VIII. Nevertheless it is a fine sword and whether King John bestowed the privilege of a civic sword is not of great moment. There is good reason to believe that parts of the sword are very old and it may well be that it is what the antique dealers would describe as a 'made-up piece'. The 'Red Book of Lynn' is a treasure of which there can be no doubt; its first entry is dated 1307 and it is one of the earliest paper books in existence.

These and the other civic treasures may seem to have little bearing on the history of Lynn as a port: but the esteem in which they are held, and they deserve a whole book to themselves, is significant because it testifies to the value which Lynn has always put on its unique tradition of power, wealth and dignity. Of course like other ancient towns, it has had its less edifying episodes, but Lynn has an atmosphere which is all its own and as Belloc wrote, "Every man that lands in Lynn feels all through him the antiquity and the call of the town".

Defoe says,

> "It is a beautiful well built and well situated town at the mouth of the river Ouse, and has this particular attending it, which gives it a vast advantage in trade, namely, that there is the greatest extent of inland navigation here of any port in England, London excepted. The reason whereof is this, that there are more navigable rivers empty themselves here into the sea, including the Washes, which are branches of the same port, than at any one mouth of waters in England, except

the Thames and the Humber. By these navigable rivers the merchants of Lynn supply about six counties wholly and three counties in part, with their goods, especially wine and coals, viz., by the little Ouse they send their goods to Brandon and Thetford, by the lake to Mildenhall, Barton Mills and St Edmunds Bury, by the river Granta to Cambridge, by the Great Ouse itself to Ely to St Ives, to St Neots, to Barford Bridge and to Bedford, by the River Nyne to Peterboro', by the Dreyns and Washes to Wisbech, to Spalding, Market Deeping and Stamford. Besides the several counties into which these goods are carried by land carriage from the places where the navigation of those rivers ends, which has given rise to this observation on the town of Lynn, that they bring in more coals than any sea port between London and Newcastle, and import more wines than any port in England, except London and Bristol; their trade to Norway and to the Baltick Sea is also great in proportion and of late years they have extended their trade farther to the southward.

Here are more gentry and consequently is more gaiety in this town than in Yarmouth or even in Norwich itself, the place abounding in very good company.

The situation of this town renders it capable of being made very strong and in the late wars it was so; a line of fortification being drawn round it at a distance from the walls, the ruins or remains of which works appear very fair to this day, nor would it be a hard matter to restore the bastions with the ravelins and the counterscarp upon any sudden emergency to a good state of defence, and that in a little time, or sufficient number of workmen being employed, especially because they are able to fill all their ditches with water from the sea in such a manner as that it cannot be drawn off.

There is in the market place of this town a very fine statue of King William on horseback, erected at the charge of the town. The Ouse is mighty large and deep, close to the very town itself, and ships of good burthen may come up to the quay, but there is no bridge, the stream being too strong and the bottom moorish and unsound, nor for the same reason is the anchorage computed the best in the world, but there are good roads farther down."

This gives a very fair picture of Lynn in the eighteenth century and it is obvious that it was still a place of importance and dignity from both the mercantile and social aspect. It remained so for a long time to come and although there were times when for one reason or another the shipping trade languished, the town has never declined as a market town, a business centre and an urban community. But the foundations of all this lie farther back in time and we must retrace our steps to the days of the Plantagenets. A town which during its long history has been granted no less than eighteen charters with an urban society based upon the integration of church and trade guild linked with every important seaport in north-eastern Europe and beyond, was a power to be reckoned with.

From its earliest beginnings Lynn must have depended upon the harvest of the sea for its very existence. Through all the vicissitudes of foreign trade one thing endured and still endures—the craft of the fisherman. Anything that lives in the sea and can be eaten is fair game to the Lynn man. For many years one has tended to think of shell-fish, cockles, mussels, shrimps as the main concern of the Wash fisherman; but soles, smelts and cod are still brought in. In the reign of the first Elizabeth, Wash oysters were sold at Stourbridge Fair in Cambridge and we are told that they were often of the size of a horse's hoof; but it may have been only a little horse! At Snettisham and below Boston there were 'scalps' but whether these were oyster scalps is not certain; the same term is used of mussel-beds.

To this day the Lynn boats lie in the Fisher Fleet — not as a young gentleman of the B.B.C. said recently, the "Fisher Fleet Creek". Fleet means a creek and Lynn is full of them, Purfleet, Surfleet, Whitefriars Fleet, St Mary's Fleet, and others. Some have been filled in and one, Colwayners, or Colville, Fleet was vaulted over as far back as 1585. But before some amateur etymologist enthuses over 'Bus Fleet' which looks so temptingly like Buss Fleet, it would be well to utter a warning. This was formerly Mill Fleet which was filled in and is now the omnibus station, appropriately re-named by common usage! The name Nickere Fleet is a little obscure; it has been suggested that this was a corruption of *nikr,* an Icelandic word which passed into Anglo-Saxon, meaning a water-goblin. Hence perhaps, "Old Nick".*

---

*There was a Danish phrase for a drowned man, "Nikken togham bort"—Nick took him off.

Formerly most of these fleets provided berthing for vessels and there was a town ordinance of 1697 which prohibited any vessel of twenty tons or upwards being laid in the Mill Fleet, Dowshill Fleet, Whitefriars Fleet or Purfleet, otherwise than on ancient or accustomed "shipseats" — what nowadays we should call mud-berths.

A very important factor in the growth of Lynn as a seaport was its connection with the Hanse, that enormously powerful 'consortium' of German towns to which we have referred in connection with the 'Steelyard'. In the beginning the Hanse or Hansa was the association, *hansa* simply means a league or band, of the chief German trading cities. Originally this consisted of Lübeck, Bremen and Hamburg; but eventually it included most of the towns in the Baltic area as well as such Flanders towns as Ghent, Bruges and Antwerp. From beginning as a trading association it became so powerful that it was virtually beyond the control of the Emperor and became what amounted to an Imperium. In all its member towns there was a Kontor, which was a close corporation in itself, and even in England there was a kontor at London and a depot at Lynn. These local headquarters came to acquire almost the status of embassies; they secured special privileges and exemptions from certain fiscal dues. Nowhere was their power so pre-eminent and ruthless as in the Baltic itself which the Hanseatic League treated as its own private sea. To help them to control this area they enlisted the services of a bloodthirsty band of sea-wolves, compared with which the Vikings seem something like the Band of Hope.* Eventually their excesses forced the Hanse to enlist the help of others to suppress them in equally bloodthirsty manner. The whole history of the League is beyond the resources of this book; but the effect of its activities upon the merchants of other countries seeking to trade in the North Sea and especially the Baltic was far-reaching. English ships were constantly being attacked, their crews imprisoned or murdered and their cargoes seized. Protests were made, reprisals, usually by a withdrawal of privileges, were taken and the King was urged to protect his subjects on their lawful occasions. At the same time he was usually anxious to avoid a complete rupture with the Hanseatic

---

*Originally these Vitalienbrüdern or Victual Brothers had been taken into the service of the League to take food and stores to Stockholm at a time when Sweden was under blockade by Margaret, Queen of Norway. From this blockade-breaking role the Vitalienbrüdern soon developed into pirates who would plunder any ship venturing into the Baltic—even those of their own masters.

Towns, because as often as not, he was in debt to these wealthy merchants. Edward III on more than one occasion pawned his crown jewels to secure the money of which he was so constantly in need for his wars with France.

Meanwhile the Lynn merchants who ventured into the Baltic were at risk not only while at sea but also while they were ashore, as witness this incident recounted in Hakluyt's *Voyages.*

> ". . . . . . the marchants of Lenne doe avouch, verifie and affirme, that about the feast of S. George the martyr, in the yeere of our Lord, 1394, sundry malefactors and robbers of Wismer and Rostok, and others of the Hans, with a great multitude of ships arrived at the towne of Norbern* in Norway, and tooke the said town by strong assault, and also wickedly and unjustly took al the marchants of Lenne there residing with their goods and cattels, and burnt their houses and mansions in the said place, and put their persons unto great ransoms: even as by the letters of safeconduct delivered unto the said merchants it may more evidently appear to the great damage and impoverishment of the marchants of Lenne: namely, Imprimis they burnt there 21 houses belonging unto the said marchants, to the value of 440 nobles. Item, they tooke from Edmund Belyetere, Thomas Hunt, John Brandon and from other marchants of Lenne to the value of 1815 pounds."

It is evident from this that there was a considerable colony of Lynn merchants at Bergen where there was in fact a kontor of the League.

This kind of thing was constantly happening and whenever the King of England intervened, the Hanseats had a counter-claim all nicely tied up and ready to be presented alleging some enormity for which Englishmen had been responsible. And be it remembered that the English were not backward in harrying the Hanseatic ships when opportunity offered — but not when they were in Baltic waters!

It was said in Elizabeth's day, "There be no laws on the Spanish Main" and the same could have been said of the German Ocean two centuries earlier.

---

*Bergen

Nevertheless the presence of the Hanse merchants in Lynn ensured a constant and profitable flow of trade. The warehouse which was at one time the 'steelyard' is to be seen in St Margaret's Lane today. Incidentally, the earlier name of this lane was 'Muckle Lane', which was itself a euphemism for Muckhill Lane, that being the approach to one of the town muckhills which from time to time would be shovelled into the long-suffering Ouse. From this we learn that the mediaeval sanitation of Lynn approximated very fairly *mutatis mutandis* to the sewerage systems which are still to be found not far from some of our pleasure beaches today.

The Hanseatic League eventually died by reason of its very strength, its tyranny succumbing to the rising power of national self-sufficiency — and to more sophisticated methods of borrowing money by impecunious princes. In 1597 the Emperor Rudolph forcibly expelled the English Merchant Adventurers from Germany, so the following year Queen Elizabeth ordered the Hanseats to leave the London Steelyard in fourteen days!

Meanwhile, Lynn's prosperity had continued to flourish quite apart from the trade which came through the Hanse. As we look at the merchandise passing in and out of Lynn through the centuries we glimpse some illuminating and sometimes surprising sidelights on social progress. For instance we are prepared to note that in 1325 we were exporting 'wadmal' which is a coarse cloth used for the working clothes of the poor, lining horse collars, and the like. When however we learn that we were also exporting say, which was a fine textured woollen cloth, the generally accepted belief that English weavers could not produce anything like that until Edward III introduced the Flemings, suffers a rude shock. We were also shipping out 'worth' which was a merchant's name for worthstead or worsted cloth, as well as nettlecloth, a coarse cloth made of nettles which, believe it or not, when retted like hemp will make an excellent canvas. Up to quite recent times patches of nettles were deliberately encouraged to grow on many farms for this very purpose. The Germans have a word for it, *nesseltüch.*

Wines, silks, bowstaves and playing-cards were imported. The importing of bow-staves at Lynn is interesting because it is generally supposed that English bowyers demanded Spanish or Italian yew; but there is evidence that we were also getting

Polish yew from the Carpathian forests which was shipped on Hanseatic ships from Danzig. It is significant however that Lynn imported more wine than any other seaport, excepting London and Bristol, and for long there was a minimum quota of bowstaves to be shipped with every tun of wine. It is hardly necessary again to demolish the romantic nonsense written and sung about the virtues of English yew, which was useless for making bows!

Another import which deserves comment is that of cask staves. It seems likely that these might have been of Baltic oak which the best brewers have always demanded for their coopers to use in those civilised days when beer came to the consumer "in the wood". Now it comes in what look like glorified dustbins; and to fastidious palates it sometimes seems that this simile is not inappropriate!

There was also traffic in trane oil and this leads to speculation on the date and extent of whaling from Lynn, which is sometimes assumed to have been a prominent activity in Tudor times or even earlier. The old *Greenland Fishery Inn* which is believed to have been frequented by the whalers would seem to indicate that this could not have been earlier than about 1576. Anthony Parkhurst wrote to Hakluyt that there were fifty English ships taking cod and whales in 1578 and it looks as if this was an extension and development of the Iceland fishery where English ships had been for the past three centuries or more. That the odd offshore whale had been no rarity since mediaeval times would seem to be evidenced by the mention of the 'blobberhouse' at Cromer in 1483 and whales had frequented Norwegian waters long before that. They seem however to have become less common, whether because they had moved out into the Atlantic in search of food or for some other obscure migratory reason is not clear. The principal whaling people were the Basques and they must have killed on a grand scale; for the only part of the whale which was esteemed for food was the tongue and to a lesser degree some parts of the carcass which was sold in the French market towns around Bayonne and Biarritz. When the Basques moved across the Atlantic in the fourteenth century they gradually pushed up from the Newfoundland Banks to the edge of the ice off Greenland and we know that in 1576 some Englishmen were off Labrador on the same ploy; but there is little evidence of any real exploitation of the east Greenland and Spitzbergen waters before the end of the sixteenth century.

It is believed that the Lynn ships often came back with their catches lashed on each beam and that the whales were flensed and the blubber 'tried out' in the blubberhouses which still stood until recent times. It must have been an odoriferous homecoming. Later the blubber was tried out on the beach at Greenland and brought back as oil, but one can imagine that in that way a deal of the by-products of the catch must have been left behind. The Basques were also pioneers in the art of boiling the blubber on board, but it does not seem to have developed very far; the day of the factory ship was a long way ahead.

While all these activities were in progress the mercantile opulence of Lynn continued to grow. There is probably not a town in any part of England which can show such a wealth of architectural evidence of the cultured pride of its merchant princes. The eighteenth and nineteenth centuries were not conspicuous in esteeming the value of these majestic relics of the past; but Lynn seems to have been large enough and proud enough to have avoided the worst excesses of neglect and demolition. This is not the place to elaborate on the exceptional wealth of ancient buildings which testify to the past glories of this sea gate of England; but be it remembered this reflects the maritime importance of what was once and to a large extent still is a proud town.

The Guildhall was once the hall of the Guild of the Holy Trinity; St George's Guildhall, is now a venue for the Lynn Festival of Music and Drama; St Margaret's Church, with the two huge monumental brasses which are interesting not merely for their size and workmanship but because they are in the same tradition and possibly by the same Flemish craftsmen as three others at Lübeck, Stralsund and Thorn, observe the Hanseatic connection. Formerly St Margaret's had a third brass of comparable size; but it was stolen by a dishonest sexton who sold it as scrap metal for five shillings and then, so 'tis said, hanged himself in somewhat tardy remorse! The other great church in Lynn goes by the modest title of St Nicholas' Chapel; it is nearly as large and magnificent as St Margaret's but is not a parish church. The Merchant Princes' houses, all magnificent examples of their varying periods of architecture and some with a palace-like interior courtyard, are a standing monument to the confidence and self-sufficiency of the men for whom they were built. In addition to these there is Thoresby College, built in 1500 to house thirteen priests, possibly the chaplains of the Trinity Guild. Recently refurbished as a social welfare centre the works of reparation revealed an ancient quay wall which shows that before the Hall was built a strip of land must have been reclaimed from the river.

The Custom House, which was built in 1683 originally as a Merchants Exchange, is a distinguished building of almost Dutch appearance, though built by Henry Bell, a local architect who twice served as Mayor of the borough. Nothing which he ever did as Chief Citizen could compare with the debt which the town owes him for this gem which still houses H.M. Department of Customs and Excise.

A mere stone's throw from the Custom House there stands, in New Conduit Street, the house of a former deputy Customs Collector whose son, George Vancouver, achieved undying fame as a navigator who gave his name to the island lying off-shore British Columbia, by circumnavigating which in 1791 he not only demonstrated its insular character but also laid effective claim to its status as a British possession. George was born in this house in 1758 and signed on as an ordinary seaman, under Captain James Cook for the second voyage undertaken by that redoubtable navigator. Vancouver soon showed his potential ability and having gained his Master's Certificate was given command of a ship charged with the exploration of the western seaboard of North America. Whether he ever re-visited his native town after he had made a reputation for himself is not known; in any case he died seven years later at Petersham in Surrey.

It is important to distinguish between George Vancouver the navigator and Charles Vancouver, the American agriculturist, who came to England between 1786 and 1793. In 1794 his notes on a tour of Essex and Cambridgeshire were published and as a result he was invited to write a paper on the drainage of the Fens of the Great Level.

Although the two men were not notably related and may never have met, it is not unreasonable to suspect that George was descended from one of the many Dutch engineers who, having worked with Sir Cornelius Vermuyden on the reclamation of the Fens in the first half of the previous century, made for themselves a home in the East Anglian countryside which they had helped so materially to recover from its primaeval watery waste.

Although the first "floating light" was moored at the Nore in 1742, the idea had been conceived long before that by a barber of King's Lynn, one Robert Hamblin. However the idea was received only with ridicule. How would a barber know that it would be impossible to moor a floating light which would not break loose from its moorings and constitute a danger to shipping?

Nevertheless Hamblin's ideas eventually penetrated the thick skulls of the 'experts', who doubtless got the credit for them, and by the times of the French Wars there were sufficient light-vessels and light-buoys for it to be necessary to have 'crash plans' for removing them if necessary to confuse the enemy.

In addition to the wide variety of merchandise which passed in and out of Lynn in mediaeval times there was also a considerable amount of what we should call 'passenger traffic' including pilgrims to the Shrine at Walsingham. Some have thrown doubt on whether pilgrims would have willingly faced a road journey of over twenty-five miles from Lynn to Walsingham while Wells was only five miles from the shrine. It must however be remembered that besides the large numbers who came from Europe on pilgrimage many from other parts of England might find it easier and safer to travel by water, and Lynn was linked in this way with such travel centres as Peterborough, Bedford, Northampton and Cambridge. Another factor which must not be overlooked in the social aspect of pilgrimages. At certain seasons of the year, as Chaucer has told us, "Thenne longen folk to go on pilgrimages" and the spiritual benefits which they hoped to gain were not lessened by the pleasure of travel. To start from Lynn meant that they could furbish their wardrobes in a town which could supply their every need and at competitive cost. If the pilgrim came from abroad he would be certain to find someone who could speak his language, and might very well be a fellow-countryman, and the shrewd tradesmen of Lynn would make little trouble over exchanging Flemish guilders for English groats — for due consideration, of course.

In this connection one inevitably thinks of the Chapel of the Red Mount in the Walks. It is an odd-looking building externally, not unlike a huge dovecot; but inside it is an architectural jewel, a perfect shrine in miniature with a fan vaulted roof. It is late in date, having been erected in 1485; but there is reason to believe that the 'mount' on which it stands and is partially imbedded, had some religious significance before the chapel was built. Some there be who are sceptical of the connection of this unique building with the Walsingham pilgrims; but there are good reasons for believing the tradition to be well-founded and moreover it is on record that in 1509 the offerings of the devout were four times those of St Margaret's, St Nicholas and St James in toto. Pilgrims were open-handed folk; after all, why spoil the ship for a ha'porth of tar!

But in due course came the beginning of that long and involved process which many writers dismiss tidily as the Reformation. It took a-many years to accomplish beyond recall and the story of it is at times unclear. As regards Lynn it meant that the little incidents which often bedevilled the relations between the Town and the Bishop of Norwich, at one time even getting to the point where the Bishop gained possession of the King John Sword and only relinquished it with an ill grace, were resolved. Henry VIII signified his good will to the town by decreeing that henceforth it should no more be Lynn Episcopi but Lynn Regis and King's Lynn it has been ever since. It is said that Henry did a deal with the bishop whereby he gained the manor of Lynn in exchange for the abbey of Holme which the bishop desired. At the same time Henry conferred many privileges on the town; so a good time was had by all.

James I specifically conferred Admiralty jurisdiction on the town and appointed the Mayor Admiral of the Port; but it is noteworthy that there does not ever seem to have been an oar included in the civic insignia.

In the Civil War the town declared for the King and it was in the nature of Lynn that in this they received the support of the country gentry. (Did not Defoe in his time remark on the social aspirations of Lynn folk!) However they did not receive the help they had hoped and so they surrendered after a very short siege of less than three weeks. During the siege a 16 lb. roundshot was fired at St Margaret's Church during Sunday morning service and the congregation departed the sacred edifice in haste, leaving their hats, books, etc., behind them.

Defoe remarked on the fact that the anchorage at Lynn was not "computed the best in the world". In his day ships could only moor at one of the quays of the harbour or lie at anchor in the channel and with the tidal rise and fall to say nothing of the current running, especially at spring tides, this imposed considerable limitations on the very considerable traffic which used the port.

Throughout its history many attempts have been made to improve and control the unruly behaviour of the River Ouse which, after the draining of the Fens by the construction of the Old and New Bedford Rivers and the sluices at Denver and Salters Lode, had concentrated the outflow in the one tidal channel of the Great Ouse from Earith to the sea with no inflow on flood to the Middle Level. The net result at Lynn was that the harbour was subject to silting at times of high spring tides. In 1723, which is round about the time that Defoe was at Lynn, the rise at high spring tides was over 14 feet; but when this coincided with a north-east wind the rise could reach 26 feet, forcing ships from their moorings and flooding many of the streets of the town. Moreover, at such times there would often occur a tidal bore which still happens today.

Various schemes were put forward to improve both navigation and drainage throughout the next hundred years or so, culminating in the opening in 1821 of the Eau Brink Cut which straightened and widened the channel between Lynn and Wiggeshall. In 1844 this was linked with the Fen drainage system by an outfall sluice very massively constructed with sluice gates opening on the ebb to let the drainage water out but closing on the flood to prevent the tidal water getting back to the fen drain. All went well until 4th May 1862 when the sluice, which seems to have been gradually undermined, collapsed and ten thousand acres of land were flooded. This was followed by further collapses and further flooding.

All these catastrophes produced consequent problems lower down at Lynn and many great minds were greatly exercised on the complex problems of fen drainage, river navigation and the control of tidal conditions in the Wash itself. These were so interrelated as to make one vast problem the solution of which involved not only engineering skill but expenditure of an astronomical order. In 1837, as we all know, Queen Victoria came to the throne and in that same eventful year Lord William Bentinck and a few adventurous associates put forward the preposterous plan — or so it then seemed — to enclose the whole or a great part of the Wash. The idea was to unite the four Wash rivers, the Ouse, Nene, Welland and Witham in one common outfall to the sea and the land which it was hoped would be reclaimed thereby, estimated at 150,000 acres, was to be known as Victoria county. To describe this plan as ambitious would be a vast understatement; based as it was on the technical advice of so outstanding an engineer as Sir John Rennie it deserved serious attention. Parliament reacted as might be expected; it threw it out three times before a company was formed to improve one river, the Ouse. Thereafter the scheme pursued an erratic course, a long alternation of vigorous activity, administrative and financial hold-ups, law suits with the Eau Brink Commissioners, who were not so starry-eyed as the promoters, and so forth. The more grandiose idea of enclosing the Wash was never achieved, although it is by no means dead and, as we know in these latter days it is again on the tapis. Although the work was piecemeal it did achieve quite solid and lasting improvement of the channel of the Ouse: while the task of keeping Lynn open as a port seemed to be endless, it was absolutely essential to improve the conditions under which the shipping which was the life-blood of Lynn could berth secure from the vagaries of wind and tide.

Accordingly in 1865 a company was formed to construct an enclosed dock with lock-gates and on 7th July, 1869 the Alexandra Dock was opened by the Prince of Wales. Part of the land required for this basin was taken from the existing river bed and a fresh channel cut so as to form a dead-straight canalised watercourse between training walls to the Wash two miles away. The work of excavation was a major operation in the days when the only earth-moving equipment consisted of the bone and sinew of hundreds of Irish navvies. In spite of this the task took only two years to accomplish. Fourteen years later in 1883 a second basin was made, opening out of the original one; this is the Bentinck Dock.

Besides the Docks, which being locked are not subject to tidal rise and fall, there is still ample accommodation for vessels to berth at the quays in the Harbour both on the main river front and at private wharves in the River Nar and what in Defoe's time constituted the Haven. The tide is still a fast one, especially at springs and it is often necessary for ships entering the Docks to be warped in.

In 1692 some Lynn ships were involved in the disaster which overtook all shipping off the north Norfolk coast as the result of a sudden storm which blew up. At that time about two hundred colliers returning to Newcastle from London in ballast had just left Yarmouth Roads and having little chance of weathering it ran for Lynn Deep. At the same time a fleet of laden ships were coming from the North and some ships which had left Wells and Lynn with cargoes of corn ran into the same trouble while they were at anchor, presumably to join up in convoy. Many were blown ashore, others collided and in the result over 200 vessels were lost and over a thousand sailors perished.

The 'Great Tide' of 1953 to which reference has already been made brought great disaster to Lynn when a heavy outflow of flood waters from the Fenland rivers coincided with abnormally high spring tides at the same time as gale-force winds from the North East. The damage and loss of life which resulted was the highest in Norfolk and Suffolk and Civil Defence services were rushed to the town to help cope with the first emergency of magnitude since the 1939-45 War. A dramatic reminder of these days is provided by the high-water marks incised on the wall of St Margaret's Church by the West Door.

A great part of Lynn's wealth and influence proceeded from her command of traffic coming into the town or passing up and down the Ouse and the other rivers flowing into the Wash. Much of this traffic would have been transhipped from the sea-going ship into wherry or barge or vice-versa; but in the days when the current down the rivers was freer and the channels wider and ships drew less, a large amount was in fact carried by the ships themselves. In the days when they were chiefly square-rigged they would not make much progress with a following wind for long at a stretch. Other aid they would need and towage by horses would be of little avail in the absence of a good haling way. The alternatives would be to rely on sweeps or quants and this was probably their regular standby for some centuries.

As we have seen the rivers provided slow but sure links between many towns from the Eastern Midlands to the Wash; but to no town was this of more importance than Cambridge. Long before an Address to James I recited that the river was "the life of the trafficke to this Towne and Countie", the right of the men of Cambridge to the unfettered use of their river was recognised in 1118 by a charter of Henry I. There is no doubt that while in the days of the Heptarchy the river had served as a boundary between East Anglia and Mercia it had also served as a highway with the outer world. Had not Etheldreda's marble coffin, popularly believed to have been found by divine direction, been conveyed from Cambridge to Ely by water? By the same means much of the stone and timber for the rebuilding of the abbey in the tenth

century reached the Isle. This highway had been a material factor
in the growth of Cambridge and not least in bringing about the
establishment there of what came to be one of the greatest fairs in
Europe, indeed some say that it was the greatest of them all,
outvying Leipzig, Frankfürt, even Nijni-Novgorod. The traffic
came from all over Europe, possibly even farther, and the way by
which all this merchandise reached the fair was by the Ouse and
the Cam; for by no other rivers could sea-borne goods be taken
so deep into the heart of England. There were four fairs in the
year at Cambridge; but by far the greatest was Stourbridge, held
each year from the feast of St Bartholomew, 24th August, to
the fourteenth day after the feast of the Exaltation of the Holy
Cross, 14th September. In its later years it declined somewhat in
size and area; but in the days of its prime it occupied a large
field between the river and the Newmarket road measuring a full
half-mile on each side. It was opened with great pomp and since
the Fair is so bound up with the history of Cambridge's maritime
activities it is worth recounting the procession on this occasion
as it was observed in the eighteenth century; it is very certain
that the mediaeval fairs would have been no less splendid:

> The Crier in Scarlet on Horseback
> 28 Petty Constables on foot
> Three Drums
> Banners and Streamers
> The Grand Marshal
> Two Trumpets
> The Town Music (12 in number)
> Two French Horns
> The Bellman in state with the stand on Horseback
> Four Sergeants at Mace on Horseback
> The Town Clerk on Horseback
> The Mayor in his robes mounted on a Horse richly
>   caparisoned led by two footmen called red coats
>   with white wands
> The two representatives in Parliament on Horseback
> Twelve Aldermen according to seniority on Horseback
>   (three and three) in their proper robes, the six
>   seniors having their horses attended by as many
>   Henchmen or red-coats with wands.
> The Twenty four Common Councilmen three and three
>   according to seniority

Eight Dispencers in their Gowns (two and two)
Four Bailiffs in their habits (two and two)
The Treasurers in their gowns
The Gentlemen and Tradesmen of the Town.

This procession was continued annually until about 1758 when it began to be abridged owing as it is said to the trouble and charge of keeping it in a suitable condition." Alas! What a splendid show they must have made — a worthy memorial of this great relic of a glorious past.

When this magnificent cavalcade arrived at the fair ground the proclamation was duly "cryed" in the course of which the most meticulous conditions were prescribed for the due conduct of the occasion, the prices of bread and ale, fish and meat, the exact measures and quality of these and all other commodities sold. The present-day standards of weights and measures and trades description seem by comparison to constitute a very permissive state of affairs.

And after all this pomp and circumstance, what was the scale of the fair? It was a veritable town of tents and booths with its own streets. Wool, woollen goods, glass, wrought-iron, jewellery — every trade in fact and every commodity whether produced in this country or abroad, food and drink for the thousands of buyers and sellers, as well as a "Court of Pie-powder" to adjudge on any disputes and without right of appeal to any higher tribunal.

It is easily assumed, and commonly asserted, that Garlick Row which is near the old site of Stourbridge Fair, is a survival of one of these 'trade' streets. This may be so; but it is well to utter a word of caution. Not far away is Jesus College, formerly the Priory of Saint Radegund to which foundation King Stephen granted the right to hold a fair, which became known as Garlic Fair. There does not seem any special reason to connect this with Garlic Row; but there is none the less a slight element of doubt herein which should not be readily ignored.

In 1425 the bursar of Burcester Priory in Oxfordshire bought at the fair for the priory horse collars and head stalls, red silk for vestments, deal boards and Spanish iron — quite a comprehensive shopping list!

248

All this was going on while the ships from the Low Countries, France and the Germanies lay alongside the riverbank having discharged their cargoes and ready to take back overseas the English goods which their merchants had bought.

Another Cambridge fair which brought sea-going foreign ships up the river was Reach Fair held at Rogationtide. Today Reach is a village only by courtesy, its church built by the parson of the adjoining parish of Swaffham Prior dating from 1860. Ten miles from Cambridge it was formerly a village of some importance at the northern end of the Devil's Dyke. The charter for the Fair was granted by King John in 1200 to the Burgesses of Cambridge and notwithstanding various attempts through the centuries to dispute this jurisdiction, it is still opened by the Mayor of Cambridge who scatters largesse to the local babes and sucklings in the form of coins of discreetly low denomination. The Fair is now a mere matter of roundabouts and trivialities; but it was formerly of much more consequence and it appears that the Prior of Ely had one third part of the fair, shared with Cambridge as to two parts. In 1586 Camden wrote that in the Middle Ages "ships of considerable burthen came from the sea at Lynn to Reach". They would have reached the village — or town as it must then have been — by way of Reach Lode.

While it is certain that Reach was formerly a place of some importance it would be rash to exaggerate its size and status. The mists of time can easily magnify known facts like the Spectre of the Brocken, and the 'Kingdom of Reach' about which much is said, but little is known, may be nothing but local amour-propre made the more heady over a pint-pot.

For long after Reach Fair had ceased to be an emporium for general merchandise it continued to be an important horse fair right up to the day when the horse was no longer a normal and essential partner in the daily life of civilised man.

It would, of course, be overmuch to expect that between Lynn and Cambridge relations would always have been honey-sweet. In 1286 the commonalty of Lynn preferred a complaint against the commonalty of the borough of Cambridge and the Prior of Barnwell—

> "for unjustly distraining the men of Lynn coming with their merchandise to Cambridge and the fairs of Reach and of Barnwell for stallage and toll. The attorney for the

commonalty of Lynn produced the charters freeing the townsmen of Lynn from payment of toll in all parts of England except London, on which the Mayor of Cambridge and the Prior of Barnwell admitted the exemption, were adjudged to return the pledges they had taken, and forbidden in future to distrain the men of Lynn for stallage and toll."

Nearly three centuries later in 1541 an Act was passed revoking the King's grant of two fairs to the borough of King's Lynn, on the ground of their being prejudicial to the fish trade at Stourbridge, Ely and other fairs.

Within ten years Henry VIII was dead and the young Edward was on the throne, propped up there and enmeshed in a web of intrigue woven by the somewhat disreputable collection of place-hunters around him. Apparently Cambridge and King's Lynn had been for long at loggerheads over matters of tolls and other charges levied by each on the shipping of the other. The issue having been referred to the arbitrament of the two Recorders and two Aldermen from each town, the parties came to some sort of agreement whereby the "ships, cranes, keels, lighters, boats and other vessels loden with their goods wares or merchandise" from Cambridge should go ride and pass freely by to and fro in the common stream or haven of Lynn to and from the sea or other place without paying any manner of toll or custom anchorage mereage ringage or groundage or other such like". On the other hand the Lynn ships could tie up at Cambridge at times of Stourbridge Fair at certain fixed rates and enjoyed certain other privileges, etc., etc.

Besides these special occasions there was always a quiet but steady stream of sea-borne vessels coming right up to Cambridge and mooring at the hythes which lay on the riverside between the Great Bridge and the Little Bridge at Newnham. These were five in number, the Corn Hythe, Flax Hythe, Garlic Hythe, Salt Hythe, and Dame Nichol's Hythe and they stretched along what is now known as the 'Backs'. There was also the Common Hythe, which still exists as the Town Quay. It is very rare to see this quay in use, although it is not many years since an enterprising yachtsman brought his auxiliary-powered ketch round from Cornwall and having with much patience and not a little skill negotiated the occasional shallows from Ely, moored her at the Town Quay — to the consternation of the latter day Bumbles at Guildhall.

In order to negotiate the Great Bridge it would have been necessary for craft to have masts in tabernacles and that this must have been so is evidenced by early prints showing their masts above the Bridge. Alternatively they could have discharged into lighters or unloaded at the Common Hythe.

At all times there was regular barge traffic to Cambridge from Ely or Lynn and until the construction of the railway coal and turves were invariably taken to the town in this way. Even later still the sight of this traffic could have inspired Tennyson to write:

> "By the margin willow-veiled
> Slide the heavy barges trailed
> By slow horses —"

As road communication improved and the network of iron roads brought speedy, sure and cheap transport for men and goods, the rivers slipped into decay; the banks were neglected, the locks and weirs became unusable and, especially in the Fen country, the watercourses which had been the very life-blood of East Anglian trade, were regarded more as works of drainage than as living links between man and man. With the changes in the use of the rivers they themselves, like living beings, developed loose and unruly habits and gradually this reacted on their estuaries and the ports which men had made and which in turn had so potently shaped the lives of men.

Bibliography

Addison, William	—	Suffolk (County Books), 1950.
Anderson, Romola and R. C.	—	The Sailing Ship, 1947.
Arnott, W. G.	—	Alde Estuary: The Story of a Suffolk River, 1961.
——	—	Orwell Estuary: The Story of Ipswich River, 1954.
——	—	Suffolk Estuary: The Story of the River Deben, 1950.
Ashe, Geoffrey	—	From Caesar to Arthur, 1960.
——	—	King Arthur's Avalon, 1957.
Astbury, A. K.	—	The Black Fens, 1958.
Baker, B. Granville	—	Blithe Waters, 1931.
——	—	Waveney, 1924.
Bede	—	Ecclesiastical History of the English People.
Belloc, Hilaire	—	Hills and the Sea, 1906.
——	—	On Sailing the Sea (Mariners Library) 1951.
——	—	The Road.
Benham, Hervey	—	Down Tops'l, 1951.
——	—	Once Upon a Tide, 1955.
Benham, Sir William Gurney	—	Colchester, 1951.
Brøndsted, Johannes	—	The Vikings, Penguin, 1965.
Burne, Lt-Colonel, Alfred H.	—	More Battlefields of England, 1952.
Callender, Geoffrey	—	The Portrait of Peter Pett and the Sovereign of the Seas, 1930.
Capper, D. P.	—	Moat Defensive, 1963.
Carr, G. G.	—	Sailing Barges, 1951.
Carter, George Goldsmith	—	Sailing Ships and Sailing Craft, 1969.
——	—	Looming Lights, 1945.
——	—	Forgotten Ports of England.
Chatterton, E. Keble	—	Sailing Ships, 1909.
Clark, Roy	—	Black Sailed Traders, 1961.
Clarke, G. R.	—	History of Ipswich, 1830.
Clodd, H. P.	—	Aldeburgh: The History of an Ancient Borough, 1959.
Cobbett, William	—	Rural Rides, Edit. James Paul Cobbett, 1853.

Collingwood, R. G. — Roman Britain, 1923.

Cooper, Charles Henry — Annals of Cambridge, 1842.

Cooper, Major E. R. ("Suffolk Coast") — Suffolk Coast Garland, 1928.

—— — The Steelyard at Woodbridge (Transactions of the Newcomer Society), 1939.

Crouch Marcus — Essex, 1969.

Defoe, Daniel — Tour through the Whole Island of Great Britain, 1721—1726.

Dixon, Douglas — The King's Sailing Master, 1948.

Dutt, William A. — Highways and Byways in East Anglia, 1901.

—— — Norfolk and Suffolk Coast, 1909.

Ecclestone, A. W. & J. L. — The Rise of Great Yarmouth; the story of a sandbank; n.d. privately printed.

Evelyn, John — Diary and Correspondence, edited William Bray.

Ekwall, Eilert — Concise Oxford Dictionary of English Place Names, 1960.

—— — English River Names, 1928.

Fiennes, Celia — Journeys. Edited Christopher Morris, 1949.

Fitch, E. A. — Maldon and the River Blackwater.

Foord, Edward — The Last Age of Roman Britain, 1925.

Forrest, A. J. — Under Three Crowns, 1961.

Finch-Crisp, William — A Chronological Retrospect of the History of Yarmouth, 1884.

Gay, Revd. Norman — Glorious Dunwich, 1946.

Green, Charles — Sutton Hoo, 1968.

Grieve, Hilda — The Great Tide, 1959.

Grose-Hodge, Humfrey — Roman Panorama, 1946.

Hakluyt, Richard — Principal Navigations, Voyages, Traffiques and Discoveries of the English Nation, 1599. (Everyman Edition 1907).

Harris, L. E. — Vermuyden and the Fens, 1953.

Heard, N. — Wool — East Anglian's Golden Fleece.

Hedges, A. A. C. — "Yarmouth is an Ancient Town", Great Yarmouth Corporation, 1959.

Hele, Nichola Fenwick, — Notes or Jottings about Aldeburgh, 1890.

Hillen, H. J. — History of the Borough of King's Lynn. 2 v. 1907.

Houghton, Bryan — St Edmund — King and Martyr.

Ingleby, Holcombe — The Treasures of Lynn, 1924.

James, M. R.	—	Suffolk & Norfolk, 1930.
Jenkins, J. T.	—	A History of the Whale Fisheries, 1921.
Jobson, Alan	—	The Felixstowe Story, 1968.
Leather, John	—	The Northseamen, 1971.
Leslie, Major J. M.	—	History of Landguard Fort in Suffolk, 1898.
Lockwood, William	—	Woodbridge in the Olden Time, privately printed, 1890.
de Mare, Eric	—	London's Riverside, Past, Present and Future, 1958.
Mariners Mirror	—	passim.
Marlowe, Christopher	—	People and Places in Marshland, 1927.
Malster, Robert	—	Wreck and Rescue on the Essex Coast — the Story of the Essex Lifeboats.
——	—	Wherries and Waterways.
Mead, Cmdr. Hilary P.	—	Trinity House, n.d.
Morant, Philip	—	History and Antiquities of the County Essex, 1768.
Morey, George	—	The North Sea, 1968.
Morton, H. V.	—	The Land of the Vikings, 1928.
Mothersole, Jessie	—	The Saxon Shore, 1924.
Manship, Henry	—	History of Yarmouth, 1619.
Nash, E. Gee	—	The Hansa, its History and Romance, 1929.
Noon, J.	—	Ancient and present State of the Navigation of the Towns of Lynn, Wisbeach, Spalding and Boston, 1751.
Norden, John, and others	—	Maps of Orford Ness, selected and presented to James Alfred Steers, 1966.
Oman, Carola	—	Nelson, 1947.
Palmer, Charles John	—	The Perlustration of Great Yarmouth, 1872 — 5.
Pepys, Samuel	—	Diary, edit. Henry B. Wheatley, 1926.
Power, Eileen	—	The Wool Trade in English Mediaeval History, 1941.
Powicke, F. M. and others	—	Handbook of British Chronology (Royal Historical Society) 1939.
Purchas, A. W.	—	Wells next the Sea, 1965.
Redstone, Lilian J.	—	Our East Anglian Heritage, 1939.
——	—	Ipswich throughout the Ages, 1948.
Redstone, V. B.	—	Bygone Woodbridge, 1893.
Richmond, I. A.	—	Roman Britain.
Sayles, G. O.	—	The Mediaeval Foundations of England, 1948.

Scoresby, William — An Account of the Arctic Regions, 1820.

de Selincourt, Aubrey — The Crouch (Portraits of Rivers — edit. Eileen Molony) 1953.

Skeat, Rev. Walter W. — The Place Names of Suffolk (Cambridge Antiquarian Society) 1913.

Smith, J. R. — Foulness, A History of an Essex Island Parish, Essex County Council, 1970.

Steers, J. A. — The Sea Coast, (4th Edition) 1969.

Stevenson, D. Alan — The World's Lighthouses before 1729 — 1959.

Tennyson, Julian — Suffolk Scene, 1939.

Tibbs, Rodney — Fenland River.

Tompkins, Herbert W. — Marsh Country Rambles, 1904.

—— — Companion into Suffolk, 1949.

Tripp, Sir H. Alker ("Leigh Hoe") — Suffolk Sea Borders, 1926.

Vale, Edmund — Seas and Shores of England, 1936.

Victoria County History — Cambridgeshire Vol. III.

—— — Essex, Vol. II, et passim.

—— — Norfolk, passim.

—— — Suffolk, Vol. II, et passim.

Waller, Ambrose J. R. — The Suffolk Stour, 1957.

Ward, E. M. — English Coastal Evolution, 1922.

Warren, C. Henry — Essex, 1959.

Webb, John — Great Tooley of Ipswich, Suffolk Record Society, 1962.

Wedgwood, Iris — Fenland's Rivers, 1936.

Wentworth Day, J. — Coastal Adventure, 1949.

White, Archie — Tideways and Byways in Essex and Suffolk, 1948.

White's Norfolk, 1883

White's Suffolk, 1885

Willson, Beckles — Lost England, the story of our submerged coasts, 1902.

Wright, Thos. — History and Topography of the County of Essex, 1836.

Ziegler, Philip — The Black Death, 1969.

Index

The Wash, 230,ff
    —Barrage, 244, 245.
Waterford, 49.
Watson-Watt, Sir Robert, 118.
Weavers, 30, 86.
Wedmore, Peace of, 45.
Wells, 228.
Welsh, 20.
Weybourne Hope, 226.
Wherry, 215, 216.
White Tower, London, 59.
William of Orange (III), 81.
Willoughby, Sir Hugh, 76.
Winchelsea, 74.
Wind in the Willows, 39.
Wingfield, Sir Humphrey, 123.
Winston Churchill, 116, 174.
Winterton Lighthouse, 225.
Witham, 45.
Wivenhoe, 61, 62, 65, 78.
Wolsey, Cardinal, 75, 97.
Woolverstone, 79.
Woodbridge, 52, 72, 120—132;
    —derivation of, 121;
    —Bread Dole, 132;

—Coal Trade, 127;
—Priory, 121, 123, 128;
—Napoleonic period, 127;
—Seaborne Trade, 127;
—Shipbuilding, 126;
—Steelyard, 129;
—Tide Mill, 128.
Wool Staple, 140, 159, 214.
Worsted, 59, 60.

Y
Yachting, 37.
Yarmouth, Great, 65, 70, 72, 205—
    223;
    —Beach Companies, 221;
    —Haven Bridge, 213;
    —and Lowestoft, 187, 188;
    —Nelson at, 220;
    —St Nicholas Church, 210;
    —and Norwich, 214;
    —Rows, 210;
    —South Town, 208;
    —Telegraph, 221;
    —Volunteers, 222;
    —Whaling.

This is a detail of the large panel, ten feet by four feet, which hangs in the Christchurch Mansion at Ipswich. Generally attributed to the celebrated marine painter, John Cleveley the Elder. The style of the central part around the Common Quay is more mellow and genial than much of his other work and one wonders if the artist may not have been his more sophisticated son, John Cleveley Junior; but on the evidence of the date assigned to it, 1753, this would be impossible, since the younger John was not born until 1745.